The
Urgent
Life

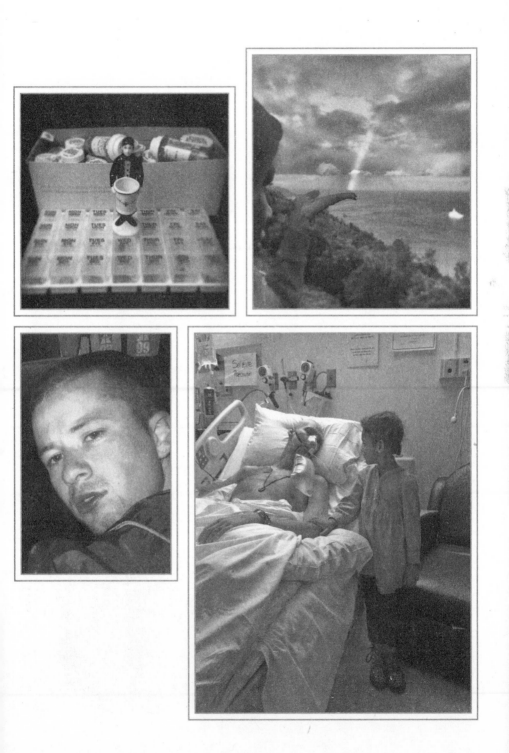

The
Urgent
Life

My Story of Love, Loss,
and Survival

BOZOMA SAINT JOHN

VIKING

LIBRARY OF CONGRESS CATALOGING-IN-PUBLICATION DATA
Names: Saint John, Bozoma, author.
Title: The urgent life: my story of love, loss, and survival /
Bozoma Saint John.
Description: [New York]: Viking, [2023]
Identifiers: LCCN 2022022454 (print) | LCCN 2022022455 (ebook) |
ISBN 9780593300176 (hardcover) | ISBN 9780593300183 (ebook)
Subjects: LCSH: Saint John, Bozoma. | Businesspeople—United
States—Biography. | African American businesspeople—United
States—Biography. | Businesswomen—United States—Biography. |
Husbands—Death. | Grief.
Classification: LCC HC102.5.S24 A3 2023 (print) |
LCC HC102.5.S24 (ebook)
| DDC 338.092 [B]—dc23/eng/20220613
LC record available at https://lccn.loc.gov/2022022454
LC ebook record available at https://lccn.loc.gov/2022022455

Printed in the United States of America
1st Printing

Designed by Alexis Farabaugh

For Lael, whose life I cherish beyond my own

I don't want to get to the end of my life and find that I have just lived the length of it. I want to have lived the width of it as well.

—DIANE ACKERMAN

Contents

The
Urgent
Life

1.

The Beginning and the End

I woke up with a start.

Typically, I take my time getting up. The alarm rings, I hit the snooze button, and then I lay back down for a few minutes, curling into the quiet before shaking off the last vestiges of sleep and stepping into the fevered rush of my day.

But that morning, I sat up abruptly, my heart heavy, my stomach queasy. I wanted to cry and vomit at the same time. It felt like something was coming.

I tried to remember what I had forgotten that was so terrible. You know how you go to bed reeling from something awful, and when you wake up, for a split second you've forgotten what filled you with such dread? I searched my mind for what that could be, for that horrible thing my memory had briefly hidden in my sleep.

But there was nothing. Everything was fine, all things considered.

Fine was a relative term at that moment in my life, because both my husband and my mother were battling cancer.

My mother's diagnosis had come first, in January 2013. The doctors had run their tests and determined that after surviving breast cancer two years before, she would now have to fight another form of the awful disease, this time in her uterus.

When Mom moved from Colorado to New Jersey to receive chemotherapy, I squeezed my suitcases into her small spare room. She'd emerge from her treatments tired to the bone, so I was there to pick her up, to coax her to eat, to help her to her bed to lie down. But we took comfort on the days in between chemo, knowing that she was getting better.

We found out that my husband, Peter, was ill in late May. It was Burkitt's lymphoma, a form of cancer so rare that the specialist consulting with his primary oncologist was based all the way in Texas. But his physicians said it was curable. The medical team was flooding his system with a cocktail of medications, and it was working. Each time the doctors took a scan to check the cancerous growths in his throat and neck, they had shrunken a tiny bit more.

Peter had always been fiercely healthy. He'd walk around Manhattan with a light coat in the middle of winter and never even catch a cold. The cancer diagnosis jolted us, but we were confident he would survive.

So as strange as it might have seemed that I felt good while two of the people I loved most were ill, I was actually in a strong place emotionally.

Until that Wednesday morning.

I wanted to call my sisters or one of my best friends, Leander, but what would I say? And would giving voice to the fear manifest something awful that hadn't yet happened? Could silence short-circuit it, prevent whatever *it* was from coming into existence?

I reached for my phone. I needed to know if anyone else was feeling the same sense of doom, that something awful was imminent. But instead of making a call, I reached out to the void.

I was fluent in social media, but I wasn't one of those people who shared her most intimate thoughts there. I didn't vent about politics on Facebook or do Instagram videos on climate change when I spotted litter in Morningside Park.

But now, I was going to try to express my feelings of foreboding in 140 characters or fewer. My tweet was simple and vague.

"I feel uneasy," I wrote. "Does anybody else?"

I got one response back from someone I barely knew. Yes, she said. I feel it too.

I got out of bed and prepared to go to work, figuring my early-morning angst would fade. But I couldn't shake it. Not when I dressed, not during my fifty-minute drive to my office in Westchester County, not as I sat at my desk looking at marketing strategy decks and going through the other motions of my day.

I'd checked on my mom before I left the house. She'd rested well the night before and was eating breakfast and reading. And when I called Peter at the hospital, he was in a good mood too. His oncologist would be in later that morning to go over his latest scans.

I grabbed some lunch and was sitting at my desk when my phone began to buzz. It was my mother-in-law.

"Can you come to the hospital?"

She and Peter's sister, Debra, had come from Massachusetts when Peter first got sick and were staying at my apartment in New York City. They went to the hospital every day, and there was nothing unusual about my mother-in-law calling me at work and asking me to stop by. She'd phone because Peter was asking for me or to see if I could bring something random, like one of his sweatshirts or the rosary beads of hers that she'd forgotten at the house.

But when I asked her why I needed to come to the hospital now, in the middle of the workday, she wouldn't say.

"I just need you to come," she said again. "Right away."

I couldn't avoid it anymore. The feeling I'd been trying to bury with phone calls and spreadsheets and storyboards began to bubble up and overflow. My mind began to get fuzzy. I couldn't catch my breath. Panic was smothering me. I wanted to run, but I couldn't move.

I don't know what I said to my mother-in-law before I hung up the phone. But I knew I did not want to go to the hospital. I couldn't.

I managed to stand up, work my way out of my cubicle, and stumble toward the office of my colleague Chad.

Chad and I didn't really socialize outside of work, but we were confidantes at the office, talking about the latest office politics, reviewing creative campaigns, sharing a laugh to break up the day. At the time I hadn't really told with any of my colleagues that Peter was ill. But if I could talk to anyone about it, I knew it was Chad. I walked into his office and quickly shut the door.

"Peter's been sick," I told him in a rush. "He's been getting better. But his mother just called me from the hospital and told me I need to come. I don't want to. I know something's happened. I'm afraid."

Chad was sitting behind his desk.

"Whatever it is, you can handle it," he said. "You will be okay. Take it one day at a time."

He stood up, walked around his desk, and gave me a hug.

I have a photo of that moment. Someone in the office figured it would be funny to snap a picture. It was taken as we embraced, my leopard pumps edged up against his black loafers.

Little did that person know that they were capturing my last flicker of normalcy, the last moment before my life would shift into a new dimension, tipping into an abyss.

Chad said I could handle it. But could I? To find out, I'd have to face it first.

"Go," Chad said gently. "You can do it."

As I walked away, I tried to gather strength from his words. I did have some power, the power to look at the situation and decide what to do about it, the power to figure out the best way to respond.

Maybe Peter had a bad reaction to one of the medications. We'd be by his side as the doctors figured out what changes needed to be made. Maybe one of the growths hadn't shrunk this week, but perhaps we could talk about surgery and having it removed. It was a temporary setback. There might be better news with the next scan.

It was a fifty-five-minute drive from my office in Purchase, New York, to Memorial Sloan Kettering in Manhattan. The whole ride I tried to keep my panic at bay. I was counting numbers. I was thinking about the groceries I needed to buy to refill my mom's refrigerator. I tried to daydream. Anything that would take me out of the moment.

I finally arrived. I passed the front desk, where nurses and physicians huddled and scurried, and approached the hallway where Peter's room was located. Before I turned the corner, I could hear his mother and sister talking. They spoke in hurried, frantic whispers.

I started to sweat. My palms began to itch. I didn't want to enter that hallway. But I had to face it.

My mother-in-law saw me. I saw her. And without a word, I knew.

"Oh, Bozoma," was all she said.

What I'd felt was coming had arrived.

. . .

"Hey, you may look like royalty, but you're not the queen, so please hurry up!"

I whipped my head around. You could feel the people in line behind me collectively catch their breath. There were a couple of *oob*s, followed by some nervous laughter. Even folks who didn't know me knew that something sharp was about to come out of my mouth.

It was October 2000. Little did I know I was about to meet the man I would love for the rest of my life.

I was working for Spike Lee's Spike DDB, a cutting-edge advertising agency that was a joint venture with DDB, a legendary pillar of Madison Avenue. Despite the collaboration, Spike wasn't leaning on anything DDB had to offer, so we were basically our own self-contained entity. Pretty much the only interaction between the two agencies happened in the cafeteria.

That particular morning, I was there ordering my breakfast. I am detail-oriented when I'm purchasing anything, whether it's curtains for my bedroom or a pair of shoes. I am very precise, so I was making sure my breakfast sandwich met my specifications.

"Two well-done fried eggs on a cinnamon raisin bagel with four strips of bacon," I recited. "And no cheese."

That was when the loudmouth behind me grew impatient and told me to hurry up. He didn't know who he was dealing with.

"Who said that?" I snapped.

I saw him, a guy tall enough to play for the New York Knicks literally trying to duck behind somebody who was barely five feet tall. He sheepishly peeked his head around his human shield.

"Are you serious?" I asked, looking at him. "Man, you don't know me."

I turned and continued with my order.

"Make sure the bagel is toasted dark . . . and that the bacon is very well done."

People were really laughing now. When I finished and moved over to the side to wait, the heckler stepped out of the line and walked over.

"I'm so sorry," he said. "I get angry when I'm hungry, and I needed my breakfast."

His name, he said, was Peter.

He was a white guy, about six five with reddish-blond hair, green eyes, and eyelashes so light, they almost looked like they weren't there. He was well built, with broad shoulders. And though he'd started out a bit rude, he now seemed courteous.

But he was also wearing this heavy gold chain. I didn't see a lot of white guys running around with their shirts open, wearing necklaces that looked like a prop from a 1980s Run-DMC video. That told me all I needed to know.

I can't take this man seriously, I thought to myself. I immediately dismissed him and turned back toward the people making my breakfast. A few minutes later, I grabbed my sandwich and left.

A couple of days had passed when I was back in the breakfast line again. And so was Peter. Once again, he was rude, but this time that rudeness wasn't directed at me. Instead, he walked past the two people waiting in front of me, cut off the person standing at the counter, and proceeded to order the exact same sandwich, down to the slightly burnt bacon, I'd ordered the day we met.

This fool here, I thought, shaking my head.

He walked back to me.

"I ordered your breakfast to make up for what I did the other day," he said.

"That's fine," I said coolly, "but you cut off these other two people."

He looked amused. "I can't win with you. What can I do?"

I told him nothing and wished he would step aside and let me get my food so I could move on with my day.

"Let me take you to dinner," he said.

Now I knew he didn't know who he was dealing with. I wanted to tell him no. I wanted to tell him *hell* no. But suddenly I had a thought that would basically achieve the same goal.

"Well," I said, trying to keep my lips from edging into a smile, "if you want to get to know me, you'll read my favorite book."

I could see confusion crease his face. "What book is that?" he asked.

"My favorite author is Toni Morrison, and my favorite book is *Song of Solomon*," I said. "If you read that, you'll know me better."

Toni Morrison's words had captured me from the moment I'd read *The Bluest Eye*, her first novel. Her works were elegant and difficult, layered with metaphor and meaning that stretched the edges of the imagination and pushed me to ponder the boundless ability of love and ingenuity to transcend bigotry and the confines of the mundane. I had to read *Song of Solomon* four or five times before I could even begin to grasp all of its complexity.

I was cracking up inside. I figured that was the end of him.

Well, a week or two later, I was sitting at my desk when the receptionist rang my phone.

"There's a white guy at the front door looking for you," she said.

White guy? Spike's agency was on the third floor of the building. Again, we were a cloistered little group, Spike's own domain. No one dared come there if they didn't have specific business, especially not a six-five white man wearing a gold chain. But when I went out front, there Peter was.

"What are you doing here?" I asked.

"I finished the book," he said.

I think my jaw may have hit the floor. "No way," I said to him, shaking my head.

"I promise you, I did," he said. "Let me take you to dinner and we can talk about it."

I was dumbfounded. I was an English and African American studies major who'd attended Wesleyan University, and I knew there was no way that this man could have read anything by Toni Morrison, let alone *Song of Solomon,* in a week and been ready to talk to me about it. I decided to call his bluff.

"Okay," I said. "Let's go to dinner."

The following evening, we met at an Italian restaurant on the Upper East Side. We sipped a little red wine, and I decided to wait until after we'd eaten our appetizers to finish Peter off, embarrassing him about his complete lack of understanding of what Ms. Morrison had written, if he'd even gotten past the first couple of chapters.

It turned out that Peter had not only read the book, he had tremendous insights into the story. Beyond that, he had a profound interest in the African American experience. We talked about the systemic racism that infected every aspect of American life and the particular dangers that Black men faced just by their very being.

He was unexpected, and I realized he had so much more to offer than I had initially given him credit for. I was floored and enraptured. It was November 9, our first date, and I swear that I fell in love with him that night.

Peter asked me to go out again the next evening and after seeing a movie, we went for a drink and began to talk about our families. We could not have been more different.

He was very proudly a second-generation Italian American. His maternal grandfather had come from Italy when he was seventeen years old and built a successful construction business in Worcester, Massachusetts, where most of Peter's family still lived.

Peter was the youngest of six kids, and there was a significant gap between him and his oldest sister, who was almost the same age as my mother, so it was like he had two moms growing up. He was babied and adored.

Peter's upbringing loomed in stark contrast to mine. I was the child of Ghanaian immigrants. My father, Appianda, was a member of the Nzema people, who call the southwestern region of Ghana home. My mother, Aba, was part of the Ahanta tribe, who hail from a swath of the southern coast that stretches from Sekondi-Takoradi to the capital, Accra. I was the oldest of four daughters, and I rarely let my sisters forget who among us had been born first. When I wasn't deciding what games we should play, I was defending them at school.

My mom had been a model in London before marrying my dad. She would eventually work as a seamstress and in retail sales, but during my childhood she was a stay-at-home mother able to pick up and pack up our family whenever my father's career demanded it.

My dad served in the Ghanaian government in the late 1970s and early 1980s and then went on to be an executive in numerous Christian organizations. His shifting jobs made for a peripatetic childhood.

I was born in Middletown, Connecticut, but before I could walk, and after my father finished attaining his doctorates at Wesleyan University, our family moved back to Accra, Ghana's capital. He became a lecturer at the University of Ghana, teaching anthropology and ethnomusicology, before becoming a member of Parliament, representing his native region. When a coup led to my father's imprisonment, my mother, sisters, and I fled to Washington, D.C. A year later, when I was six, we moved to Pasadena, California, followed by a move to Nairobi, Kenya. Finally, we briefly returned to Ghana before settling down in Colorado Springs, Colorado, when I was twelve years old.

Unlike Peter, who'd grown up in a largely Italian American working-class community, I spent my teenage years navigating spaces where most people looked nothing like me. I was one of the few Black children in my neighborhood and in my school. But my parents taught me to never downplay who I was. We were proudly Black, proudly African, and we carried our Ghanaian culture to the edge of the Rockies, cooking up jollof rice and fufu with soup, listening to my dad lecture on global politics and the radically transformative spirit of Kwame Nkrumah, and listening to music by Alpha Blondy.

Peter's and my differences—in our upbringings, in our cultures, in our family histories—fascinated me. I'd never dated anyone quite like him before. We quickly became inseparable.

Many days we'd meet in front of our office building and decide on the fly where we would go that evening. We might take the subway to his place or pick up some food near where we worked. I lived in Jersey City, but more often than not, after shutting down a local bar or going to hear some music, we'd head to his apartment on Manhattan's Upper East Side, which, despite Peter's hovering roommates, was far more convenient, and much nicer, than mine.

I can't tell you how many times I had to buy clothes on Madison Avenue as soon as the stores opened, because I hadn't made it home the night before. Our romance was moving at what felt like warp speed, and by my birthday on January 21, I couldn't imagine a life that didn't include Peter.

That evening, he took me to dinner with my friends. It was a restaurant we'd been to before, one that we both enjoyed.

I'm not a person who blows off the anniversaries of my trips around the sun. I want balloons, phone calls, best wishes. So, I was sort of waiting for the surprise, for the magical thing. After all, I'd been dating Peter for two months by then. Whatever that might be wasn't apparent at dinner. I was a little disappointed but still hopeful.

We went back to his apartment. Before we walked in, he made me close my eyes and wrapped a handkerchief around them in case I peeked. He steered me across the threshold, then untied the blindfold.

All I saw was a sheet covering something bulky in the corner of the room. I thought, *What the hell is that?* Jewelry would have been nice, but what was under the sheet was definitely not a small box. At this point, I would have been good with a bouquet of flowers.

He walked over to the mysterious object sheathed in white, looking incredibly nervous.

"Your gift is under this," he said, beads of sweat peppering his brow.

I didn't say anything, but I thought to myself, *He'd better be sweating.* There was no gift wrap, nothing special or fancy. The guy made a decent living and was usually so romantic. This was not what I'd envisioned.

I edged closer. Peter looked like he was going to throw up, fidgeting, pulling at his fingers. I started feeling a little mischievous in the midst of my growing disappointment. I slowed down my walk. Peter became flushed and red.

My God, I thought. *Is he going to pass out?*

Finally, I pulled the sheet off. And my heart exploded.

It was a painting—Peter's interpretation of *Song of Solomon*. He'd never picked up a paintbrush before, but he put on canvas his vision of Toni Morrison's words, depicting Sugarman—the subject of the song, the evocation of Solomon—as he took flight.

It was the most beautiful gift I'd ever received. No one had ever been that considerate of me, that thoughtful. I burst into tears and couldn't stop crying. For the first time, I told Peter that I loved him, that I'd never met anyone like him. I had known since our first date in that Italian restaurant that he, and this, was something I was lucky to find even once in a lifetime.

He said he loved me too, that he'd never felt this way about anybody before. *Song of Solomon* had changed his life, and so had I.

We agreed right then and there that we would get married. We'd been dating for not even three months, so of course it was probably too fast. Perhaps we were irrational. Perhaps we were dizzy and high, and the buzz would wear off long before we ever said *I do*. But in that moment, it was what we both wanted.

It was going to be the two of us. Always.

· · ·

I stood in the hospital hallway, my mother-in law sobbing in my arms. I asked her what was happening. I looked at the closed door to Peter's room. I needed to know before I opened it and went inside.

"Just tell me," I said, holding her, "so I can be prepared."

She shook her head. Peter wanted to tell me himself.

Though his room was big, it felt cramped from all the equipment. There was a heart monitor, a gauge for blood pressure, stands filled with his various medications grouped in clusters. There was also a large chair so he could have somewhere to sit when he got tired of lying in his bed. It faced a window, and he was perched there now, in the hospital gown he hated so much. He turned his face toward me.

"Oh, Bozoma," he said, echoing the words his mother had just uttered.

I ran toward him. It was only a few steps, but it felt like it took an eternity to reach him. I was leaving shards of myself along the lino-leum floor, trying to bridge the gulf. His arms were reaching out. He usually had so many cords around him, infusing him with his medicine, monitoring his vital signs, that I'd treated him delicately, like the pieces of china his mother collected and that she'd helped me pick out for my bridal registry years before.

But in that moment, I didn't care if I tripped or ripped out every cord from every machine. I just threw my arms around Peter and held on tight.

I suddenly realized how much weight he'd lost. He had been a sturdy guy, and hugging him before had felt like grabbing hold of a tree trunk. Now, I felt like I could have wrapped my arms around him and myself at the same time, he was so thin.

I didn't need to see his eyes to see the truth. I knew it in my soul. It had awakened me from my sleep.

"What is happening?" I asked, gently pulling back. "What did they say?"

"I'm not going to make it," he said. It was matter-of-fact, just like that.

I'd known, but now that he said it, it didn't make sense.

"I don't understand," I said.

So, he said it again. And again, each time in a slightly different way. The medications weren't working. The tumors were aggressive and growing. He might have only a couple of weeks left.

Finally, we both just started crying. When minutes had passed and we again pulled apart, he reached for a piece of paper on the nightstand. There were several. He was always so organized. Even at a moment like this, he was making plans, putting things in order.

"You know I hate lists," I said, and for a moment we both smiled.

My eyes were still overflowing with tears, so it was hard for me to focus. Finally, they cleared enough that I could decipher the bold letters at the top of the sheet he handed me. "Boz," it read.

So, this was my list. At least I could try to concentrate for a few seconds on what he wanted me to do. I was quickly learning the comfort that could be found in distraction.

At the top, right under my name, was the most immediate of tasks, the one that was most important to him, and to me.

"Cancel the divorce," it read.

Before all this, we had been on the brink, our storybook romance derailed by tragedy, by misunderstanding, by the tedious differences that plague all couples and sometimes rip them apart. We were going to split up.

But now, though I wanted to crumble and pull back into myself, I had to summon the strength to do what needed to be done, to cancel the divorce and fulfill the many other wishes he'd scribbled on my list.

I had to face what was happening.

That was the first lesson, one I had begun to learn when I woke up that morning with that feeling, and when Chad urged me out the door: that when you feel fear, instead of running, you have to shine a light on what scares you. Whatever it was that filled me with terror as I sat at my desk, that left me clutching the steering wheel as I drove to the hospital, that made it nearly impossible to put one foot in front of the other as I walked down Sloan Kettering's corridor,

I had to open my eyes and face it. Everything always seems so much worse in the dark—so much worse when you don't know what it is.

To overcome our greatest fears, we have to confront them, like a child lifting the covers, grabbing a flashlight, and peering under the bed to make sure that the boogieman isn't there after all.

Or maybe he is. But at least now you can see him fully. Knowing what you are up against, you can brace yourself, then gather the energy for the fight.

I looked into Peter's eyes again. The eyes I said yes to when he asked me out the first time. The eyes I said yes to when he asked me out the very next night. The eyes I had also sometimes refused, but said yes to so many times.

In them, I could see my past and my uncertain future. I could see the faces of the daughter we were raising together and the daughter we'd lost. I could see myself when I met him at twenty-three and myself at that moment, at thirty-six.

In his eyes, I saw a question. Was I ready for the fight ahead?

I wasn't sure. But I said yes.

2

Common Ground

I 'm not sure how long it took to absorb the initial shock of Peter's news. Minutes, maybe? There was so much to do. How to begin? What was the next step? How did we go on?

Fortunately, Peter had his lists. He always had lists for everything—keeping a notepad by our bed, little boxes sketched next to each errand, so he could tick off his progress, like a first-grader's report card.

Make breakfast? Check. Do four sets of push-ups? Check. Call the boys and figure out where we're watching the game? Check, check, check.

I didn't do lists. If the task was important enough, I figured I'd remember it. Maybe I'd tap some notes into my phone. But when I was done, it was over, mission accomplished. Out of sight, out of mind. I didn't feel any need to document it, to put an exclamation point at the end of each sentence.

That was why Peter never made me lists. He didn't even jot down reminders for me on Post-its. But at the hospital, in that moment, Peter was in solution mode. He needed a list to organize his own thoughts, and I think he was thoughtful enough to want to give me something to do. He didn't want me to have time to sit, to think, to conjure in my mind all that was coming.

I'd never been so thankful for that sheet of to-dos. It was probably the only way I was able to function. If I had deviated from it, I think I would have fallen apart. My list even had the little boxes next to each chore.

But he reinforced one of those tasks with words.

"I want to see everybody," he said.

I pulled out some paper and a pen and started writing the names of everyone I needed to call. Peter wanted to see his four brothers, Michael, Stephen, David, and Neil, who hadn't yet made it to the hospital. We needed to reach out to our good friends who'd made us the godparents to their son Allen and discuss guardianship of our daughter, Lael. She would have only me once he was gone, after all, and since it was now all too clear that anything could happen, we needed to put things in order.

I took notes, straining to see through my tears. I couldn't stop to mourn. We might have as little as two weeks left together, a matter of days. We needed everyone to know. We wanted everyone to be there.

"Call your sisters," he said, "your cousin Tina; my guys Mecca, Will, and Priyesh; all my nieces and nephews."

And, Peter insisted, we needed to call my father.

I finally opened the door and asked Peter's mother and sister to come into the room while I went out to the hallway.

I don't even remember what I said, how I stopped my fingers

from shaking long enough to tap into the contacts in my phone and click their numbers. But the urgency of my mission helped me focus.

The calls became mechanical, like the voice relaying the news was somehow detached from my body. There was no time to deal with tears, not those of the person on the other end of the phone or my own. There was no time to absorb the gasps or to wait for the pregnant pauses to pass.

"Peter's diagnosis is now terminal," I said. "He wants to see everybody, so try to make it to New York as soon as you can. Please. Hurry."

It was the same script I delivered to my father. He was typically a man of few words, and that day, that call, was no different. But within hours, he was on a flight from Atlanta.

It wasn't the first time he'd jumped on a plane at a moment's notice to see Peter after an unexpected phone call from me.

• • •

In the summer of 2001, Peter and I had been dating about only eight months when we decided to move in together. We spent so much time in his apartment trying to eke out a bit of privacy as we dodged his roommates that we decided we wanted to have a home of our own. But I dreaded telling my father.

We signed a lease for a place on Eighty-Ninth Street, off East End Avenue, near Gracie Mansion, where the mayor of New York City lived. We planned to move in August.

"You've got to tell your dad," Peter said one afternoon, as we stuffed plates and pillowcases into cardboard boxes.

He was right. But I had avoided disappointing my dad my entire life. I knew moving in with my boyfriend was going to upset him. When I finally decided to make the call, I actually wrote a script to make sure I got out everything I needed to say in case I panicked on the call.

"Hi Dad," I jotted down. "I wanted to let you know that I'm in love with Peter, he's in love with me, and we've decided to move in together."

My father was in China at the time on business for his Christian nonprofit company. When it was evening there, and I figured he would be in his hotel room, I rang his cell phone.

"Hi Boz?" he said, a question in his voice.

I can still feel the sweat trickling down my arm. I quickly recited my script.

Because my dad is a man of few words, when he speaks, you listen intently and follow his direction. You don't fling back questions. You don't argue. But his silences can be even more daunting. He was quiet for what felt like the longest minute ever.

Then, he spoke.

"Why would you shame us like that?"

I didn't have an answer. That wasn't in the script. And to my father, neither was Peter. Dad had plans for me. And marrying a white American man was not part of the vision.

"We belong to the church," he continued, slowly, emphatically. "This is not the way Christians behave. We don't live out of wedlock. You're the eldest. You must set an example for your sisters. You cannot do this."

It was exactly the response that I dreaded. But there was no going back. I was grown. My whole life, I had done everything my father wanted me to. And I wanted to be with Peter. That desire overwhelmed everything else, including my fear of letting my father down.

"I'm doing it," I said.

"You will not," my father replied, more forcefully this time. It went back and forth like that for a bit.

Then, finally, Dad hung up on me. I didn't know it, but he was on his way to New York.

. . .

When I came into the world on January 21, 1977, I was the first daughter born to a man who desperately wanted a son.

My father, Appianda Arthur, was born to Enokpole Moses and Bozoma Arthur. Enokpole, the king of Eastern Nzema Traditional Area, also known as Sanzule, had four wives, and Bozoma was the youngest. But when my father was two years old, Bozoma passed away, leaving my father to be absorbed into the larger family. He went to live in the home of Bozoma's sister. It wasn't easy. He says that throughout life he was dogged by a profound loneliness, the only child born to his mother and father, he was a motherless boy surrounded by mothers.

Our tribal culture is matrilineal, so you belong to your mother's people. Heirlooms and wealth flow through your mother's bloodline. But boys are still greatly valued. In some instances, they are the ones handed the family business. And as in so many cultures, having a son is believed to be evidence of a man's virility. Given the rootlessness he felt as a child as the nearly forgotten son of a king, my father desperately wanted a boy to teach, to raise, to guide.

But after me, the girls kept coming. There was my sister Alua. Less than two years later, Ahoba was born. Then, in 1982, my mother became pregnant again. Her final pregnancy came during a turbulent time.

That year, a military lieutenant named Jerry John Rawlings over-threw Ghana's civilian government led by the president, Hilla Li-mann. My father, along with many of his fellow lawmakers, was taken into political detention. My mother, carrying her fourth child, fled the country with me and my two sisters.

We left in the middle of the night, our departure furtive and rushed. Mom dressed my sister Alua and me in matching maroon-colored velour dresses. I loved that outfit. As we slipped our feet into our shiny black patent-leather shoes, careful not to disturb the lace socks so carefully folded over our ankles, it seemed like we might be going to a party.

But it soon became clear we weren't. My mother and the few friends who had come to our house to help her pack spoke in whispers. On the ride to the airport, Mom told us to be very quiet and to behave. I didn't need to be told twice. The firm set of her jaw, the fierce focus I could see in her eyes, warned me that she was in no mood to be messed with, and that I, the oldest, also needed to keep my younger sisters in line.

I don't recall much about the flight, but I remember the screams of my youngest sister, Ahoba, when at some point she wanted her coco, a Ghanaian breakfast porridge made of cornmeal. There was none. Mom had lost the thermos somewhere along the way. And there was nothing I could do to comfort Ahoba, who finally sat in silence, tears flowing down her face.

When we landed in Washington, D.C., we were met by my father's best friend from graduate school, Chris Weaver, who is also my godfather. He'd paid for our plane tickets and petitioned for the visas we needed to enter the United States.

I can't imagine what it was like for my mother to have to escape from her home, pregnant and traveling with three small children.

But I do recall she cried every single day, waiting to get news about my dad and knowing that even though we were welcome in my godfather's house, we couldn't stay there forever.

I didn't know it at the time, but it was the first lesson I would have in how to cope with bone-deep fear and loss. We'd left behind our home, our country, and who knew when we would return. But my mother had to focus on a higher purpose—saving her family—and barrel through.

I also believe that for both my mother and my father, there was something else that buoyed them through such a moment of terror—the thought of bringing a long-awaited son into the world.

My father didn't say much about the months we were separated and what he endured trying to get back to us, but I know that the one touchstone he had in his prison cell was a Bible. At that time, he wasn't a Christian. He was still steeped in the native religions of Ghana, the idea that our long-dead ancestors continued to look upon us with their spiritual gaze and that there was magic in our midst.

But as his colleagues were tortured and killed for being part of a government no longer in power, my dad held on to that holy book. He read, and he prayed.

"If there's a God up there, and you're listening," he said, "if I can walk out of this prison with my arms and my legs and my senses intact, I'll believe in you all my life and serve you."

Several months after his arrest, Dad did walk out. He was released and fled the country, going to Liberia before eventually making his way to Washington, D.C. And my father kept his word, returning to us a changed man.

My mom, so traumatized by what she'd lived through and thankful that we were all back together again, converted to Christianity soon after. After that, we just had to wait for my baby brother, who was about to arrive.

I don't think either of my parents actually said the words "We hope it's a boy." But they must have, because all of us—our family in London and Accra, my godfather in Washington, D.C., my sisters and I—knew they wanted a son, my father most of all. There had been so much emotion when he returned, the tense relief that he had escaped something horrific, the desperate desire to get back to something normal, that we just assumed that after having three girls, Mom would deliver a boy, my father's gift for having survived such an ordeal.

I remember the phone call from the hospital the day my mother gave birth. When my godfather called my sisters and me, we yelled out almost in unison, "What's his name?"

"Well," my father said. "It's a girl!"

The forced jubilation in his voice couldn't hide his disappointment. We all felt it. And Mom and Dad knew something we didn't, that after four children, there wouldn't be any more babies.

But then something beautiful happened. My father embraced things as they were. Though tribal identity comes through the mother, it's the man who names the children after his parents and their siblings. I, for instance, was named Bozoma after my father's mother, while Alua was named for our father's oldest aunt, and so on.

Under that tradition, the new baby should have been named for his aunt who was next in line. But my father changed it all up, causing all sorts of cultural explosions in our family. Instead of his mother's sister's name, he named the new baby Aba, for my mom, in appreciation of all she'd been through. Years later, after my parents' marriage staggered and ultimately fell apart, my mother still said that was an unexpected honor she would always cherish.

What's more, my mother's name is given to a girl born on a

Thursday, but my baby sister was born on a Tuesday, so even that was a shift. Dad had thrown all norms to the wind.

From then on, Dad's goals shifted toward making us strong girls who would grow up to be powerful women. And as the eldest, I was to be the standard-bearer, the role model for my sisters and chief heir to my father's aspirations.

. . .

I don't remember a time in my life when my dad wasn't adamant about our education. I enjoyed math, tackling diagrams and graphs in geometry, and science, loving how mixing chemicals caused a reaction that turned liquid amber and blue. I thought I might want to pursue medicine, and that definitely pleased my father. But the ceiling was high.

"You can't be a nurse," he would say, nodding approvingly when I told him I'd gotten an A on my chemistry final. "You can only be a doctor."

I also loved to draw and design, sketching capes and jumpsuits that reflected my sense of middle school chic. But graphic arts were also out of the question. If I wanted to pursue a creative career, it'd have to be architecture. Whatever career caught our interest, Dad wanted all of us, but especially me, to reach for the highest peak of that profession.

"You're the eldest," he'd say, when I competed in a track meet or when I chose what Advanced Placement class I would take in high school. "You're the example for your sisters."

Looking back now, the pressure to be the best at everything I tried was constant. Not being the best would not only have disappointed him, it would have been almost sacrilege, an affront to our ancestors to fail the expectations that had been set for me.

But I didn't have that awareness at the time. I don't recall a moment in my childhood when I even wanted to do something that was contrary to what my dad desired. When I decided to try out to be the cheerleading captain in high school, a position of leadership and school spirit, he approved. When I ran for student government, he was proud. I wouldn't have done it otherwise. I couldn't distinguish between what I did because it was expected of me and what I truly wanted to do in my heart.

That feeling of duty continued when it came time for me to go to college. My father had attended Wesleyan University in Middletown, Connecticut, earning two doctorates, in anthropology and ethnomusicology. His thesis can be found to this day in the university's stacks. It's dedicated to me: "For my eldest daughter, so that she may grow up to appreciate the culture of the Nzema people."

So. No pressure.

I was Ahanta, like my mother. Fanti was the language we spoke at home, making my father's dedication even more poignant and pointed. He wanted to make sure I remembered that I was also a daughter of his tribe and I represented them with every action I took.

Though I was interested in Georgetown and Stanford, Dad wanted me to go to Wesleyan. While he did allow me to visit a few different schools, you can guess what was first up: his alma mater. We visited during Sons and Daughters Weekend, when all the lectures and activities were focused on children of alumni whom the university hoped would continue their parents' legacy.

After that visit, the school waved its cardinal red and black flag, wooing me constantly with letters and phone calls. So even though I received eight acceptance letters, getting into every school I applied to, I chose Wesleyan.

It ultimately wasn't that difficult a decision. I didn't hate it. And it was a well-regarded university. I didn't feel like I was giving something up. The desire to go someplace else wasn't as important to me as making my dad happy.

While I was away at college, the daily phone call from my father was as much a part of my routine as labs, lectures, and lunch in the student center. This was the late 1990s, before the ubiquity of cell phones, and Dad had bought a landline phone for my room. He knew my class schedule and what times I went to the dining hall to eat, so he also knew exactly when to call. Everybody in the hall knew that if they heard my phone ringing, and I was not in the room, to run and come find me because my dad was on the line and would keep calling until I picked up.

Given my family's hope I would become a doctor, I took plenty of science courses. In between organic chemistry, biology, and introduction to physics, I even continued to take Latin, which I'd begun studying in the ninth grade, in part because it helped me decipher the technical jargon so often used in medicine. But I majored in African American studies and English literature. Those were my real interests, and I didn't want to go to medical school, no matter my parents' aspirations. I just hadn't told them yet.

My sister Alua followed me to Wesleyan, which made my father even prouder, and because I wanted to stay close to her during her senior year, I decided to stay on campus after I graduated, getting a job in the admissions office. It was a double win because I had a justification to put off explaining to my folks that I didn't want to pursue a medical degree.

I did everything to postpone the conversation I knew was coming.

At Alua's graduation, though, I finally stopped beating around the bush. It was such a joyful day, I figured my father couldn't get too upset.

"I want to move to New York, for a little while," I told my parents. "Maybe for a year or so, and just figure out what I want to do."

"I don't know what that means," Dad said incredulously.

I remember the feeling of that conversation more than the rest of the words. There was my dad's extreme disappointment and his worry about how I would take care of myself. I'd told friends that I wanted to do something completely unexpected, like going into the music business or pursuing a career in fashion. But I couldn't tell my parents that. They'd find those prospects fanciful, frivolous.

I was leaving a job in the admissions office to do what? Putting off going to medical school to live where?

Now that I think about it, I have to give my father some credit, because even though he didn't approve, he didn't tell me *not* to go. He didn't try to stop me. He could have threatened to disown me. He could have said he would bar my sisters from ever speaking to me again because I'd become a bad role model. But he did none of those things.

However, after being away from home for five years, I felt a new determination. For the first time, Dad's disappointment alone was not enough to make me change my plans.

That conversation marked a shift in our relationship, a step toward my becoming my own woman, a transition from my doing everything he wanted me to do even without his telling me to do it.

Of course, he still offered a bit of advice.

"Don't get distracted by men or the party life," he said. "You want to go there to figure out what you want to do, so concentrate on that. And remember, a year from now, it won't be too late to apply to medical school or even a graduate program."

It was the first time I was disobedient. Little did Dad know that it wouldn't be the last.

. . .

I arrived in New York City in May 2000, and Peter and I met in November. By the time my parents came from Colorado for a visit in February, I'd been head-over-heels in love for months.

I hadn't dated much and had never introduced any guy I was involved with to my very Christian, very conservative parents, not even my college sweetheart, Ben. But Peter was going to be in my life, so I knew it was time for my parents to meet him.

I planned a dinner at my Jersey City apartment. Peter arrived, a little nervous but still his avuncular self. We didn't hold hands or kiss. That would have felt too awkward. But the way we interacted, the fact that they were meeting him at all, must have tipped off my mother to how serious this relationship was. She knew to be nice to him. She was cordial and gracious. I think she knew that I was in love without my saying a word.

My dad was his typical formal self. But he could see that there was something there too, that this was no fling.

After Peter and my parents said their goodbyes, Dad turned to me.

"How seriously do you like this guy?" he asked, peering over his eyeglasses.

"Well," I said, wondering how truthful I should be, "I like him a lot." I didn't say anything about love.

He paused. "I don't know about people who aren't like us," he said. "You should be careful."

I knew that "us" didn't just mean that Peter was white, though that was certainly part of it. He also was American. Dad wanted me to marry a Ghanaian man, which I thought made no sense. He'd brought us to the United States, and I'd spent half my life in Connecticut and Colorado. Where exactly was I going to meet a Ghanaian guy?

BOZOMA SAINT JOHN

But remembering my dad's parting words at my apartment made me super nervous when Peter and I decided to move in together that following July. I spent weeks literally throwing up when I thought about how I was going to break the news.

I didn't want to let my father down again. I had figured he would forgive me for not going to medical school if I racked up a different professional success. But so far, getting coffee for Spike Lee wasn't quite it. And now, while Dad was in China on business, I was calling to tell him that I was about to live in sin with my white American boyfriend.

The morning after that tense conversation when I finally told him our plans and he hung up on me, I went to Peter's office and relayed my dad's reaction.

"Oh no!" he said, looking like someone had slapped him. "What are we going to do?"

"We can't do it! But I want to do it! Can we do it?" I said.

We were like two kids who'd broken a window and didn't know whether to confess, smash our piggy banks to pay for the damage, or run.

We'd signed a lease, and I still wanted to live with Peter, but I didn't know how to resolve the tension with my dad.

Peter and I decided to sort it out later. I had to go to work. I took the elevator down to the third floor and was sitting at my desk, focusing on proposals and anything else that could take my mind off my dilemma, when my phone buzzed.

It was Peter.

"Hello."

That was my first clue something was wrong. Peter never said hello. He dived right into whatever news he wanted to share, about an account he was working on or a new lounge he heard about that he wanted to check out.

30

"Your dad's here" were the next words out of his mouth. He sounded tense and scared. I'd never heard him sound like that before.

I thought either I was hallucinating or he was.

"Oh God! Are you sure it's my father?" I asked in disbelief. "I just talked to him yesterday. He's in China."

And then the voice, resonant and familiar boomed from behind him.

"Bozoma, I'm here in Peter's office."

Now, let me say here that it's my dad who gave me the nickname Boz in the first place. He never called me by my full name. So, he had flown to New York at a moment's notice, all the way from Beijing, cutting his business trip short. He'd headed right to my boyfriend's office. And now he was calling me Bozoma. I was in trouble.

"I'm on my way," I said, jumping up from my desk. But Dad shut me down.

"This conversation is for men," my father bellowed.

He sounded like a character from a bad '70s sitcom.

"Okay," I said, trying to get a handle on my thoughts. "I'll give you fifteen minutes and then I'm coming up."

Peter sounded so afraid I didn't want to hang up the phone. But I did. I looked at the clock, counting every second. Finally, I left my office.

When Peter opened the door, the air was stale with tension. I walked over to hug my dad, and his body barely budged.

I don't know what happened during those fifteen minutes, the span of time between my getting that call from Peter and then taking an elevator up five flights. Peter didn't reveal it to me, not then, not ever. But somehow, he and my dad had reached an uneasy peace.

"I have given my blessing for you to live together," my dad said. "But I don't like it. I think it's disrespectful, and I don't know why a man would come into another man's house and take his daughter without asking him for permission."

Peter and I stood there, silent.

"I'm going to leave."

And with that, Dad picked up his small bag, walked out of Peter's office, and flew home to Colorado.

When I look back on that day, it's startlingly clear to me that sometimes even those who love you most, who have the best of intentions, fail to understand what you need because of their own limitations. I was starting to learn that while my father could urgently offer his opinion, he couldn't really advise me, because my life, my journey, was mine alone.

Your greatest counsel is your voice within. Some people say it's your spirit talking, or your gut, or your intuition. Whatever you call that murmuring, it can quiet everyone around you and allow you to tap into your truth.

Right then, the voice inside me was pushing away the girl who'd always tried to please her father and, instead, was beckoning the woman straining to light her own way to come in.

The next time Dad and I spoke, Peter and I were unpacking boxes, settling into our new apartment. Dad and I made small talk. He didn't even acknowledge that Peter and I were living together.

Still, Peter and I had done it. Score one for Team PBoz.

3

A Little Bit at a Time

The nurse walked into Peter's hospital room, her tray cradling a few of the pills he had to take constantly. Handing him a tiny Dixie cup filled with water, she watched Peter place the tablets in his mouth. Satisfied, she grabbed the tray and began to walk away.

But then she hesitated.

"Take it one day at a time," she said finally, looking first at Peter, then at me.

She headed toward the door and was gone.

"Take it one day at a time."

I heard that from the doctors at Memorial Sloan Kettering as I steeled my hand so that when I clutched Peter's, mine wouldn't shake. I heard it from my colleague Chad, whose office I'd retreated to after I got the call from the hospital, fear and sadness rattling my mother-in-law's voice.

It's what my friends would tell me when I called them for reassurance often in the middle of the night. Even the woman at the hospital reception desk tossed out the phrase, eyeing me with pity as I rushed past her to Peter's room.

I supposed it was better than "It will be okay," especially when it became clear that no, it wouldn't, and might never be again. But it had become a litany, a throwaway line that sounded profound yet really had no meaning—a shield meant to protect the sayer from grappling with my grief rather than a balm to give me comfort.

Take it one day at a time? What did that even mean? I was living second to second, distracting myself for minutes, maybe an hour, before reality flooded back in, overtaking me. I would stay there submerged before I found a task where I could shift my focus, allowing me to regain my bearings and come up for air.

All right, I thought. *You say to take it one day at a time? Well, let me show you what my days are really like.*

I grabbed my iPhone. Peter was lying in his hospital bed, wan, weary, wanting to go home, but somehow upbeat. We were watching the New England Patriots play the Denver Broncos in a *Monday Night Football* matchup. Given our hometowns, it was obvious where our loyalties lay, and in our past, we'd always had a great time when they duked it out on the field, shouting, boasting, and needling each other over every touchdown and play.

That day, the Broncos were winning, a rarity. Rarer still was this interlude for Peter and me at this point in our lives.

We'd fallen in love instantly and gotten married less than two years after our first date. But unlike our courtship, our marriage had been fraught. Starting a family and imagining a future together meant we couldn't paper over misunderstandings about how each of us, a

Black woman and a white man, experienced the world. And when we had to weather an overwhelming tragedy, the loss of our first-born, it was too much for our love to bear. We eventually separated, living apart for almost three years, much of it on different sides of the Hudson River. I couldn't remember the last time we'd watched a game together. And it was doubtful we'd ever get another chance to sit side by side, cheering on the Broncos and the Patriots.

At that second, I wished I could grab the moment in midair, cup it in my palm, and relive it whenever I wanted. But I couldn't. Once a second ticked by, it was gone forever. All I had was my camera to freeze a memory, to record a reflection, to keep what was vanishing alive.

One day at a time.

I raised my phone; got the blue, red, and orange uniforms blurring together on the TV in focus; and clicked the button.

• • •

Death had always shadowed me. By the time I was eight, all of my grandparents were dead. The only grandparent I ever knew was my mother's mother. I can't easily recall her name, only that everyone—her five daughters, her grandchildren, the postman—called her Mama. One thing that I do clearly remember is that she was very, very scary.

Statuesque, with black hair tumbling down her back, Mama was formidable, a force to behold and endure. My mother and I inherited our steel from her along with our blade-like cheekbones. Still, once you got past our sharp edges, my mother and I were softer. We sat together and laughed. We even kissed each other goodbye. I don't remember Mama ever giving anybody a kind word, let alone a hug.

She spoke in abrupt bursts, just long enough to tell you to pipe down or to pick up your toys. There was no pleasure in her conversation, only direction and purpose.

And yet Mama baked bread. Warm, wonderful, delicious bread that she made in a clay oven that sat in her front yard. She was renowned for it, and those loaves became her main source of income and a path toward a sliver of independence. My grandfather, a builder who constructed many of the buildings in Ghana's capital, Accra, provided well for his children. But Grandfather—tall, wealthy, larger than life—had many wives and even more girlfriends. Polygamy wasn't common, but it was accepted in Ghanaian culture, and he took full advantage. Mama was no doubt unhappy with her situation, and so she didn't treat anybody very well, including her own daughters. But she'd carved out a space that was all her own, selling baked goods that were warm, soul-filling, and so different from the woman who'd made them. Even when I was seven years old, the irony of that juxtaposition was not lost on me.

By my eighth birthday, Mama was gone, her stern voice nothing more than a murmur I'd occasionally hear in my dreams. Her passing wasn't surprising, or, given her coldness, especially sad. After all, my grandfathers and other grandmother had left the world before I was born, so death had always been around. I knew that dying young, dying prematurely, wasn't inevitable. But it was certainly possible.

Years later, when I was seventeen, I was sitting in my bedroom watching an episode of *Beverly Hills, 90210*, a fluffy teen melodrama that was must-see TV for my friends and me. One of the lead characters, Brenda, played by the actress Shannen Doherty, did a self-exam of her breast. That captured my attention. *Maybe*, I thought, *I should do one too.*

I stood in the shower the next morning, the soap bubbling down the drain as I examined my left breast. And there it was. A tiny lump.

I freaked out. I don't know if I even turned the water off before I grabbed a towel and yelled for my mother. The fear on her face when I told her what I'd felt, what I'd found, made me even more afraid. She called my doctor and made an appointment.

A couple of days later, sitting in the office after he'd examined me, the doctor said they would have to do a biopsy to determine whether the lump was benign or malignant. But we couldn't schedule it right away. I would have to wait roughly a month for my procedure.

While death had always hovered, near enough that it wasn't unfamiliar, I had never feared it would actually touch me. I was seventeen, in my final semester of high school, and the road ahead seemed endless. I wasn't one of those teenagers unsure about their destiny, about whether they wanted to go to college or straight to work, to see the world or stay close to home. I had a solid plan. I would go to Wesleyan, then forge a career, maybe not in medicine like my father hoped, but doing something that could make a mark.

But when I felt that tiny mound beneath my skin, for the first time I thought maybe my plans, my future, weren't so secure after all. For the first time, it felt as though I could die young, die prematurely, and that it wasn't inevitable, but it was possible. Even for me.

I thought about that lump every moment of every day. When I took a shower or sat on my bed putting on lotion, I would push the skin up around it, its outline carved in sharp relief, and stare, wondering what it was. Was it innocent? Would it kill me? I felt like I was being assaulted, that my body had been invaded. As I sat in class trying to absorb formulas or moved in sync with the other cheerleaders during our after-school drills, that lump would shove its way into my thoughts. It got to the point where I could feel it without touching it. It took on a life of its own.

Time moved faster after the procedure. We got the news quickly that the lump was a benign cyst.

But I was still afraid. My doctor told me that even though I didn't have cancer, I should remain vigilant, on the lookout for any new growths. "Get a mammogram every year," he said. "Schedule it on your birthday so you don't forget."

It felt macabre to mark the celebration of every year I'd been alive with an exam that reminded me of my mortality. But I dutifully scheduled my next checkup for January 21 the following year, and on or close to that date every year after.

. . .

I always followed rules, eager to be the good Ghanaian daughter. I was the girl perched in class before the bell rang with minutes to spare. While many of my friends called the adults in their lives by their first names, I greeted them with *ma'am* and *sir.* My classmates noticed.

One day, Eric, the beautiful quarterback on the football team, turned to me, a ninth grader sitting in tenth-grade math, as we engaged in our regular classroom ritual of passing our assignments forward.

"Do you always have your homework?" he asked, incredulity wrinkling his brow.

His words didn't compute, and not just because I was distracted by his hazel eyes. It had never occurred to me that I could not have my homework. That just wasn't possible.

That is, until after I found that lump. While other kids might have snuck their first blunt in middle school or crept out of the house to meet friends as soon as they hit their teens, I waited until my last days of high school to finally rebel.

My rebellion wasn't enough to totally derail me. I had a whole stack of college acceptance letters taped on my bedroom wall. But I began to skip classes. C's were scrawled in red ink across the tops of essays and tests where I was used to seeing A's. Eric turned to me one day, and for the first time I had no paper to give him.

I was no longer just lying about a sleepover with a friend when I was really going to a party. I also began to sneak out at night, climbing out the window of my basement bedroom. My best friends, Summer, Joniquea, and Danielle, would pick me up a block or two away, and we'd meet the rest of our crew in the woods, where we'd chug Jack Daniel's and puff cigars. I'd barely make it home before morning. Soon there were days when I didn't go to school at all. I'd grab my backpack, walk out the door, and head to the house of a friend whose parents were at work to listen to gangster rap and watch music videos all day. Track practice was done for the year, but I would have gladly skipped that too.

When the unexcused absences began to pile up, I think my guidance counselor chalked up some of my misbehavior to senior fever, the affliction that grabbed hold of twelfth graders who'd taken their SATs, received their college acceptance and rejection letters, and now no longer gave a damn.

But I wasn't misbehaving simply because it was fun. My antics were a way to distract myself from the anxiety I feared might consume me, to rise above my melancholy. For the first time I was worried about illness, about death, about having to wrestle with forces that were beyond my control.

And who could I talk to about that worry? Not my mother. She'd shown glimmers of concern after I first found the lump, but mostly she was stoic, and I knew she expected the same posture from me. And I couldn't talk to my friends. They were different from me now.

My worries were greater than a grade on a midterm or whether I'd get a date for prom. I spent my eighteenth birthday resting on a couch after having a procedure on my breast. I'd had a glimpse of terrible things. Summer, Jonikquea, Danielle, and all the rest were still, blissfully, blind.

Finally, my guidance counselor called me into his office to find out what the hell was going on. He also asked my mother to come in and discuss why her oldest daughter, so smart, so popular, so certain, was suddenly struggling to get a B and missing assignments and classes.

For the second time in just a few weeks, I saw a look of fear cross my mother's face.

"What is wrong?" she asked as we drove home from school following our meeting.

I couldn't tell her. I didn't know how to articulate how I felt, what I now knew. That youth was no guard against death. And how whenever I tried to forget, a scar on my left breast was there to remind me.

Death hovered, always. It crept in, robbing my father of his mother before he could speak. It snatched Mama, leaving her clay oven forever untended and cold. I'd sidestepped death for now. But I knew it would keep taking.

4

The First Loss

After spending hours at the hospital with Peter, I decided to head back to my apartment. I wanted to change my clothes.

I needed to catch my breath.

The news of his terminal diagnosis left me with no appetite, but I fixed some spaghetti for Lael before pouring water for her bath and putting her to bed. Then I lay down beside her, desperately wanting sleep to come. I would have done anything for a few hours where I didn't have to think or even dream. But my thoughts kept returning to the terrible truth I'd learned in the hospital that day and all the unthinkable moments and tasks that were still ahead.

Finally, I got up and wandered over to the bookcase in my living room. There sat works of literature I'd discovered at Wesleyan, classics that dazzled me with their melodies and prose.

Love Poems, by Nikki Giovanni. *I Know Why the Caged Bird Sings*, by Maya Angelou. *The Fire Next Time*, by James Baldwin.

They were required reading for my college courses, but I continued to reread them on my own. They'd always given me so much joy.

Now, in the midst of my terror, I turned to them again.

I plucked a book from a shelf, lay down on my couch, and let Nikki Giovanni's odes to love lull me to sleep.

. . .

"What are you doing at Clark?"

This white boy had to be out of his mind. There he was, sitting at X House, the hub of Black student life at Wesleyan, asking why I'd become a resident advisor at Clark, a mostly white dorm.

I was living in Clark because it was the only dormitory that had an open resident advisor position and I needed money. I was cobbling together my tuition with a combination of student loans, financial aid, and checks I made from working two or three jobs. When I wasn't coordinating fire drills and enforcing quiet hours at Clark, I checked out books in the main library as well as the space dedicated to African American studies adjacent to X House. I was also that Black girl on a largely white campus who could do hair, nails, and even mend clothes in my dorm room for a few extra dollars. But none of that was Ben's business.

"What are *you* doing *here*?" I asked him.

That was more of a rhetorical slap than a real question. I knew why he was there. Ben was always around the Black kids on campus, a wealthy white boy from Geneva, who spoke French with a British accent and wanted to be a rapper when he grew up.

That evening, we were sitting near each other during one of X House's many poetry slams. Ben was getting ready to perform. He just laughed at my dirty look and snippy reply. A little while later he took the stage and rolled out his rhymes. He was actually quite the lyricist. I'd heard him perform many times before, and I enjoyed hearing his bars flow.

I lingered through a handful of other poets—a girl named Khadine who performed a pantomime during her spoken trills, a guy named Umi whose sleepy eyes belied his ferocious delivery—then I put on my sweater and prepared to walk home.

"Hey, Bozoma," Ben said as I headed for the door. "Can I walk you back to Clark?"

· · ·

Compared to Colorado, Wesleyan was a multicultural oasis. The school was predominantly white, based in Middletown, Connecticut, which was as vanilla as its name. But the college took its liberal arts focus literally, teaching a canon that centered around the voices of Chinua Achebe and N. Scott Momaday—not just those of old white men. In the middle of campus sat el-Hajj Malik el-Shabazz House (X House), named for the great thinker, orator, and activist better known as Malcolm X. I discovered it before my first day of freshman year and immediately applied on the housing forms to live there.

If Blackness was something you could measure on a Richter scale, I was off the chart.

English literature was one of my two majors, but I soon became immersed in my other emphasis, African American studies. At most hours of the day, you could find me at the library dedicated to Black thought. It was cramped, with barely enough space to pass between the rickety desks and the stacks. "Are they serious?" I asked myself the first time I saw it. It was almost a cliché that they would dedicate such a dim, shabby space to the study of Black scholarship. But

I loved riffling through those shelves, plucking out tomes penned by Baldwin, Brooks, and DuBois, then sitting down and devouring their words late into the evening. I also performed in Wesleyan's West African dance troupe. And I was head of the Ujamaa Organization, a group that amplified the voices of Black students on campus.

It was the mid-nineties, the era of Rodney King's beating and O. J. Simpson's verdict, and a moment—not unlike the period after the murder of George Floyd nearly thirty years later—when the spotlight was on anti-Black racism and systemic injustice. Despite its liberal leanings, Wesleyan had problems similar to virtually every other majority-white campus in America. My freshman year there were maybe four Black male students, who were arrested by the Middletown police and kept overnight in jail for ridiculous infractions, like walking down Main Street without identification. Ujamaa demonstrated in front of the police station, protesting that blatant bigotry. We held weekly meetings and called on local civic leaders and Wesleyan alumni to address the discrimination that we faced.

When we weren't agitating, we were throwing bomb-ass parties. There was a sweaty bashment every weekend in X House's basement. And there was a spades game every day all school year long. I didn't know how to play when I got to Wesleyan, but I learned in my first week. There was no way I was going to be left out of those marathon sessions, where we paired up and smacked down cards, talking trash, howling with laughter. We were a community—engaged, aware, but always ready to blow off steam and have a damn good time.

Wesleyan also introduced me to the first young Africans in the U.S. whom I wasn't related to. Unlike me, they were from the boroughs of New York City, where they had a bustling community all their own, as well as international students who hadn't grown up in the U.S. at all. But I felt a bond with them, and not just because of our literal roots.

The foreign students were outcasts in a way, straddling two worlds, not fully belonging to either. On holidays, they'd often have to stay on campus because home was too far away and expensive to get to for a short break. I related to them because my father had once been in their shoes and I'd grown up hearing his stories about how hard it was, how he was so homesick those first few months on that very same campus, he wouldn't eat. Dad lost so much weight that the skin began to sag on his long, narrow frame, and he would hallucinate about Ghana.

Eventually, my dad was taken in by the families of a couple of his Jewish friends. They fed him matzoh ball soup and brisket, and he'd join them on high holy days, washing down potato kugel with tiny glasses of Manischewitz wine. My father said that their passion about tradition, about ritual, about family, felt familiar. It felt African. And it made Connecticut's winters a little less cold.

I believed I could do for the African students on campus what my father's Jewish friends had done for him, providing comfort and friendship. I also wanted to be a bridge between them and the young African Americans on campus who didn't always automatically feel a connection, though we all shared a far-off history.

Nana Kwabena was from Ghana. He and I would whisper to each other in Twi and Fanti, laughing and gossiping about classmates who even within earshot didn't have a clue what we were saying. Lemu was a graduate student from Cameroon, and Georgina was another Ghanaian who was a year ahead of me at Wesleyan and who had grown up in New York. We'd party until early morning, then arrive bleary eyed to our first classes. Our tiny group was like an annex to X House, a separate circle within our Afrocentric hive.

But I most identified with the Black American students. I had grown up in the U.S., this conflicted country so scornful of the dark-skinned people who etched the contours of its culture, who gave it its swagger, and challenged its soul. I was proud to be part of a strand in that complex, awesome history.

Yet, like my international classmates, I too sometimes felt like I was on the outside looking in. Many of the Black students were from New York, and they had cultural touchstones all their own.

"I had to walk a mile when the G wasn't working, all the way to the Slave," Kevin, a freshman who grew up in the Bedford-Stuyvesant neighborhood of Brooklyn, said one day after returning from winter break.

"The G?" I asked. "The Slave?"

Kevin dismissed me with a smirk, then returned to his conversation with the couple other New Yorkers sitting at our table. He couldn't be bothered to try to translate or explain. It was often like that. A mention of a party spot over here, a neighborhood over there, or some legendary moment in Brooklyn lore that I was totally clueless about.

At those times, I was left with questions and not just about the places and memories that they were referencing. Were there aspects of Blackness that I didn't get? It was true that I didn't know anything about being Black on the East Coast. I just knew about Blackness among the mountains of Colorado. Was there a difference? Was there something I'd missed? Were there codes that I couldn't unlock, aspects of Black identity that would always be foreign to me? I didn't know. It made me feel a little insecure.

But there was a language that we all spoke, that all of us understood. And that was hip-hop.

Rap was the bumping backdrop to our on-campus lives, electrifying our parties, stoking fierce debates during our games of spades, and putting us in a trance as we floated on the melody of a newly discovered mixtape. We'd argue through the night. Who was more influential, Public Enemy or Grand Master Flash? Was Queen Latifah really the greatest female rapper of all time? Or might that be Lil' Kim?

No conversation was more heated than the battle over East Coast versus West Coast rap. And I was fearless in the face of East Coast snobbery when I was talking about my greatest of all time, Tupac Shakur.

I was obsessed with Tupac, the child of a Black Panther who found his voice on the streets of Oakland before blowing up and becoming a movie star as well as a rap icon. He was murdered in 1996 during the start of my sophomore year, leaping in death from luminary to legend.

The East Coast cabal was always singing the praises of the Notorious B.I.G., the other protagonist in a hip-hop tragedy who took on the trappings of Shakespeare when he was murdered less than a year after 'Pac. But Tupac Shakur, with his doe eyes and dope lyrics, was my number one. I loved him so much that I even taught a class about him.

I'd heard about a lyrical poetry course offered at the University of Southern California that focused on Tupac's music. I didn't see why Wesleyan couldn't do something similar.

I approached one of my American studies professor, Jeffrey Kerr-Ritchie. If anybody could understand the relevance of such a class, it had to be him. He was biracial, with short dark curls. And he had a tattoo on his right forearm. Everybody had a crush on him and tried to take his course just to get a dose of his beauty and brilliance twice a week. We would pile into his class, and when he rolled up the sleeve of his button-down shirt, we'd salivate watching the edge of that tattoo slide in and out of view.

But when I asked if he might be willing to teach the class, he didn't mince words.

"I have no interest in that at all," he said curtly. "But if you write the curriculum and petition the dean to put it on the schedule, I'll sponsor it."

It was like a dare. I'm sure he thought I'd just drop the idea and move on. But this was about Tupac, so in between classes on the American labor movement and Black feminism, I wrote a sixteen-week curriculum for a course I dubbed simply, "Tupac, His Life and Times."

I set up an appointment with my class dean. Fidgeting nervously by his desk as he pored over my syllabus, scanning the topics and potential assignments, I waited impatiently for his decision.

"Well," he said, peering over his silver wire-rimmed glasses, "we can't give students full credit for this."

My heart sank.

"But it can be an elective worth half a credit," he continued. "And since I don't think any of the professors have time to fit this into their current schedules, how about you teach the class?"

I marched right over to Professor Kerr-Ritchie's office. When I told him the course had not only been approved but that I would be the one teaching it, his mouth dropped. I think it was the first and only time I ever saw him look a little uncool.

I had thirty-two students when we offered the course for the first time in the spring, as well as a waiting list with the names of at least a dozen more who wanted to get in. I taught at seven p.m. Tuesdays and Thursdays because during the day I was carrying a full course load of my own.

There was nothing else on campus quite like it. Instead of the typical classroom, we clustered in the lobby of X House, students splayed on the floor or sprawled on the threadbare couches. We brought potato chips and donuts to share, and even Professor Kerr-Ritchie would occasionally stop by to listen and chime in to the discussion.

Unlike other teachers, I chose to do the homework right along with my students. For one assignment I asked the class to write down the lyrics of a Tupac rap that hadn't gotten radio play. The task was to take a stanza from the lyrics and interpret what he was trying to say, dissecting Tupac's poetry the same way a student might parse the meaning of words penned by William Butler Yeats or Walt Whitman.

This was before the internet, when you could summon the lyrics of a song by clicking on Google. You had to track down those obscure recordings, then spend hours listening. I picked "Only God Can Judge Me," a hip-hop hymn to fearlessness and self-determination, and I hit play and rewind until my finger was sore, trying to get the lyrics down and wondering halfway through why the hell I gave this assignment in the first place.

But the effort was worth it. Class lasted an extra hour because it took so much time for everyone to rap, then talk about their respective lyrics. Yet we were all having such a good time, no one complained and everyone stayed until the end.

I taught my class on Tupac for three semesters, and nearly twenty-five years later, people still remember it. Not long ago, I put a post on Facebook about a class I was teaching at Harvard called "The Anatomy of a Bad Ass," on the art of boldly building a personal brand. One of my Wesleyan classmates, Jason, reached out.

"I hope you include some assignments like the ones in your course on Tupac!"

I hadn't thought of it. But I definitely started looking for those notes.

. . .

Well before Ben walked me home for the first time, we'd been in each other's orbit because I briefly dated one of his friends, Leevert.

I use the term *dated* loosely. It was hard to claim Leevert, who strolled through campus with an LA strut and a fade haircut so tight, he looked like he'd stepped out of a Benetton ad. I'd never had a boyfriend before, and rocking with Leevert to the beats of EPMD at an X House party gave me a thrill, thinking that out of all the girls on campus, Leevert had chosen me.

Never mind that during the day he fist-bumped me like a friend. Playing platonic in public, then sneaking kisses in his room after dark felt romantic, like we were having an affair. I fell for him hard.

It took me several months to realize that our under-the-radar trysts were less about passion and more about staying in the shadows so all the women Leevert was juggling wouldn't find out about one another. When word filtered back to me about all the other girls he was dating, I broke it off. I returned to campus after summer break very much single.

I moved into Clark dormitory for my RA job but still spent most of my free time at X House. And despite Leevert's playboy ways, I remained hopeful that one day I'd find my Black prince. While the white girls on my floor flocked to dark theaters to swoon over Jack Dawson, the poor artist played by Leonardo DiCaprio in *Titanic,* I was dreaming about Darius Lovehall, the cutie-pie poet brought to life by Larenz Tate in the classic romance film *Love Jones.*

Darius declared his ardor for Nina, played by Nia Long, with scats and rhymes. That's what I wanted. Black love, a *Love Jones* love, my own co-starring role in a cocoa-hued fairy tale. Instead, I found Ben.

After our encounter at the poetry slam, he seemed to show up wherever I was, outside my dorm, in the campus center. I thought it was cute that someone so confident and brash in front of an audience was too shy to just come out and say he wanted to see me. Finally, Ben suggested we go to lunch. I was flattered and intrigued. I said yes. Our love affair had begun.

We went to concerts on campus and spent nights in our cluttered dorm rooms debating the bona fides of Too Short and DJ Quik. During open mic night, I abandoned my typical perch in the back of the X House basement to bask in the front row, snapping my fingers furiously to the beats of Ben's rhymes.

Ben was romantic, bringing me cups of hot chocolate on bitter winter nights. I didn't tell my family about my new love, knowing that my father wouldn't approve of my taking time away from my studies for any man, let alone one who was white and wanting to be a rapper. But unlike my previous entanglement with Leevert, my new relationship breathed in the daylight. Ben and I kissed before class, walked hand in hand through campus, and cuddled under trees on the Hill. We were inseparable.

It wasn't Black love, but it didn't feel that far off. Ben mostly hung around with Black students who embraced him as one of their own. We lived and loved inside that safe, ebony campus bubble. We were never in the real world together, but we dreamed of it. We imagined the adventures we'd have carving out a future in Manhattan, the alphabet soup of subway lines becoming as familiar to us as they were to the New York classmates who scoffed at my ignorance.

Ben didn't rap about cars or girls or money. He delved into the esoteric and the spiritual, the metaphysical and philosophical. And love. He wasn't derivative or patronizing, cribbing experiences that he couldn't relate to. He was fully in his lane, never pretending to be anything other than the rich white boy from Geneva that he was.

Ben was buoyant when he was spitting rhymes:

> *If I could turn back the hands of time*
> *Bo-bo I'd lick the sweat off your neck*
> *Mad scared I could eva lose you*
> *Your love is crucial*
> *Relationship unfinished like your tattoos boo*

And in between classes, when we were discussing politics and literature, he was thoughtful and engaging.

"Think about it, Dino," he'd say, using the nickname he'd created for me. "Is it worth it for Black people to give Bill Clinton a pass because he acknowledges them when his policies feed on every stereotype to squash economic aid, and also send a whole bunch of Black folks to prison?"

He had a point. He usually did.

The nights, however, were different. Ben had a difficult time getting to sleep, and on the cusp of sunrise, restless but unable to rest, exhausted but unable to sleep, Ben would often curl up beside me in my dorm room and tell me his deepest, darkest thoughts.

"I'll never make it, Dino," he'd say, his face buried in my shoulder. "I'm not good enough. And if I can't make it in music, there's nothing else for me. There's no point in going on."

In hindsight, his melancholy was troubling. But back then, I didn't know the signs of mental illness. I just chalked up Ben's moodiness to his being eccentric, to his being creative, and to his being desperately in love with me.

He tells me stuff he would never tell anyone, I'd think during moments when I was alone. For me, a girl who, until her senior year in high school, could honestly say she'd never done more than kiss a guy, it was unbelievably exhilarating and cool.

One night, when Ben was unspooling the reel of thoughts racing through his mind, I gazed at him intently, struggling to keep pace. I've always been known for my stare, and to this day, people often comment about the intensity of it, how it can make them feel like a thief caught sneaking away under the streetlights.

Ben's stream of consciousness suddenly stopped.

"Why are you looking into my soul?" he said angrily. Before I could figure out how to answer, he stood up and stormed out of my room. I was stunned.

Ben didn't speak to me for four days. He wouldn't return my calls, and when he spotted me in a hallway, he'd quickly turn and walk the other way. When the thaw finally came nearly a week later, he just showed up at my place, like nothing had happened.

I wasn't having it.

"What was that?" I asked him. "How could you just walk out and then not talk to me for days?"

"Oh, I don't know," he said casually as if he could erase the memory of his bizarre tantrum with the wave of his hand. "I was just feeling kind of weird. Forget it. Want to go get dinner?"

I didn't understand. But I was so relieved that he was speaking to me, I ignored my unease.

It was actually surprising that Ben had let me roam campus for days without his hanging by my side. He was very jealous, and when he was overcome by one of his dark moods, he'd accuse me of not loving him, muttering how it might be better for both of us if he just disappeared.

Again, looking through the telescope of time, I know now that Ben's behavior was troubling, that it was manipulative and possibly even abusive. But in the moment, I focused instead on how badly he clearly needed me. I would kiss his cheek, or press against his chest, trying to convince him how much I loved him.

I believed his words flowed from insecurity, not illness. And why would I have thought otherwise? Before Ben, the only person I'd ever known who'd experienced depression was me.

. . .

I began to struggle emotionally after my health scare at the end of high school. Before then, I'd always thought depression manifested solely in a person's mood and their mind. But I felt it in my bones. Activities that used to animate me were suddenly uninteresting. And I'd often leave my breakfast or dinner untouched because I had no appetite.

I carried that numbness to Wesleyan, where it became startlingly clear that these feelings weren't going to just go away. I didn't bother discussing them during my calls home. There would have been no empathy. Mom would probably just tell me to pray; worse, my father might tell me I had nothing to pray about.

"It's okay. Just focus on your studies," I could hear him saying. "Do you know what your people have been through? You're not depressed. You're very privileged."

But when I finally went to the campus health center a few weeks into my freshman year because I wasn't feeling well, the physician on duty quickly surmised that I was depressed. I thought he was going to assign me a counselor who would drill down to the roots of my anxiety and fears. Instead, he prescribed Prozac.

The green-and-white pills left a metallic taste in the back of my throat, and I would try to douse the bitterness with a glass of orange juice or sips of 7Up. They were awful, but at least they made me feel a little bit like the girl I might have been if I'd never watched that episode of *Beverly Hills, 90210*, like the young woman I would have grown into if I hadn't discovered that tiny lump in my breast.

I took a pill every day as soon as I woke up. It was my armor, a secret weapon that somehow made me feel more confident about facing the day. Still, it was no elixir. While it kept me from sinking too low, it kept me from feeling the highs as well. I felt protected, but no joy.

It was the simple things that I lost, like the surge I felt back home in Colorado during Friday-night football games, cheering along with the roar of the crowd. I'd watch the Wesleyan Cardinals pick up yards on the football field and I'd play the part, leaping from my seat to participate in the wave or poking a foam finger in the night air. But in reality, there was no rush, no excitement. I felt nothing.

Before Prozac, I'd pick up a novel and get lost in the story, feeling the emotions of the characters as I immersed myself in their world. I still enjoyed books, but whereas I once could experience the passion Janie felt when she first laid eyes on Tea Cake in *Their Eyes Were Watching God*, now I was just an observer, like a fan watching a TV show. It was as if I was wrapped inside a cotton ball. Nothing could bruise me. But I couldn't feel the good stuff either.

I didn't like that purgatory. But it was better than having the blues and sleepwalking through the day.

Ben would watch me take my daily dose and shake his head. "You don't need those, Dino," he'd say. "You're fine."

That was our ballet, each of us trying to reassure the other. Each of us believing we could talk the other into being happy, into being well. If only.

. . .

After junior year, my relationship with Ben would warm, then cool. During the warmer moments, we'd resume our fantasy about living together in New York. Then, Ben's grades hit rock bottom and Wesleyan told him that he had to leave. Our Manhattan dreams became more urgent. He wanted to move there when he left campus, and he said I should join him after graduation.

Ben's parents back in Switzerland put an end to all that. What was he going to do in New York with no job and no prospects? They agreed to get him his own apartment, but he'd have to come home to Geneva.

After he moved, he called often, but sometimes we reached out to each other with a simple email.

"I think we've both been thinking about the 'L' word for a while and you said it," he wrote after I had told him I loved him. "I haven't said that word to anyone for so long I don't even know what it means but I do know that I like it when you say it to me."

"Yo, you should come here this summer. Serious, give it a try!" he wrote in another message. "Can't you tell your pops you're visiting a friend in Europe or touring or some shit? Tell him to come too. We can all chill in the same bed. Even if you just come and stay for 24 hrs. It will be worth it . . . Gotta go. You touched the depths of my perverted emotions, Dino. I'm about you. Love you more, Ben."

But it wasn't long before the messages and phone calls began to grow dark, and I started to fear that something was seriously wrong. Burrowed in his apartment, Ben tried to work on his music. But depression would sweep over him like a wave, washing away his desire to rap, to write, to create. He drank constantly and seemed to always have a blunt close at hand.

"Things in my head, Dino, they're not right," he said during one of his calls to me when it was the middle of the night in Geneva. "I have wild thoughts. Bad thoughts."

I asked him if he'd seen a doctor and told him medication might help. But he brushed me off, repeating what he'd always told me, that none of that was necessary. It was all very disjointed, how he could recognize something was off but would not take the steps to do anything about it.

And then there was "Diego," Ben's name for the imaginary lover he said I was sneaking around with behind his back. His jealousy ramped up with his anxiety, and he began to constantly accuse me of cheating.

"Diego must be in Hawaii," Ben said when I mentioned that after graduation, I might try to find a job in a place that was warm and vaguely exotic, like the island state. "You know I can't make it there! What hard rapper is from Hawaii? You're going there to hang out with your other dude."

After a while, it began to feel like Ben actually believed Diego was real, that he'd heard me call his name in the middle of the night or found him lying in my bed. As Ben's obsession grew, I sometimes wished there *was* someone named Diego—calm, stable, secure within himself—who would scoop me up and whisk me away.

One night, Ben called to tell me that a girl had been at his apartment.

"She left her bra here," he said tauntingly.

It was such an odd, cruel detail to throw out. "Why would you tell me that?" I asked him.

"If you can cheat, so can I!" he shouted.

I was hurt. I was angry. But mostly I was getting scared. Ben didn't seem rational. I didn't know what to do.

I'll love him harder, I thought when I hushed my anger about his alleged affair. *With every other sentence, I'll tell him how much he matters to me, to his friends, to his parents.*

But even though I wanted to pull him closer, he just seemed to slip further and further away. Until one day, he began calling me incessantly.

"You don't love me," he mumbled. "What's the point of being together if you're going to just sleep with somebody else?"

It was the same conversation we'd had a million times. My nerves ragged, I called my girlfriends Leander and Clare, and they suggested I get out of my apartment for a bit and go to dinner with them. I didn't have a cell phone, so when Ben called yet again, I told him I was heading out for a while and he wouldn't be able to reach me.

"Leander and Clare? Yeah, right. I know you're going out with Diego," he shouted.

Again, with that damn Diego. *I wish there was a Diego,* I thought. *Then I wouldn't have to deal with your ass.*

"I've gotta go," I said instead. "I'll ring you when I get back if it's not too late."

I put on a jacket, grabbed my purse, and clicked off the TV. As I shut the door behind me, I heard the phone ring.

I could have turned around and answered. But I was so tired. And that's what haunts me.

. . .

When I got back to my apartment a couple of hours later, the red light was blinking on my answering machine. I grew tense. I had told Ben I was going out, so why had he continued to blow up my phone? This had to stop. I pushed play.

There were four, maybe five messages, each more anxious and desperate than the last.

"Where are you?" Ben asked in the first call. "Call me back."

"You haven't called me back!" he said in his next message, left not more than fifteen minutes later. "I really need to talk to you."

The next time I heard his voice, Ben admitted he was unraveling. "I don't feel good," he said, his voice pleading and scared. "I'm leaving my apartment. You have to call me."

In the last message, Ben told me where his fragile mind had led him. He was standing on a bridge in the middle of Geneva. For the first time that day, he sounded almost calm.

The water was moving fast, Ben said, like it was anxious to get to where it needed to be. He'd called his good friend Dave, who also lived in Geneva, but not until he'd made his way to the bridge. Ben said he knew if he'd called from his apartment, Dave would have headed there to try to stop him.

The river below was the quickest way to end it all, Ben reasoned. He'd never survive a plunge into that water, rushing so furiously.

"Bye, Dino," he said. And he hung up.

He couldn't have jumped, I thought, my mind leaping between fear and disbelief. I dialed Ben's number. As soon as I spoke to him and confirmed he was all right, I was going to tear into him for scaring me like that. It wasn't funny. It wasn't cute.

I dialed, and dialed, and dialed. I hoped he was just mad and try-ing to punish me for going out, for not staying home and soothing him. But with every call I made that went unanswered, every call that went straight to voicemail, a feeling of dread swelled up inside me.

I called Jeremy, one of Ben's closest friends when we were at Wes-leyan.

"Nah," Jeremy said repeatedly, like he was trying to convince himself as well as me. "Nah, nah, nah. He wouldn't do that."

"Yeah, right?" I said, wanting to believe him. Ben had always been dramatic and moody. But he'd never tried to hurt himself.

I just needed to hear his voice.

Hours passed. Finally, I shakily dialed Leander, who lived two floors above me. She convinced me to call Ben's parents. I don't think I could have summoned the nerve to call them without her prodding.

Ben's parents and I had never met. They'd never visited him on campus, but he said they knew about me. I had to call Jeremy to get their phone number. My voice trembled after his father said hello.

"This is Bozoma, Ben's girlfriend," I said. Had he heard from him?

"No," he said, concern creeping into his voice. "Why?"

I hadn't rehearsed this. I couldn't bring myself to tell him what Ben said.

"He left a message that kind of scared me, but hopefully every-thing's okay," I blurted out in a rush. "I've just been trying to reach him. Here's my number. Can you make sure he calls me when you catch up with him?"

An hour later, Ben's father called back. What exactly had Ben said?

I couldn't speak it. So, I played him Ben's last message. He began to wail.

The sound of his pain sparked the anguish burning inside me, but I tried to calm him. Ben was sad and scared, but he wouldn't go through with it, I told him. We just had to find him.

We knew the name of the bridge, and Dave didn't live that far from it. Maybe Ben was there, sitting on a bench, sad, lonely, but alive, gazing out at the water.

Dave raced to the bridge. But Ben wasn't there. His family called local authorities, who searched the water.

In the following hours, when my thoughts grew dark, I fought to find the light. If Ben wasn't on the bridge, then maybe he'd headed home. If they hadn't found his body immediately, maybe there was a chance he hadn't jumped. But then Dave called and confirmed they'd found Ben's body.

Then, there was no more hope, no more denial.

Then, I broke inside, sank to my knees, and sobbed.

. . .

When it came to attending Ben's funeral, I didn't have much money, but I did have a credit card that I'd been lured to open by one of those representatives who set up tables on campuses to get cash-strapped students started on the road to debt. I'd resisted using it but was glad I had it then so I could buy a last-minute round-trip ticket to Geneva.

Ben's parents insisted that I stay with their close friends, and not at a lonely hotel. His parents were wonderful, somehow warm and embracing in the midst of overwhelming grief. Ben had been their only child. Taking my hand, introducing me to their relatives and friends, I think they were looking for answers, and they hoped that maybe I had them. But I didn't. Not one.

I stayed only a couple of days, eager to get away from their sadness and back to my Middletown apartment, where I could mourn
alone. Before I headed back, I met with Dave. I wanted to see the
bridge.

He walked me there. I'd pictured some intimidating structure,
like San Francisco's Golden Gate, or maybe a picturesque European
span that had welcomed lovers and travelers for a hundred years.
But it turned out to be just an ordinary overpass, spare and unre-
markable.

I couldn't cross it. I couldn't bring myself to walk to the center
where Ben probably stood before leaping. I lingered at its entrance
and gazed at the water instead. It looked rough and cold, just like
Ben told me.

. . .

Often people say that when a person dies by suicide, those left behind are angry with their loved one for taking his or her life. But I
was never angry with Ben. I was only angry with myself.

I felt like I'd failed him, and that conjured a very specific type of
grief, a grief that was violent and sharp. Because along with the sadness came a feeling of responsibility. A feeling that somehow, I could
have prevented his death.

If only I had turned around, set down my purse, and picked up
that phone one last time. Surely it wasn't asking too much to take a
few more anguished calls so that I could save him. Maybe if I had
said one extra word, if I had found a different way to say I loved
him, I could have led him away from the darkness.

Maybe. Maybe. Maybe.

That Thursday night, at the dinner with Leander and Clare, they'd wanted to talk about Ben like girlfriends do.

"Do you really like him?" Leander asked.

"Why are you putting up with all his mess?" she and Clare asked, almost in unison.

I didn't want to admit my feelings. I didn't want to look weak, to admit that someone who worked my nerves so badly was also someone I couldn't get out of my system, a man I believed I couldn't live without.

We were sipping fruity drinks that were far too sweet, the sugary alcohol warming my blood and slurring my speech.

"I don't know," I said dismissively. "I don't really like him that much. I could take him or leave him."

But that was a lie. I loved him passionately, urgently, deeply. And my dishonesty that night has dogged me ever since. It's made me superstitious, because I fear that my denial set something loose in the universe that the truth could have put back in place. Or maybe it made God want to punish me, because in the end, I was weak. I was in love, but also exhausted, tired of always having to hold Ben. And for a second, I just wanted to put him down.

Now, years later, when a friend asks me about somebody I'm not supposed to love, about a situation that I'm supposed to be bigger than, I tell the truth about what I'm feeling. Instead of faking bravado because I fear looking weak, I say the truth out loud, because I believe words have power, that words have consequences. And I don't want my dishonesty to set off a reverberation in the universe that I can't stop. I don't want to be punished. Not like that, again.

I still have Ben's final messages. I recorded them on a little tape that in the age of thumb drives I can no longer play. But for years, when I still had a cassette player, I listened to them constantly, imagining what I would have said if I had been there to receive his calls.

It's like when someone snubs you at a party, or you get into an argument with a stranger. You replay the confrontation over and over again in your head, wishing you'd said something different, thinking of the scalding reply you'd unleash if you got the chance to do it all over again. I was obsessed, dreaming up an alternate reality, one where I'd been home when Ben made that last call from his apartment, of a parallel plane where I answered the phone when Ben was there shivering on that bridge.

It wasn't logical. I know now, when I separate emotion from reason, that I couldn't have saved Ben if he didn't want to save himself. If he hadn't jumped then, he might have jumped the next day, the next week, the next year. And I know all the musings in the world won't bring Ben back.

I had to forgive myself. But it took years, and I still haven't done so completely. I've had to learn that too is okay. Every wound doesn't heal the same. The same grace we're often so eager to give someone else, we have to be willing to offer ourselves.

Ben's death was not the last time in the face of tragedy I would feel I could have done more. I would have to learn what I could control and how to let go of what I could not.

5

Love in Black and White

Peter wanted to go home.

After the doctors determined that there was nothing more they could do, Peter's oncologist suggested he remain in the hospital. But Peter felt if there was no therapy, no medicine that could make him well, he wanted to get out of there.

Our family and friends had heeded my calls to spend time with Peter, driving from Massachusetts and Pennsylvania, flying in from Colorado and California. So when it was time to move Peter home, there were more hands on deck than there were items to gather as we stuffed photographs, shirts, and blue jeans into duffel bags; piled them into my car and taxis; and headed to New Jersey.

We were rolling about twenty deep. There was Peter's best friend and Lael's godfather, Mike Metzger, who we called Mecca; a bunch of Peter's Alpha Sigma Phi brothers; and Peter's parents, siblings, nieces, nephews, and a smattering of our close friends.

And what was the first thing we did when we got to Peter's apartment? What we'd always done when we got together. We partied.

When Peter and I lived together, before and after we were married, spontaneous gatherings were a weekly routine. In Manhattan, folks live on top of one another, so socializing spills out of those matchbox-size apartments into the bars and restaurants that peek out from virtually every storefront. But Peter and I often entertained at home, even when we lived in a studio apartment where the only thing separating the living room from our bed was a bookshelf.

Our parties were ridiculous fun. On a Friday or Saturday night, we'd make some calls or friends would randomly stop by. We'd order pizza and heat up leftovers, eating, laughing, and drinking until the sun cast a sheen over the East River.

The day we brought him home from the hospital, by the time Peter, his parents, and I pulled up to his place, a bunch of our friends had already stopped at the liquor store and picked up beer. We sent someone else to get Chardonnay and Cabernet Sauvignon for the wine drinkers, and I ordered a smorgasbord of Chinese, Italian, and Indian takeout.

I took a picture of Peter and his boys downing shots of some liquor. Someone else snapped a photo of Peter, me, and Lael sitting on the floor. That's still one of my most treasured photos. I posted it later on Facebook with a three-word caption: "This is us." It was my telling the world that no more explanation was necessary. This was us. Still together amid all our brokenness.

Improbably, incredibly, it felt like a celebration. Peter's frat brothers were teasing and embarrassing him with raunchy stories about old times. There were toasts, giddily and simply made "to Peter." It was like being back in that cramped studio apartment on a Friday night. It felt good because we all hadn't been together in so long. A neighbor down the hall hearing all the noise as they tossed trash down the chute would never have guessed that this was literally the worst day of our lives.

I poured drinks, posed for pictures, and filled paper plates with shrimp curry and chicken samosas. At times, I probably appeared to be happy. But looking back, I think I must have been in shock, a ghost floating around the room, watching, hovering, but not really present.

Late in the evening, tipsy, tired, we had to sober up enough to figure out where people would sleep. Several of our friends had driven straight to the hospital from the airport, so there'd been no time to line up hotel rooms. We hastily began trying to find couches and beds, at my mom's apartment, which was nearby; at my place in Manhattan, where Peter's mom and dad had been staying; at the apartment of my girlfriend, who had a pullout sofa and a pile of blankets to spare.

In the midst of all the chaos, panic intruded once again. Should I stay? Should I go?

We'd spent so much time apart during our separation. If Peter had only days to live, I should be with him, I reasoned, lying by his side, ready with a cool towel if he got a fever, leaning into all the time that we had left. But then I thought maybe he should have time alone with the other people who loved him, his mother and father, his brothers and sister.

So many questions. So many decisions. In the end, I decided to leave.

As weak as he was, Peter insisted on walking me to my car. We left the apartment, the revelry still going strong. We stood briefly in silence. Now that we'd decided to reconcile, our love felt brand-new, urgent, and somehow tentative. We were eager and also a little shy. He drew me in for a hug. Then he kissed me.

We hadn't kissed in nearly three years, not since our marriage began to fray and Peter moved out. So, in some ways, it was like a first kiss, yet also different. No butterflies welled up inside. It felt deeper. It felt like forgiveness, like he was forgiving me for all the things I'd done to hurt him, and I was forgiving him for dying, for leaving us with little time to love.

Going forward, I knew that there could be no more days like this, living life on the fly. We had to prepare. We had to greet what we knew was coming with a plan.

. . .

That kind of mindset was so unlike me. I was always the impulsive one, lacking in patience. If I had a craving, I wanted to taste it. If I had an idea, I wanted to put it in motion, not tomorrow but right now. It might be a job that I coveted, a car I had my eye on, or an acquaintance I declared after our first meeting was my new best friend.

But after Peter's terminal diagnosis, I felt my impatience had to feed a purpose. I needed to slow down, to be thoughtful, because time was running out. There would be no do-overs.

After we separated, Peter had gotten a new apartment in Edgewater, New Jersey, while I got a place on 115th Street and Fifth Avenue in Manhattan. But in light of his diagnosis, we decided to live together again and to move into my place in the city, which was a little closer to the hospital and, in my opinion, a whole lot cozier and comfortable.

I lay awake at night trying to figure out all the things I'd need from Peter that he'd soon be unable to share, like his passwords and log-ins. I needed them for everything, from his Facebook page to his iPhone. And as painful as it was to talk about, there was a funeral to plan. Were there certain songs Peter wanted played at the service? Who did he want to deliver the eulogy?

Those were hard, practical things that Peter typically understood. But as our days together wound down, our roles slowly began to reverse. Peter, the brooder and list maker, started to cast planning aside. I was preparing for the end, while Peter seemed to be drifting into a dream world where our future was vast and wide.

One afternoon we sat down at the dining table, our bank statements and insurance policies splayed out in front of us. A friend had referred us to a financial planner who was on speakerphone, helping us sort through tedious tasks like account transfers and powers of attorney. We hadn't told the planner about Peter's prognosis, only that he was battling an illness and we wanted to put things in order.

"I'd like to put money in a more aggressive stock account," Peter said, "but maybe we can watch the performance over the next few months and if it's really tanking, we can switch it to bonds or something safer."

"You may need to let the money ride a bit longer than that," the planner said, "but sure, we can revisit this in six months and see how you feel then."

Awkwardness hung in the air. I looked down at my hands, then at Peter. We didn't have six months. We had to make decisions we were both comfortable with right now.

"That sounds like a great idea," Peter suddenly blurted out.

I grew rattled. Did he just not want this finance guy to know what we were grappling with? We wrapped up the call, and I turned to face him.

"We can't wait," I said quietly. "We need to decide on an account we think is best today."

Peter looked at me, his eyes bright and hopeful. "Let's make a plan," he said. "But let's also put a meeting on the calendar for six months from now. Want to get some gelato?"

He enveloped himself in that optimism. For the first time in years, he, Lael, and I were all living under one roof, and Peter would constantly say how happy he was that our family was finally back together. Maybe, Peter mused one afternoon, we could look into moving farther upstate to the 'burbs and buy a house. Or at the very least we should think about one day getting a second home where we could go on weekends in the summer, maybe in Cape Cod, or closer, down the Jersey shore.

The set of notes he'd written, full of activities he wanted us to do, like going to an amusement park or having Vietnamese food at our favorite restaurant on the Upper East Side, suddenly seemed like a run-of-the-mill schedule instead of a bucket list. After we completed one of those excursions, Peter would talk excitedly about how he couldn't wait to do it again, though he had to know that was likely the last time we'd ever ride that roller coaster or eat pho looking out the window onto Second Avenue.

Maybe it was meant to protect me. Maybe it was meant to protect himself. Perhaps he thought that if he believed hard enough, he could make it so our ending hadn't been written. That he could stretch the band of time far enough to exceed all the doctors' expectations. But I began to feel like Peter was losing touch with reality. And it infuriated me.

There was no six months from now. There might not even be tomorrow. There was only today. Fate had made the decision for us.

I know that it sounds uncaring. Peter was the one facing the imminence of dying. But I was contemplating how to keep going, how to raise our child and exist without him. I felt that I was teetering at the edge of the abyss by myself, forced to be the reality check while bearing all the responsibility.

"Why are you not real with me?" I'd mutter to myself. "We don't have enough time for this bullshit."

Then there were those things Peter simply would not do. Like writing cards for Lael.

The thought must have been sparked by one of the blogs or websites I scanned late at night, trying to distract myself. The idea was for your loved one to write notes for the special moments they might not be here to celebrate, like an elderly grandparent leaving words of wisdom for a newborn grandson to absorb on his wedding day. I knew the weaker Peter became, the harder it would be for him to do things we took for granted, like holding a pen firmly to write down his thoughts. So, I asked Peter to write a bunch of cards to leave for Lael.

I envisioned the pink envelope Lael would open when she lost her first tooth and the lemon-colored note she would read on her first day of school. There would be a card for when she turned sweet sixteen, and others for when she got her driver's license or sat in her dorm room during her freshman year in college. I asked Peter to write what he would like her to know and to sign each one.

He just wouldn't do it. He kept putting it off, telling me he would get to it later. Even as he ticked off the final experiences he'd hurriedly written down and dreamed for himself, he wouldn't do this one thing I so wanted from him for Lael.

I understood that unlike a fishing trip on Lake George or a hike in the Poconos, contemplating what you would say to your child from the grave was overwhelming. But sometimes you had to face the hard choices. You had to take on the wrenchingly uncomfortable and just do what needed to be done.

What we were going through was far more serious than anything we'd ever experienced. Still, Peter's denial reminded me of something else that had always divided us. How there were so many things he didn't have to see, didn't have to deal with, that I, as a Black woman in a white-dominated world, couldn't afford to ignore. I had to do the work and contemplate the worst. I had to know the openings and the exits too. I had to anticipate, to be alert, to be ready.

Peter never did write those cards. I wish he had.

. . .

I spent my preteen and teenage years at the edge of the Rocky Mountains, starkly aware that not only was I Black, I was African. In part that's because my family didn't want me to forget. And in part it was because the world outside wouldn't let me.

With every fresh school year, I encountered the same problem. The teachers could never pronounce my name.

Sitting in class, I would brace myself, waiting. Since my last name was Arthur, I would be at the top of the attendance list and I grew to expect the teacher's awkward stumbling, as much a part of the semester's first day as the waxy sheen of the hallways and the autumn leaves beneath my feet.

"Umm," the teacher said, furrowing a brow. "Boo-Zee-May?"

It was amazing how they would mangle my name, sticking vowels where they didn't belong, stretching syllables like they were playing with a fat piece of bubble gum.

Boo-Zee-May? Really?

It would happen again whenever there was a substitute teacher. *Here we go*, I'd think as he or she paused, then took a deep breath as if they were about to swim a fifty-meter relay and not just read a child's name jotted in a ledger.

"Oh boy," he or she might say. "I know I'm going to mess this up . . ."

But when the school day ended, and I made it back to 1342 Adams Drive, I was thoroughly cocooned in a Ghanaian home. There we spoke Fanti, the language of our people. And unlike some immigrants who were eager to assimilate by tucking their traditions out of sight, my family reveled in their duality. When my friends came over, we didn't order pizza or make meatloaf. They sat with my parents and sisters at the table and ate fufu and light soup.

When we moved one last time, in the summer between seventh and eighth grade, to a different school district within the same town, I met the set of classmates I would be with through the twelfth grade. They were kind and even protective. After a while I no longer had to correct the teachers who stumbled over my name. I had a whole crew ready to do that for me. None more fiercely than my best friend Summer.

Green-eyed and blond, Summer had looks that mirrored her name. We'd met the year before, but it was in the ninth grade that we formed a bond. We'd both had a growth spurt over the summer, and when we spotted each other at the start of ninth grade, legs up to our chins, towering over the crowd, it was like we shared some cool pact, telepathically declaring we were going to stomp through this joint together. Instantly, we became best friends, matching up our class schedules, gossiping by our lockers, and hanging out every afternoon.

In high school I checked many of the boxes emblematic of an all-American life. I became captain of the cheerleading squad. I ran track. But I also became even more aware of my Blackness. Every marker that represented moving from adolescence to adulthood, all the rituals that marked my coming of age, made it plain and clear that I wasn't, and never would be, a pretty little white girl.

My deep-colored skin meant I had no chance of ever being elected to the school's homecoming court. That was for Summer, whose beauty was so dazzling, when she walked into an opposing school's gym, chatter dropped to a murmur as everyone stared.

I ran for but never got elected to the student council. And when it came time for the prom, no one asked me to go. I attended the dance with the handful of other girls in school who were Black, like me.

Somehow, I didn't take it personally. I remember once when I was fourteen standing in the mirror. I looked at my almond eyes, my coffee skin, my coiled hair, and thought, *You are so damn dope.*

It wasn't like my parents told me I was beautiful. The Arthurs didn't hand out excessive compliments or even say "I love you." It was more a matter of deduction, like the math problems I breezed through in algebra. I could see I wasn't ugly. I could strike up a conversation with anybody and aced every school assignment. I was obviously witty and smart and clever.

So, I reasoned that rather than there being something wrong with me, I had just been dropped in the wrong place. People liked me well enough in this snowy-white 'burb, but they didn't quite get my flavor. My Blackness, my Africanness, put me on a different frequency, and there had to be another place beyond that wintry corner of the country where I would fit perfectly and be fully seen.

I dreamed of having a Black boyfriend, but there were few prospects to choose from. The one Black boy in my grade, Donny Coram, hovered a bit over five feet, and I was five ten by my fourteenth birthday. We would have looked, shall we say, awkward. Joey, part

Black and part Korean, had crushes on the white girls. My only other options were a couple of freshmen who sat gooey-eyed as they watched me cheer, but in my mind, they were way too young.

The closest I ever came to a relationship was with Joe Johnston, who happened to be white. We'd bonded over a love of hip-hop and basketball, and sometimes after school we'd head to his house, turn on the TV in the den, and watch Aaliyah and Nas videos on Black Entertainment Television, the rap and R & B alternative to MTV.

I didn't think he had any romantic interest in me. I figured he liked Summer just like every other boy in school. He wouldn't be the first one who'd initially befriended me trying to get close to her. That was why, when Joe called me a few days before Christmas and asked what I was doing New Year's Eve, I figured he was just snooping to find out where Summer might be when it was time for a midnight kiss.

Normally, my answer would have been that I wasn't doing a damn thing. I had to do most of my socializing during the school day or right after the bell rang because my parents didn't allow me to go to parties. When I did get to hang out late, it was because I'd spent the night with one of my girlfriends, giving me an excuse to duck out of my mother's line of sight.

As it so happened, Summer and a couple of our girlfriends were planning to go to a New Year's Eve house party somewhere in the mountains. Maybe it was because college and my eighteenth birthday were around the corner and I felt on the cusp of being grown, but for once I felt emboldened, and instead of asking to go to a sleepover so I could attend a party on the sly, I opted for the truth and straight up asked my mother if I could go. For reasons I didn't understand but I also didn't question, she said yes.

So, I told Joe that Summer and I were going to ring in 1995 at some fabulous house just outside of Colorado Springs.

"Cool," Joe said. "I heard about that party too. See you and Summer there."

That bash was a teenage fantasy, a house full of kids spending the night together with no grown-ups around. There was even a hot tub, its steam billowing and curling in the frigid air. No one had thought to bring swimsuits in the middle of winter, so we sank into the water stripped down to our underwear.

I'd always loved pretty underthings. That night I was wearing the frilly bra and panty set, colored white and cream, that my mom had bought me for Christmas. I closed my eyes, basking in the heat. When I opened them, I caught Joe staring.

No boy had ever looked at me like that before, with a mixture of admiration and longing. My stomach began to flutter. *It can't be,* I thought. *Could he possibly like me and not Summer?*

Joe got in the tub too, and we all continued to guzzle red plastic tumblers of beer or Jim Beam and Coke. I'd snatched sips of alcohol before, but never like I did that night. By the time I climbed out of the hot tub and made my way to one of the bedrooms, I could barely see or walk. I was chilled to the bone, my teeth chattering. Joe trailed behind me.

"You can't lie down in those wet clothes," he said. "You've got to dry off."

"I just want to go to sleep," I slurred, entering the room where my overnight bag sat flung in a corner. Joe grabbed a couple of towels from the bathroom and wrapped them around me. Then he led me to the bed, covered me with blankets, and lay down beside me. That was all. He just took care of me.

I don't know how long we slept before Summer burst through the door. She was going to kill Joe.

"What did you do? What did you do?" she screamed, punctuating each word by punching him.

Jumping up and grabbing my clothes, I was sober enough by then to explain that nothing had happened and to leave Joe alone. Later that day, when we were all safely back home, Joe called to apologize and to say he hadn't tried anything.

I told him I knew. That made me like him even more.

Our feelings remained unspoken, but after that night, Joe and I hung out all the time. I knew that he liked me too, but for whatever reason, Joe never tried to kiss me. We were just buddies who loved to be close to each other.

Though Joe's mother knew me from the frequent afternoons we spent watching TV at their house, my mother didn't meet Joe until I had the biopsy on my breast several weeks after that New Year's Eve party. Joe called while I was recovering and asked if he could stop by. I felt so touched that he wanted to come over, and I really wanted to see him. So, I asked Mom.

Maybe she felt bad because I had been so fearful before the surgery. Maybe she was facing the fact that I was growing up. But again, she surprised me. Dad wouldn't like it, she said, but Joe could come by while my father was at work.

The day Joe came to visit, he brought me a bouquet of tulips he'd picked up at a grocery store. Mom pursed her lips, said a curt hello, then disappeared into the kitchen. Joe and I sat there in the living room, quiet and suddenly awkward. My heart fluttered. Not because I was in love, but because for the first time, a young man had come to my home wanting to woo me. For the first time in my life, I had a suitor. I felt, I knew, that I was crossing some sort of threshold.

By August, I was getting ready to leave for Wesleyan. Joe and I were at yet another house party, this one held on an evening that was warm and sultry.

I'd had enough of our coy dance. Joe was going to a different college, I was going clear across the country, so I figured, hell, this was it. I pulled him toward me. He kissed me back. We left the party soon after, zooming off in his four-wheel drive. I lost my virginity that night, in the downstairs bedroom of a home that belonged to one of Joe's friends.

Afterward, I felt a belonging that was unfamiliar. Not only had I been initiated into the world of sex, I'd been wanted in a way I'd never known before. I was no longer everyone's best Black friend, in the circle yet lingering on the periphery at the same time. For once, I was the focus of desire, a pretty young thing worthy of romance too.

For a couple of years Joe and I hung out like old times whenever we returned home from school. But eventually we lost touch. It wasn't quite a romance, but whatever it had been, it was over.

. . .

At Wesleyan, my quest for Black love had a fresh start. There certainly were more possibilities than I'd had at Liberty High School. Then I ended up falling in love with Ben, who nevertheless moved easily through our collegial Black world. It wasn't until Ben's funeral that I felt his whiteness.

His parents were caring and friendly. And besides his cousin Alex, with whom I instantly sparked what would become a decades-long friendship, Ben's extended family members were aloof. I was always aware of my darkness, being the rare Black girl in Colorado Springs. But at that service in Geneva, I truly felt othered. When I was introduced, Ben's aunts and uncles recovered their composure enough to be polite, but their platitudes couldn't wipe the surprise from their eyes. I wondered if they would have reacted differently if I'd been a pale Swiss girl. Would they have shrugged off their stiffness and grasped my hand instead?

In Ghanaian culture, it's families who get married, not individuals. The man's father goes to the woman's father to ask for her hand. Sitting through the funeral, feeling so alone in my grief, I promised myself that I would never again be in a situation where the family of someone I loved would be able to reject me, where I would feel like an outsider from our first meeting.

A few years later, I met Peter and broke my pledge.

. . .

Peter's and my love was challenged constantly: on subway platforms, in the street, at the club, and even within our own families.

In 2001, not long after I'd introduced my mother and skeptical father to Peter during a small dinner at my apartment, Peter took me to Worcester for Easter to meet his family for the first time.

Peter, the youngest child, was born eight years after his next oldest brother. His sister, Debra, close to my mother's age, looked at Peter like a son. He was adored and spoiled. When the car we'd rented pulled up to the front door, the family rushed out to greet him. I, meanwhile, could feel the coolness directed at me like a sharp breeze.

Everyone was pleasant but formal. As we made small talk over fruit cups, my stomach tightened and my mind raced. I knew Peter had never dated a Black woman before, and I sensed his family's judgment. They wanted to believe I was just a passing fancy. Soon enough, he'd return to his senses and take up with some nice Italian American girl, like the ones he'd grown up with. At least, they hoped he would.

"I don't think they like me very much," I said to Peter when we were alone upstairs, resting before dinner.

"What do you mean?" he said, taking off his sneakers and stretching out on the bed. "Sure they do. Don't be so nervous."

But it all felt so strained, like we were going through the motions, doing just enough to get to the other side of the long weekend. I didn't want to feel like an outsider every time Peter wanted to visit Massachusetts for a holiday or his parents decided to come to New York. I wasn't sure about this, about us. I was looking for the exit.

When I woke up the next morning, I slipped on a T-shirt and a pair of leggings and opened the door. Peter's parents lived in an old house that had belonged to his great-aunt. It was the kind of house where nothing could hide. Every creak, every whisper, seeped into every other part of its three weathered floors. Standing near the top of the stairs, I could hear Peter and his sister speaking in rushed, hushed tones. It definitely sounded like an argument. I struggled to hear what they were saying. Of course, they were quarreling— about me.

"It can't be that serious, Peter," Debra said. "My God. How long have you known her? A few months?"

"Yeah, it's very serious," Peter said defensively. "I love her."

"She's nice, Peter, but . . . Is she really your type? I know you. Just take your time."

My heart was breaking. I'd barely slept the night before, already missing Peter even as he lay on the other side of the wall, in the next room. I didn't want to spend my life proving myself to people I thought would never accept that I wasn't white. It had been a won-derful few months, but Peter and I had to live and love in the real world. I no longer thought I could do it. I stood there listening, sick to my stomach, but also more certain.

Yet Peter kept fighting.

"She's brilliant," he said. "I've never met anyone with a mind like hers. And I'm happy every moment that I'm with her. Like, every single moment."

He was extolling all my virtues, even some I didn't realize I had. He loved me. He wanted to be with me forever. I was both a little embarrassed by his gushing praise and feeling more in love than ever. I leaned forward to hear more.

Then. *Creeaaak.*

That damn landing. The argument below stopped abruptly. They knew I was there. They knew I'd been listening.

Oh God, I thought. *What am I going to have to deal with now?*

I walked down the stairs as if I had just emerged from my room. But if I hadn't overheard the quarrel, I could have guessed some-thing was wrong by how weird everyone acted. Peter's sister was standing by the refrigerator, her face flushed, as she tried to find a mug, a plate, anything to pick up. And Peter's mother, who I guessed had been a silently nodding bystander, was fiddling with a coffee-pot that didn't have any coffee in it.

"Good morning," I said in a voice as chipper as I could muster.

Peter just stood there, frozen, probably because he was a terrible liar. If he ever played strip poker in college, I imagine he would have had to creep back to the dorms in his boxers having lost every bet.

Then he burst out laughing. Debra began to laugh too. It broke the tension. It also unearthed some of Mama's steel that was firmly embedded inside me.

"I wasn't trying to eavesdrop," I said looking straight at Debra, "but I heard a little of the conversation. I want you to know something: I have deep questions about this relationship too. This isn't easy for Peter and me. It's not easy for my parents."

Peter stopped laughing.

"But we are definitely in love and we're going to fight for this. So, everybody else is just going to have to get used to it."

It's a conversation I would have preferred not to have. It was a declaration that I would have preferred not to make. But sometimes you have to deal with the wrenchingly uncomfortable.

Sometimes you have to do what you don't want to do.

Peter, relief washing over his face, walked over and hugged me. His sister, looking stunned, just stood there nodding. And Peter's mother kept her quiet post by the sink.

"Mrs. Saint John," I said, smiling, "may I please have a cup of tea?"

· · ·

In New York City, you can breeze through a dozen cultures just by walking down a city block. Héctor Lavoe, Madonna, and Jay-Z all crooned the soundtrack to the city. You would think there at least, where bagel stores sat above jazz clubs, and crowds resembled a movable, living rainbow, a Black and white romance would blend in easily.

But it didn't.

You would think Peter and I, an Italian American man who loved a Ghanaian American woman, would have been swept up in that diverse city's embrace.

But we weren't.

It was hard with our families. It was hard with some of our

friends. It was hard with strangers. Sometimes it seemed that there was no peace anywhere.

Most white men mostly eyed us with curiosity, arching their eyebrows before turning back to their conversations. They never said anything, were never rude. I could just see the question in their gaze.

Peter's friends, meanwhile, were wonderful from the start. Their own dating choices were mostly limited to women who looked like the girls they'd grown up with. For a short while, Peter's good buddy Will Price dated a beautiful woman from Spain who spoke Catalan, but that was about as exotic as any of them ventured. Still, if any of Peter's crews expressed misgivings to him in private, I didn't sense it. They just seemed incredibly happy and excited that he and I had found each other.

But countless times, as Peter and I rode the 1 train to Greenwich Village or took the Forty-Second Street shuttle across town, we would encounter Black men who were downright hostile.

I could see Peter struggle, to both claim me but to also not invite a stranger's wrath. He wasn't afraid. Peter was an imposing guy. If it were a white guy saying something snarky, I'm confident that Peter would have spat something in our defense and stepped to the jerk.

But ever since our first date, when we'd spent hours discussing Toni Morrison's *Song of Solomon*, Peter and I had engaged in conversations about the experiences of Black people in the United States, and particularly those of Black men—humiliated, disrespected, and living constantly under the specter of violence inflicted by the police, the government, and, sometimes, one another.

Peter had also lived in New York long enough to know its frantic energy made nerves as taut as a trip wire. The strain it took to eke out a living and simply survive meant situations could go from playful to violent in an instant. So, when Black men talked shit—"Hey,

Queen, are you confused?," "When you get tired of him, I'll be waiting for you to come back home"—Peter would usually glare, hold his tongue, and hold me tighter.

All the jousting didn't make me feel desirable. I didn't think, *Wow, everybody wants me.* Instead, it made me sad. And resentful.

Black men had often rejected me. When my girlfriends and I occasionally traveled to another campus for parties in college, the Black fraternity brothers left me to spend the night nursing a drink or swaying by myself in the corner. When I was alone on the street, they'd barely nod if they looked my way at all. Leevert, the Black guy I dated my freshman year, didn't even claim me as his girl, and the few other Black men I dated when I moved to New York seemed to lose interest quickly. The closest I got to Black romantic love was watching it play out in front of me on a movie or TV screen.

So why now all of a sudden did brothers want to challenge Peter? I realized that it wasn't really about me at all. It was the principle of the thing. They were bothered that I was with somebody who wasn't one of them. Even though I didn't want anybody but Peter, that realization stung.

One afternoon, Peter and I were waiting for the train. It had been a good day. We'd stopped at a restaurant for lunch and tossed back a couple of glasses of champagne. As we stood on the platform, a Black man, tall, in a hurry, walked toward us. Peter was oblivious. But I sensed the man's anger.

I wrapped my arms around Peter's waist, warily watching as he drew me in tightly for a hug. Then, so fast I could barely catch my breath, the stranger grabbed my right arm and tried to pull me toward him.

Shock flashed across Peter's face, then rage. Peter wasn't quick to anger, but when he got mad, it was volcanic.

"What the hell are you doing?" he screamed, lunging toward the guy.

I jerked myself away from both Peter and the stranger, throwing up my hands to keep them apart and ward off the clash. The guy clearly wanted trouble. We didn't know who he was or what he would do, and it wasn't worth finding out in the name of our wounded pride.

As quickly as he'd grabbed me, the guy backed off. "You're a punk anyway," he snarled, before stomping away.

Was I the punk for being with a white man? Was Peter a punk for being with me? It shouldn't have mattered which of us was the target of a rude, random guy's venom. But somehow it did. It felt like a condemnation of our choice and also a violent reminder of how awful the world could be. There was always the possibility of a man like that, possessive, aggressive, lurking around the corner.

The whole incident couldn't have lasted more than a few seconds. But it was enough to destroy our day. We were shaken, the sparkle of our champagne-fueled buzz fizzled away. We sat in uncomfortable silence on the subway, then fumbled for random bits of chitchat when we got home. We never talked about that day again. Ever.

• • •

Peter wasn't the first, but he was for sure the whitest man I'd ever dated. Unlike Ben, or even my kinda-sorta high school boyfriend Joe, Peter had no connection to Blackness at all.

Except for a Black woman at the office he started to confide in when he decided to woo me, Peter didn't have any Black friends. And while I loved hip-hop and neo soul, he was a metalhead who in a mellow mood chose to rock out to Pink Floyd. He not only didn't know the words to Black Sheep's "The Choice Is Yours," he couldn't even recite the lyrics to "Rapper's Delight," one of the most mainstream rap odes ever written.

My girlfriends didn't get it. The first thing they wanted to know, of course, was the typical girlfriend stuff—how was this white boy in bed? The next question on their minds: When was I going to move past the swirl and get back to trying to find my Black Prince Charming?

We'd be sitting around chatting when Peter popped up with some corny slang none of us spoke.

"That's rad!" Peter might blurt out when my girlfriend Kadian, a fashionista, mentioned a celebrity she'd seen walking down Fifth Avenue. Kadian and my other girls would cut me a look as if to say "Is he for real?" before continuing on with their conversation.

But as uncool as Peter was, my girlfriends also saw how well he treated me. Peter wouldn't just walk me to his front door and kiss me good night when I had stuff to do in New Jersey and needed to get back to my apartment. He'd ride the subway and PATH commuter train with me for an hour, paying my fare, then turn around and go back home so I could get some rest. He called when he said he'd call, did what he said he'd do. Peter was a gentleman. There were no games, no drama. And my girls appreciated that.

He was also a good sport. Peter would accompany my girlfriends and me, decked out in our pumps and short skirts, to Nell's, a legendary club in downtown Manhattan. Peter couldn't dance, so he'd stand by the wall, watching us whirl to dance hall and hip-hop. I'd occasionally break from our group to grind against Peter, declaring that I was his and he was mine, before rejoining the throng. When my girls and I took a break, thirsty and wrung-out, Peter would head to the bar and get us all drinks.

Sipping my rum and Coke, trying to hear my own thoughts over the bass that made that sweaty basement pulse like a heartbeat, I'd look at Peter and think how I wished I had the confidence of a white man. Early in my career I had to steel myself to enter a conference room where I'd be not only the only Black person, but the only woman. I had to learn to be audacious, to walk with power.

But there wasn't any place Peter didn't feel comfortable, no place he felt he couldn't go. We'd be standing in front of Nell's, Peter the only white person in a line full of Black people that stretched around the corner, and he wasn't self-conscious at all. He didn't seem to notice if folks stared, or if his jeans and stiff button-down looked a little square and out of place at a New York lounge. Once inside, he'd have a great time, just watching me and my friends dance as he rocked awkwardly to the music.

Peter didn't get the cues, the signs, because he didn't have to. Whereas my antenna had been honed practically in the womb, sensitive to the microaggressions and slights that nicked like paper cuts, invisible to an outsider while leaving me scarred and sore.

I knew the cabdriver had seen my upraised hand when he sped past me and picked up the red-haired white woman standing half a block away instead. I felt the sting when a delivery person assumed I was the receptionist instead of the executive, the young associate instead of the chief marketing officer. That's what it was to be a Black woman.

. . .

One afternoon, Peter and I were in SoHo, browsing through the racks of some luxe boutique. Besides Peter and me there were a couple of white girls around my age who were shopping as well.

Peter was so excited, imagining me in a Mossimo tunic over here, a slinky Dolce & Gabbana minidress over there.

"What about this?" he kept asking. "And this! And this!"

Honestly, I didn't want any of the items he was picking out, but I enjoyed seeing how excited he was about designs he thought would look beautiful on me. Eventually the white girls who were shopping turned to get a look at this woman Peter was so giddy for.

They gazed at me from my head down to my shoes, then rolled their eyes and looked away. I don't think there's any Black equivalent to "Becky," the generic name for a white girl who thirsts after Black men. But I knew that there were some white women who weren't happy that a fine white guy like Peter was dating a Black woman. Their disapproval was typically subtle, because frankly, I think they took one look at me, six feet tall in my stilettos, and worried if they stepped out of line, I'd beat some ass.

But these chicks were brazen. There was no way in hell I was going to let them get away with their attitude.

"Yeah! That's my man!" I said loud enough for strangers passing outside to hear.

Peter looked up, confused. Of course this whole scene went right over his head.

"What's going on?" he asked.

I put down the scarf I was touching and walked out. Peter followed.

"What's the matter?" he asked again.

"They saw me with you and rolled their eyes!" I told him, exasperated.

"What?" he asked. "I didn't hear them say anything. Why are you mad?"

That pissed me off even more. He seemed to think I was over-reacting, but of course he didn't have to understand. I, on the other hand, didn't have that luxury. I had to demand respect, because if I didn't, plenty of people were more than happy not to give me any.

Once again, our day was ruined by an outsider's ignorance. But this time I was the only one upset. Peter was incredulous.

He tried to hold my hand. I swatted it away. He touched my hair. I tugged my head back.

Peter continued to try to soothe my feelings when we got back to his apartment. "Want something to eat?"

"No," I said, shutting him down and turning on the TV.

"I really think that yellow sweater we were looking at would look good on you."

I ignored him.

Then he smiled.

"No one ever said that about me before," he said.

"What?" I asked, annoyed that he kept trying to break the ice when I wanted to sit in my funk.

"No one has ever said I'm their man."

What on earth was he talking about? He'd had girlfriends before. Plenty, from what I understood.

"White girls don't talk like that," he said. "No one ever yelled something like that about me to the world. I liked it."

I looked up. And just like that, I got it.

Peter didn't know. He didn't know that you don't try to hold back a Black woman, standing strong in a storm. He didn't understand that it's unacceptable for a woman to hint that another isn't good enough to be with her man.

Peter just didn't know the rules. I would have to teach him.

The storm passed. I took his hand in mine. And finally, I smiled too.

. . .

On the day Peter and I were moving into our first apartment on the far east side of Manhattan, I walked by the doorman at Peter's building. He was Ghanaian, and he behaved like a doting and sweet uncle. Whenever I would visit Peter, he'd greet me in Fanti. That day, he again spoke to me in my mother's language.

"Come back down," he said quietly. "I want to talk to you by yourself."

I rode the elevator to the apartment, where Peter, his roommates, and I were taping up boxes.

Oh my God, I thought. *What does he want to tell me? Does Peter have another girlfriend? Has he been cheating on me?*

I turned right around, telling Peter that I needed to run back down to get something out of the rental car. I rode to the lobby filled with trepidation.

"What is it?" I asked in Fanti as I approached my Ghanaian friend.

He looked at me with kind eyes. "I know your parents are far away, so I'm going to be your family right now," he said. "I want you to be happy. Are you sure this is what you want to do? These people are not our people."

I was so relieved he hadn't said Peter was two-timing me that I just grabbed him in a bear hug.

"This is the man I want," I whispered, on the edge of tears. "But thank you for caring."

"All right," he said, patting my back. "Take care of yourself."

I rode the elevator back up to Peter's apartment, feeling much lighter than when I had ridden down.

But the voices of my father, of Peter's sister, and that dear, sweet doorman faintly echoed in my head. At every turn Peter and I had to defend why we wanted to be together. What was the universe trying to tell us?

6

Romance Interrupted

I lay in bed. Listening.

It was morning. I could have slept another hour before my alarm went off. But Peter had gotten up to go to the bathroom.

I used to be a deep sleeper, able to doze through car horns blaring outside my walkup's window or my roommate's amorous adventures in the bedroom next door.

Now I hovered at the edge of dreams, unable to succumb or commit. I was roused whenever Peter moved, and if he didn't, I'd pop awake then too, checking that he was breathing, making sure he was okay.

Since coming home from the hospital, Peter couldn't stand for very long, maybe five to ten minutes at the most before he needed to sit and rest. I glanced at the clock, then squished my head against the pillow. Minutes passed. I checked the clock again. Peter was taking a really long time.

Finally, I got up and knocked on the door.

"You all right?" I asked, knowing how annoying that question could be, like when your mother checked on you when you were a kid, announcing to the entire household that you were taking an extra-long squat, which could mean only one thing—you were going to need to open all the windows and pull out the air freshener.

Peter responded meekly. "Well," he said. "No."

I opened the door slowly, afraid of what I might find on the other side.

Peter was sitting on the toilet, his pajama pants around his ankles. He looked confused, like he didn't know what was going on.

"What's the matter?" I asked nervously. Was there blood? Did his stomach hurt?

"I can't stand up," he replied.

"Did your legs fall asleep? That's what happens to me when I'm on there for a long time. You know I do my best thinking on the toilet!"

I was trying to keep the mood light. Peter tried too, shooting me one of his crooked smiles.

"No," he said. "I don't have the strength to get up."

This was our life now. Opening doors scared of what you'd find. Being thrust into situations you'd never encountered before. Asking questions when you feared what the answers would be.

"Here," I said. "Let me help you."

I positioned myself in front of him, bending slightly. I told Peter to hold on to me to get his balance. He grabbed my forearms. Then. Nothing.

This was a man who used to be able to easily lift me off the ground, carrying my nearly six-foot frame over murky puddles in the middle of Manhattan. Now, he didn't have enough strength to use me as a ballast to pull himself off the toilet. I was terrified.

I used my physical power to pull him up instead. It wasn't quite like lifting Lael, but Peter had lost so much weight, he actually wasn't much heavier. I tugged him up quickly, so he didn't have to sit there knowing I'd felt his weakness.

"Oh, thank God," he said once he was on his feet, fumbling awkwardly to pull up his pants. He knew he hadn't suddenly gotten a jolt of strength, that if I hadn't been nearby, he would have been stuck in that bathroom for who knew how long. But neither of us wanted to think about that.

I leaned over to flush the toilet and we made our way back to bed.

. . .

When I told my parents I wanted to try living in New York after my sister Alua graduated from Wesleyan, they still held fast to their med school dreams. My mother flew to Connecticut to help me pack and made the roughly two-and-a-half-hour drive with me from Middletown to Manhattan. But she and Dad weren't going to help me financially. I was on my own.

I knew exactly one person in New York, a Wesleyan student who'd graduated the year before and was then a film student in a graduate program at Columbia. She was sharing an apartment up in Harlem and said I could crash on her couch. I had exactly three months to find a job, so I signed up for a temp agency my first day in town.

The deal was that in lieu of rent, I'd cook for my friend and her roommate. That was good and bad. The upside? I could eat the groceries they bought without chipping in. The downside? Since they were both out during the day, I cooked only dinner, and that meant I ate only one meal a day.

My roommates had more money than I did, but we were on a sliding scale of broke. As a result, there were certain luxuries we had to live without, like a phone. With no landline and no cell, the only way I could check on possible temp gigs was to head to a public phone and call in.

A booth sat at the corner of 125th and Broadway. With a handful of quarters, I would seal myself inside every morning and dial the agency at 7:30 a.m. sharp. If they didn't have anything for me, I'd call back at 7:45. It went on like that for the next hour, with me making calls every fifteen minutes. If nothing turned up by 9:00 a.m. when the workday had begun in most offices, I'd head home to the apartment.

During those fifteen-minute lulls, I'd duck into a restaurant called Floridita. It was a shabby but homey joint, renowned for serving heaping plates of Cuban food. The main dining room wasn't open that early, but the Broadway entrance, across from McDonald's and underneath the subway tracks, served breakfast in the mornings. I'd find a stool and sit.

The smell of sizzling eggs and fresh baked bread would make my stomach rumble like the 1 train flying above. But the only money I had was a few dollars and that handful of quarters.

A woman manned the counter. I guessed she was older because of the gray hair that whitened her temples, but her face was smooth and kind. I knew that she knew I was hungry.

After a couple of days watching me go back and forth to the phone booth, she slid me a hot buttered roll. At first, I refused. I couldn't afford to spend two dollars on a breakfast snack when I didn't have a job. But she wouldn't back down.

"No, no," she'd say, shaking her head. "You have to eat."

So, I took out two dollars, the price I saw on the menu, sipped a glass of water, and ate the roll.

It calmed my grumbling stomach. Tasting that buttery goodness, I told myself that I'd never take the magic of a hot roll for granted again.

When I walked in the next morning, I planned to just drink water and save my money. But the friendly lady at the counter gave me another roll.

"For free," she said, turning around before I could protest.

It became our routine, that piece of hot bread feeling like a gift every day.

She didn't speak much English, but after a week or so, she finally asked what I was doing. I told her I was calling into an agency, hoping to find a job. From then on, she became my cheerleader.

"Today is the day," she would say brightly when I took my seat.

I did land gigs here and there. I was sent to a dog groomer on the Upper West Side, where I grabbed puppy shampoo and blow-dried a bunch of English bulldogs who barely had any hair. I spent three days at *National Geographic*, alphabetizing files. Those jobs were good for giving me a few dollars, but they were hardly putting me on the path to the full-time position I needed to get my own apartment, let alone paving the way to a career that would allow me to wriggle out of graduate school and launch my new, fabulous life in New York.

If I got a placement, I'd rush in to Floridita to retrieve my bag, wave at my newfound friend, then rush to hop the train.

"How'd it go?" she'd ask when my two- or three-day assignment ended and I was back at her counter.

"Okay. But it's over now," I'd say.

I resumed my round robin between the phone booth and the stool.

"No?" she'd ask when I came back.

"No," I'd say, grabbing my glass, dejectedly.

"Don't worry," she'd say. "Tomorrow's the day!"

I'd been in New York maybe six weeks when the daily tension of calling the agency, sitting at Floridita, and enduring more days than I wanted to count of going back to that empty apartment made me start to believe that nothing solid was going to pan out. Maybe New York should have remained a fantasy. Maybe I'd need to go to grad school after all.

One Wednesday, I called the agency, preparing to head back home since it was already a quarter to nine. But they had a job for me. The head of an advertising agency had just fired his assistant, and they needed a fill-in as soon as possible to answer the phones.

"What agency?" I asked, not really caring since I was just relieved to get the job.

It was Spike DDB, a start-up founded by the legendary director Spike Lee.

I flew into Floridita.

"Today is the day!" I yelled. "I got a good one!"

My friend clapped her hands and glanced toward the ceiling like she was uttering a prayer. I should have kissed her. Instead, I grabbed my purse, waved, and flew out of there.

Thank God those were the days before Instagram, because I would have been roasted for my outfit. I looked every inch who I was: a Colorado Springs girl who went to college in suburban Connecticut and was now trying to do my best impression of a Manhattan corporate chick on a budget.

My gray polyester suit had black stitching piped along the edges.

I'd pulled my hair back into a tight chignon, and I wore little pearl drop earrings. I cringe at the memory, but at the time I thought I looked prim and professional.

I was excited but nervous. Spike Lee was a supernova. Starting in the 1980s, he simultaneously kicked off a renaissance in Black film while calling out Hollywood on its bullshit of excluding Black film-makers and audiences.

His groundbreaking films included *She's Gotta Have It*, which celebrated Black women's sexuality; *Malcolm X*, a biography of the iconic Black nationalist; and *Do the Right Thing*, which was so im-pactful, the Library of Congress chose to preserve it in the National Film Registry. Spike also produced riveting documentaries, includ-ing one about the four little girls murdered in a Birmingham church bombing in 1963. Now he'd ventured into advertising in a partner-ship with the global ad powerhouse DDB.

Spike was boldly and fiercely Black, launching and gilding the careers of actors like Denzel Washington, Halle Berry, and Samuel L. Jackson. I figured the agency sent me because I was probably the only Black temp they had on file. No matter. I couldn't believe I'd caught a break like this.

When I arrived at the office, the other employees weren't at work yet. So, it was just me. And Spike.

He gave me a look.

"You who they sent?" he barked.

"Yes, sir," I said, in a voice about three pitches above how I nor-mally spoke.

He stared some more.

"I can't believe they sent me Miss America," he clucked.

That snapped me out of being starstruck real quick. Spike was about five six. I straightened myself up to my full height and decided to let Spike Lee know who he was dealing with. To this day, Spike still tells the story.

"I'm not Miss America," I harrumphed. "I have English literature and African American studies degrees from Wesleyan. *And* I'm premed."

Spike didn't respond to the rundown of my credentials. He just walked into his office and shut the door.

I panicked. *Damn,* I thought. I figured I'd just screwed myself out of the first promising gig I'd gotten in New York. But when Spike's door remained closed, I took that as a good sign. I set myself up at a desk, and when the phone started ringing, I answered it.

The next day the agency told me that they wanted me to go back. The gig would likely last a couple of weeks or until Spike could find an assistant to do the typing, note-taking, and other tasks he required. I knew I didn't have any of those skills and I wasn't going to pretend that I did, but I was glad to ride this train as long as I could. I reported to the office at 8:00 a.m. sharp every day. Spike, for his part, barely acknowledged that I was there.

One morning, a few days after I'd started, Spike walked by my desk with a stack of pages under his arms.

Maybe it was naiveté. Maybe it was my gut. Maybe it was Mama's steel. But I spoke up.

"Is that a script?" I asked.

Everyone's head whipped around, including Spike's.

"Yeah," he said. It was the screenplay for a new film he was about to premiere called *Bamboozled.*

"Can I read it?" I asked.

Spike paused.

"You sure you can handle it?" he finally said.

Time to remind him again who I was.

"Sure," I said. "I'm a literature major. Zora Neale Hurston and Toni Morrison are my favorite writers."

Spike smirked and dropped the script on my desk.

"Read it. I want it back in a couple days. Let me know what you think," he said as he walked away.

I didn't realize what that smirk was about until I got home and settled in on the couch. It turned out to be heavy reading. The story was about a young, well-educated Black man trying to get a foothold in TV production. He winds up working on a contemporary minstrel show complete with folks wearing blackface. It was another incisive commentary on Hollywood, simultaneously skewering its stereotypical portrayals and the American audiences that eagerly ate them up.

I stayed up all night, not only reading the script but correcting grammatical errors and making notes in the margins with a red pen. I did the same the next evening. When I returned to work on Friday morning, I waited for Spike to arrive.

As usual, he started to pass by without a word.

"Good morning!" I said, picking up the script and gesturing toward him. "I finished it."

He looked at me like I had transformed into a talking pumpkin.

"I made some corrections. To the grammar. And I added some notes."

The other folks in the office froze. I didn't know what I'd done wrong, but clearly, I'd crossed some invisible line.

Spike snatched the script out of my hand so hard he almost took my arm off. He stormed into his office and slammed the door.

The other staffers wouldn't even look at me, and when I caught Leah, a freelance art buyer, peeking at me, she just shook her head.

Oh man, I thought. *This time I'm fired for real.*

I thought about calling the temp agency to tell them I'd be free again on Monday. Instead, I just sat there, holding my purse, trying to decide if I should flee the guillotine or wait for it to drop.

I must have sat there an hour and a half before Spike spoke up at last. He didn't even bother to open his door.

"You made some good notes," he yelled. "You should stick around."

And that was it. My career had begun.

At first, I was Spike's assistant, mostly running errands. My days were filled with mundane tasks ranging from picking up Spike's dry cleaning to keeping his son and daughter occupied when they popped by the office. But in between, I started making suggestions for certain campaigns, and when Spike realized I could write, I occasionally became a coordinator, putting together short proposals.

Spike and the rest of his team pretty much kept to themselves, ordering in or bringing lunch back to their desks. But as I got my feet wet, jotting copy and drafting pitches, I wanted to know more. I'd head up to the cafeteria for my cinnamon raisin bagel with two fried eggs and crispy bacon in the morning, or a sandwich in the middle of the day, and I befriended some of the other twentysomethings who worked for the various advertising agencies in the building.

As I asked questions about their roles and their titles, I quickly began to understand that I was too educated for the job I had. Spike's kids were adorable, but I didn't work my way through college and earn a degree in two majors to spend my days helping them write poems to recite in front of their classmates.

Spike was the founder and CEO of his agency, but a lot of the day-to-day management fell to the agency's president. She couldn't stand me, and I literally needed therapy to get over the games she used to play. But I had a good rapport with Spike. And I had my gut instincts. They'd worked before. I figured they'd work now.

"You need someone who's the go-between for you and the clients, making sure everyone's on the same page and nothing's lost in translation," I said to him one afternoon. "How about you hire someone else to be your assistant and let me become an assistant account executive?"

Looking back, I can see it was a ballsy move. I didn't know what that wretched woman who didn't like me was whispering in Spike's ear. And I'd never talked up a marketing campaign before. There was a chance I might stumble over the jargon or not understand the nuts and bolts well enough to give a coherent answer when the client asked a tough question.

But you have to know what you have in your quiver and what you don't, when to aim, and when to hold back. I was smart. I was charming. I was articulate. I was eager to leap for the next rung. So, I pulled out my bow and took the shot. Maybe I'd miss. But I know now that every try makes you sharper. And sometimes you hit the mark perfectly.

Spike said yes.

What was supposed to be a two-week temporary gig ended up lasting four years, all because I asked Spike to let me look at his script and boldly offered him my insights. I gained experience that paved the way for me to later join the corporate suites of Pepsi, Apple, Uber, Endeavor, and Netflix because I dared to ask Spike for a promotion and a chance.

I realize now that I always had a keen sense of what I was good at and the areas where I fell short. And being honest about my shortcomings was as important as knowing my talents. I didn't waste energy trying to pretend or bluff. I wasn't embarrassed by what I didn't know and that enabled me to be super confident about what I did.

I knew I was no Desmond Hall. He was our creative director

and just an incredible artist and writer. He effortlessly came up with one-liners that were witty and sharp. I remember one time he'd written a line about choking on potato chips for an ad we were creating to air during the Super Bowl. When Desmond presented the campaign in a meeting, he changed chips to pork rinds on the fly and it just made everyone—Spike, our team, the client—fall out on the floor laughing. It was pitch-perfect, conjuring up a completely different feeling about the product.

I couldn't do that. But I could present an argument for why the work we'd created, whatever the idea, was good. I could instinctively home in on what the client wanted and craft a pitch that catered to their expectations. That is my gift. I can convince people to do things even when they think they don't want to, whether it's a grocery store clerk who suddenly has the urge to scour the storeroom for the juice I want but he thinks is out of stock, or a client who's on the fence about a proposal we've pitched. Don't catch me at a souk in Marrakech. I will walk out with every damn thing at half the price. Even when I was a junior executive, rising up the ladder, I recognized that you could put me in a room with anybody and I'd detect their secret longing and connect it to the work. And again, because I acknowledge what I'm not good at, I step into what I'm able to do and don't hold back.

Asking to read Spike's script didn't feel like a risk because I understood the African American experience that his voice was steeped in. And I trusted that I could help Spike at his agency by making a contribution of my own.

I continued to stop in Floridita from time to time, able at last to always pay for my roll. But when I moved to my own apartment in New Jersey a few months later, heading uptown for fresh pastry didn't make sense. My fairy godmother and I lost touch.

All these years later, I wish I could find her. She fed me food and encouragement. She gave me bread and hope. That taught me another lesson. Don't wait to thank your angels. Tell them what they mean to you right then. That beautiful, loving woman saved my life. And I don't even know her name.

. . .

When I was young, I was locked in by my father's dreams. I might have been on my way to medical school if I hadn't broken free. When I shook loose of his grip, I briefly blamed him for almost diverting me from my professional purpose. But now I believe Dad wasn't the problem. It's dreams that hold you back. Not because they're too ambitious, but because they often aren't lofty enough. They go only as far as your imagination can take you. It's intuition that lets you tap into the unseen.

When I followed my gut, I found my career. And when I relinquished the space in my imagination I thought only a Black man could fill, I found Peter.

He and I ate our way through every restaurant in the *Zagat's* guide. And after we'd moved in together, we'd have spontaneous potlucks at our apartment fueled by pasta and red wine. New York, finally, was turning out to be as exhilarating as I'd hoped.

But my father's final words when he haltingly gave his blessing for Peter and me to live together created an endless loop in my mind. I couldn't shake the feeling that I was bringing shame on my family. I didn't yearn to be married, but I knew that eventually I would have to be.

Still, there was no rush. I was twenty-four years old, for God's sake. I had time.

Since Peter and I worked in the same high-rise at Forty-Ninth and Madison, we'd ride the 6 subway train together, then sometimes stop at the corner deli to order breakfast before heading to our offices. The morning of September 11, 2001, was like every other day. Until it wasn't.

The television behind the counter was on, its volume low. One plane, and then another, hit the World Trade Center. We thought our eyes were playing tricks on us.

Shaken, Peter and I went on to work, not yet understanding the magnitude of the moment we were about to live through. An hour later, the Twin Towers collapsed, and for a long time after, so did our sense of safety in the world.

We were sitting in a Manhattan skyscraper on a day when the country was under attack, but somehow my monster of a boss, the agency president who didn't like me, couldn't comprehend that. We had work to do, she said. Nobody was leaving early. I buzzed Peter.

A few minutes later, he was at my desk.

"Do you see the people?" he asked, steering me toward the window. Survivors of the attack were trudging uptown like zombies, covered in ash. "We're getting the hell out of here," he said as we defiantly headed for the door.

We joined the exodus. As we walked the forty blocks to our apartment at Eighty-Ninth Street and York, we passed people crying and praying, panicking and stunned. When I lived in New Jersey, I traveled through the World Trade Center every day, the commuter train dropping me there at 7:15 in the morning. I'd been living in Manhattan for only three weeks. If I'd still lived on my own, if I'd been running late, there's no telling what devastation I would have been plunged into.

When Peter and I finally got home, we collapsed in front of the

television, consoling each other, watching those seemingly inde-
structible towers collapse in replays again and again.

There were rumors that bombs had been planted throughout the
city. We decided that we needed to get out of New York, but trains
weren't running and all flights had been grounded. In the flurry of
calls our friends were making to check on one another, we found a
couple we hung out with who were planning to drive to New England the next day. We decided to hitch a ride with them to Massachusetts to stay with Peter's family.

During the four-hour drive, our friends told us that they were
planning to get married by the end of the year. Peter grew quiet.
The world was on fire. There was no time to waste.

"We should get married," he said. "Now."

We were already on thin ice with my father. I knew not even a
deadly terrorist attack would be enough for him to forgive us for not
having a proper wedding.

"We can't get married right away," I said. "We have to have a
ceremony."

"We'll figure it out," Peter said.

It was all very perfunctory. We'd essentially decided to spend the
rest of our lives together in the back seat of a Honda Accord, racing
to Worcester to escape a city whose downtown lay in ashes. It felt
hasty and vague.

But Peter was the guy who put a paintbrush to canvas to celebrate
my birthday. He was the dude who read *Song of Solomon* in a week
and was able to discuss it on our first date. There was no way he was
going to let a back seat proposal be the last word.

On November 9, 2001, a year to the day we'd gone to dinner for
the first time, Peter told me to pack a bag. We were going out of
town, but first we were going to have dinner.

It was a little weird. We took a lot of weekend trips but would typically leave early in the morning, not in the evening, and certainly not when we were full and sleepy from eating a big meal. But since it was our anniversary, it made sense he wanted to do something special to mark the day.

I put on a shimmery gold dress, and Peter drove a rental car to the Beekman Tower, a glittering art deco high-rise not far from our apartment. I remember being mesmerized by the pianist as we waited for dessert. I just wanted to bask in the moment, looking out at the river, listening to the lovely music. But Peter kept fidgeting. When the pianist took a break, I looked over at Peter and saw his pained face.

I was about to ask what was wrong when he gently took my hand.

"You know how much you mean to me . . ."

That was it. That was all I heard. I left my body and could no longer hear a thing. I just watched Peter's lips move.

He stood up. Did I need to stand? How were you supposed to act when you were being proposed to? I was overwhelmed.

People began to turn around and look. Everyone knew what was about to happen. Peter suddenly scrunched his six-foot-five-inch frame down to one knee and pulled out a ring.

It was a work of art. I love roses. My manicurist paints them on my nails, and I doodle them in my calendar and on random slips of paper. Peter designed the ring using that same floral curve in the setting for the stone, creating a delicate cup that held a single round diamond in its grasp. The setting was platinum, heavy enough to constantly remind me that it was there, and of the density of the love that it represented.

I couldn't figure out when he'd had the time to create it. But somehow, without my knowing, Peter had researched diamonds and consulted with different jewelers. Later he showed me the sketches he'd made.

We never left town. Peter had rented a suite a few blocks away at the Roosevelt Hotel. When we opened the door, rose petals blazed a path to the bed, and there were bottles of champagne. Before I dozed off, I replayed the evening, surprisingly thrilled that I was now officially an engaged woman.

My next thought? *Oh shit. Now I've got to get married.*

. . .

I've often struggled with ambivalence, of being more enamored of the idea of a thing than the reality. Like when I tried out for the track team in high school. I pictured myself running across the finish line, having an Olympic moment after every Saturday-afternoon meet. I won my share of races, but as I wrung out my sweaty socks, spent weekends icing my sore knees, and got up in the dark to run laps in the Colorado chill, reaching for the brass ring often left me physically and mentally exhausted. The reality was starkly different from my dream.

When Peter proposed, I finally had my fairy tale. I wanted Peter to want to marry me. I wanted the stamp of respectability my parents and friends longed for and said I should desire too. But so long as Peter and I weren't officially married, I was still somewhat free. That was about to change. I worried about the future and the unknown.

When I called to tell my parents that Peter and I were getting married, my father's response didn't exactly ease my nerves.

"Why would you want to marry a white man?" he asked. "Don't you remember what happened with the last one you were with?"

It was a harsh question. It had taken me months to finally tell my parents that the funeral I'd attended in Switzerland was for a man I loved. Not to mention that Peter had called my father and received his blessing before he proposed. Throwing that relationship and its tragic ending in my face was cruel, but I suppose it was also my father's final attempt to salvage his dreams. Maybe he'd hoped I'd change my mind and search for a Ghanaian husband after all, because white men brought bad luck.

But instead of scaring me straight, he was scarring me. I didn't need a rhetorical question to remind me of Ben's death. What I needed was reassurance that love returns, sometimes in a different form, in a different way, but you needed to always trust that you could find it again. Just because a happy ending eluded me before didn't mean that it would elude me forever. That's what I needed to hear.

I ignored my father, asking to speak to my mother instead, who was ecstatic that her oldest child was getting married. But Dad's raising the memory of Ben had summoned yet another emotion: guilt.

A few days after Peter proposed, I made a call to Geneva. I cried as I told Ben's mother, Peggy, that I was engaged. It felt right to call her because we had been tethered together ever since that horrible December day when Ben had died two years earlier. In a way, sharing the events in my life allowed her to imagine what Ben's life could've been if he'd lived. So I always called with my triumphs and even my disappointments. She didn't understand my complicated sadness during what should've been an ecstatic call.

"This is such a happy moment," she said. "Why the tears?"

I told her I felt like I was betraying Ben. I had thought of moving to Hawaii after college, maybe finding a job overseeing guest services at a luxury hotel. Ben was the one who'd dreamed of a New

York life. From the time we began dating, he wanted to spend that life with me. Now I had this thriving career in Manhattan and was about to marry another man.

I listened to Peggy's breathing on the other end of the line. If I couldn't get Ben's blessing, I thought, I'd be grateful for hers.

"It was never meant to be," Peggy finally said quietly. "You can release it. And be happy."

. . .

I wanted a traditional Ghanaian ceremony while Peter wanted a Roman Catholic wedding in a church. Rather than compromise and leave one of us feeling dissatisfied, we decided to do both. And because we didn't want to have two different anniversaries, we set the ceremonies exactly one year apart, in June.

The traditional Ghanaian ceremony came first, at my parents' home in Colorado. Ghanaian weddings are completely different from their western counterparts. For starters, the bride and groom are literally voiceless. It's the families who commit to each other, forging the bond. I coached Peter and his family about how the ceremony would go, and my mom ordered from Ghana the traditional outfits we all would wear.

Peter's mom was battling breast cancer at the time and had recently undergone a double mastectomy. Still weak from the treatment, her family was concerned about her making the trip from Massachusetts, but she was adamant. She fidgeted and fussed over her outfit, wanting to make sure her head wrap was just so, that the wide sash around her waist was tied correctly. Up to that point, we hadn't had the warmest relationship, but I loved her for wanting to show up, literally and completely.

In Ghana, when a man wants to marry a woman, his parents and siblings go to her home, knock on the door, and are turned away unceremoniously. Sometimes they're literally chased away, and they have to keep coming back, often over several days.

We didn't have time for all that. Folks had jobs and lives and things to do. So, we gave Peter a break, refusing him and his family only once. I'd warned Peter because I was afraid if he didn't know that was the way it would go, he might have a heart attack and his parents would say c'est la vie, hop in a cab, and head right back to the airport.

But I didn't prepare Peter for *everything*. What would have been the fun in that?

The next time Peter and his family knocked on the door, it opened, and they were greeted by a full house. I'm talking standing room only. Jam-packed. Stacked to the rafters. My relatives had flown in from New York, England, and Ghana, and there wasn't a spare inch on which to sit, lean, or stand.

Each of our families had a representative to negotiate the marriage. We'd assigned a friend of my parents to do the talking for the Saint Johns. He stated their intention.

"We would like to marry the oldest daughter of the house," he said. He announced the gifts the Saint Johns had brought—the dowry—to win the bride's hand.

He then asked to see the daughter—you know, to confirm that they were getting the right girl.

My mother led the bride-to-be down the stairs, veiled under a heavy cloth. Peter, sitting on the couch, was sweating bullets.

"Is this the woman you've come looking for?" Peter's representative asked.

"Yes," Peter said. At this point his shirt was drenched.

"Are you suuuure?" the representative asked again, arching his eyebrow.

"Uh-huh," Peter said, starting to look confused. What the hell was going on?

Finally, the representative whispered loudly in Peter's ear: "Look under the veil!"

Peter lifted the cloth and saw that he was about to marry my sister, Aba. I was peeking around the wall in the upstairs hallway.

"No! It's not her!" he yelled in a panic, shaking his head furiously.

The house shook as everyone exploded in laughter. My family and friends were quite pleased that their trick had gotten such a reaction.

Peter laughed nervously. His parents just looked bewildered.

Peter's representative, chewing up the scenery like a thirsty B actor, feigned outrage.

"How dare you try to trick us with the wrong woman!" he thundered. "Send this one back and bring us the right one!"

Some of my female relatives hurried over with drinks and snacks to soothe hurt feelings and quickly fraying nerves. Once Peter and his family downed some peppermint schnapps, they tried again.

This time my mother led me down the stairs, my face shielded. I could feel Peter's nervous energy as I sat down beside him. I snuck my hand out from under my veil, grabbed his hand, and squeezed. His tension eased. He could feel it was me.

The entire affair lasted maybe ninety minutes. Unlike a Western wedding, solemn and quiet, it was loud and celebratory, full of trickery and symbolism, like the bride switch, which was customary in a family with many daughters. If you could marry off the wrong one, the groom would come back to marry the right one, so the family would be done with two daughters instead of one. Our ritual, full of pomp and exaggeration, hinted at so many truths. How marriage was really a transaction, how it involved the feelings and desires of far more people than just the bride and groom.

It was also unabashed, raucous fun. Well, for my family, anyway. I think Peter's folks expected a fun, exotic celebration but were shocked by all the drama and theatrics, the chatter and the chaos.

Peter had ordered the pieces of my dowry. There was the rainbow-colored kente cloth meant for celebrations, the golden swatches for my trousseau, the purple fabric I'd wear on our anniversary, and the navy-and-white swath I'd don once our first child was born. When he unveiled the suitcase, bursting with cloth, the house roared again.

We opened a bottle of the schnapps Peter had bought by the case to pour in honor of our ancestors. Then Peter handed an envelope full of money to my father and pulled out the diamond ring he'd designed for me. The house continued to cheer. Peter beamed.

But of course, my family had to shake Peter down for more.

"That's not enough money!" yelled one uncle.

"What about her?" said a cousin, pointing at one of my aunts. "Doesn't she get a pocket piece?"

"She has three younger sisters!" tut-tutted one of my mother's oldest friends. "Don't forget them!"

There was yelling and laughing and backslapping as Peter was harassed, pushed, and pulled from every angle.

That's the way it worked. You had to pay quite a price, or you didn't get the girl. But I'd trained Peter well. He had envelopes for cousins and uncles and godparents. Finally, my father announced that he would accept the dowry.

"All is well," he said.

Now I belonged to the Saint Johns. I got up from the couch and walked over to where Peter's family sat to join them.

When the evening wrapped up, after more laughter, eating, and drinking, there was one last ritual. The women began to wail, beating their breasts, tearing at their clothes, falling to the floor. It was meant to show how much they loved me and how they would miss me so much. It was quite the show. And I'm sure Peter and his family, drained and exhausted, were glad to get the heck out of there.

. . .

In the eyes of my parents, Peter and I were married that day and no longer living in sin. But we wouldn't be married in the eyes of the law for another year, when we took our vows in a Roman Catholic ceremony in New York City on June 21, 2003.

We had one roadblock to overcome. Because I wasn't Catholic, we couldn't be married in a church. But we got the consent to do so as long as we participated in Pre-Cana, which is basically Catholic marriage counseling. Some of the lessons didn't make sense to me, so as I agreed to them, I crossed my fingers behind my back, winking at God. I figured he wouldn't mind if I lied a bit because God knew my heart and that I was doing this for love.

Unlike the Ghanaian ceremony, which was out of our hands, this wedding was all ours, so Peter and I took ownership of every detail, paying for it ourselves and choosing all the music, readings, and décor.

It was a homemade wedding put together by the hands of the people who loved us. One of my mother's sisters, Auntie Amma, was a wonderful baker like Mama. She made our cake and with the help of another one of my aunts toted the four layers all the way from London. Meanwhile my mom made my wedding dress from fabric embroidered in Ghana, flown to Colorado, and then ferried to New York, where she did the final alterations the week before the ceremony.

Our color scheme was—what else—black and white. My six bridesmaids wore dresses that resembled tuxedos, while I wore a somewhat traditional white gown with a long train. But the skirt and bodice were embroidered with the Gye Nyame, the Adinkra symbol for God. My mother thought it would add a beautiful touch of our Ghanaian culture to the American wedding. I wanted God himself to drape me and be there as I walked down the aisle on the arm of my father. Perhaps it would be the antidote to the poisoned question my dad had asked me at the start, the one that still haunted me at times: *"Why would you want to marry a white man? Don't you remember what happened with the last one you were with?"* The Gye Nyame would be my talisman, a sacred symbol that would ward off any evil forces that could hinder my marriage.

The church, around the corner from our apartment, was breathtakingly ornate, with intricate marble carvings and gold that shimmered around the altar. I remember my mother walking into that sanctuary for the first time during our rehearsal and just staring at the ceiling and pastel pieces of stained glass. I don't think she'd ever been in a Catholic church before.

"These white people," she whispered to my father in Fanti, the two of them looking around in awe. "They just do anything, even in a church. Can you imagine?"

I kept trying to shush them, though I know that only my aunts, snickering on the side, could understand them.

Peter and I declared our love in front of three hundred guests. One of my dad's very good friends, who was also a Catholic priest, assisted with the mass, which Peter's childhood priest from Massachusetts came down to New York to conduct.

Afterward, we moved the celebration to the Universalist Society on Manhattan's West Side. I wanted a reception hall that felt a little more inclusive, and the Society's hippy-dippy vibe was a nice contrast to the ornate formality of our Roman Catholic service.

My wedding party made the centerpieces, a single beta fish swimming through the roots of a plant inside a bowl. And, of course, there were roses. My girlfriend Clare went to the flower district the morning of the ceremony to buy fresh buds, and we sprinkled them along the runner in the church, on the reception hall's tables, and around the wedding cake, coloring its creamy whiteness with dollops of crimson.

When Peter and I finally got the chance to embrace, during our first dance, we chose the song "By Your Side" by Sade. It was from *Lovers Rock*, the album we'd fallen in love to, and whose title we inscribed inside our wedding bands.

Peter and I waited until we returned from our honeymoon in Mexico to tackle our small mountain of gifts. Among them was a beautiful almanac. It was from Ben's parents. The card encouraged Peter and me to discover the world.

. . .

Even though Peter's mother had taken our engagement photos and donned traditional Ghanaian dress for our Colorado ceremony, I don't think it was until we actually said our vows in front of that Catholic altar that she truly accepted our plan to be together forever. But after we were pronounced man and wife, the wall between us began to shake loose. We warmed to each other. We began to feel like family.

Peter's sister, Debra, on the other hand, still occasionally had her moments.

"Boz and Pete," she asked, not long before our Catholic wedding. "How will you raise your kids?"

"What?" we both asked.

"Umm, you know," she said. "Will they be Black or white?"

Peter and I looked at each other. Had this chick never met a multiracial person in her life?

"They'll be a human being," Peter said, shutting her down.

Fortunately, those awkward conversations were rare. And in the coming months, the drama emanated more from my side of the family, specifically my dad. Not because he disapproved of us. To the contrary, we got a little too close, because not long after Peter and I married, my father moved in.

. . .

I had known my parents' marriage was falling apart maybe even before they did. I felt it, watched it, for years. But I thought since they were good Christian people who were leaders in the church, and Ghanaian to boot, tradition would bind together what frustration and dwindling love might otherwise tear apart. They'd stay together, at least in name only, and just be miserable, forever.

Part of the tension came from my father's decisions. Dad was a constant student, restless and forever searching. That was why I disliked my own streak of spontaneity. It rang the most painful bells of my childhood, reminding me of how my dad's whims drained our savings and constantly uprooted our family.

He was always in pursuit of the shiny penny, the next opportunity, the new place that would give him more power, more excitement, more joy. He assumed that what he wanted, we wanted. The desires of his wife and children were of no consequence.

It wasn't like Dad would quit one job and get another in the same town. He'd get a new gig halfway across the world. Then it was up to my mother to stuff our lives into crates and boxes. She would have to find us new schools, to make friends with the new neighbors, to figure out how to get around a strange town and locate the market where she could ferret out ingredients for my father's Ghanaian meals. Then as quickly as Dad fell in love, the fire would flicker out, and we'd be on the move again.

Now, though he was in his late fifties and already had three degrees, Dad decided that he wanted to go back to school, so he applied to an executive-education seminar at Duke University.

This time, Mom said that she would stay behind. She was tired of shifting from place to place, and since the move would be temporary, she might as well stay put and keep the house in order. But when she refused to go, we all sensed—my parents, my sisters, and I—that something was about to permanently fracture. We just didn't want to talk about it.

I knew more than most because I'd become my dad's confidante, perhaps because as the oldest child I was the closest thing he had to a son. He would tell me all kinds of things, and I would have to manage his disappointment and sadness while also dealing with my mom's passive-aggressive bitterness.

It was tough to have any conversations with her because she wanted to blame Dad for everything. It was especially tough because this was happening during my engagement. I wanted to plan my weddings, the ceremonies that would solidify my bond to the man I loved, and Mom wanted to run down the man she believed had broken her heart. I didn't want to hear it. He was still my father, and who wants to listen to misery when you're madly in love?

I think I was so enveloped in joy from my own relationship, I never considered that maybe there were things that happened during my parents' union that broke them. That there could be devastating episodes that overwhelm all the determination you can muster, or simple disagreements and misunderstandings that can wear away your affection, like the tide.

Six months after Peter and I married in New York, Mom prepared to file for divorce, and I began to worry about what would happen when my father was done with Duke. It was a one-year program, and during his daily calls to me, I asked what he was planning and where he would go.

He didn't know.

I had to talk to Peter.

The positions Peter and I held in our families couldn't have been more different. Because he was the baby in his family, years younger than his nearest sibling, he had no responsibilities. But I was the oldest daughter in a traditionally Ghanaian family. In our culture, the oldest child takes responsibility for everyone, including their parents as they age. There literally comes a time when the mother and father are no longer the heads of the family. That role falls to the firstborn.

For me it happened quickly. I was only twenty-six, and my mother wanted to end her twenty-seven-year marriage, while my father was having a midlife crisis and rootless. I had to fix it. Peter didn't understand that at all.

"You've got to live your life," he said one afternoon after I'd hung up from a call with my dad. "Your parents are adults. Let them figure it out."

It was such a nonchalant way of existing, I thought. And it was the first time we'd disagreed over something significant. I now realize it was the earliest crack, the first moment I realized that there might be something seismic Peter and I didn't understand about each other. This wasn't simple, like our growing up listening to different kinds of music. There was a gap between us in the way we viewed family and responsibility.

I didn't understand at the time that if ignored, this type of tear can become an irreparable breach. Then, I just viewed our disagreement as an uncomfortable but not insurmountable cultural disconnect, similar to experiences I'd had as a Black girl growing up in California and then Colorado.

Peter wasn't disrespectful to his parents, but he definitely wasn't as reverential as me. I struggled over the next few months, knowing I had an obligation to my father but also knowing I didn't make enough money to set Dad up in an apartment of his own. I realized I was going to have to ask Peter if Dad could temporarily come live with us.

I pulled out all the stops. First, I cried. My tears were sincere, though I laid it on a little thick to yank Peter's heartstrings. I also made promises I doubted I could keep. Dad would be with us for just a couple of weeks, I told him, though I knew it would almost certainly be longer. Dad didn't have options. He'd left his last job to attend the seminar at Duke. Mom wasn't taking him back.

Peter didn't get it, but as was so often the case with us, his desire to please me won out. He said yes.

We rented a U-Haul truck and drove from New York to North Carolina. I'm sure as soon as we arrived, Peter wanted to turn around and run because from the moment we pulled up, Dad's self-centeredness was on full display.

As brilliant as he was, my father was also very dependent, reliant on others, especially my mother, to do the planning and worrying. That was the irony of Dad's character. He had such high expectations but demanded much more of others than he did of himself.

And he could be just plain selfish. He knew we were coming yet hadn't packed one box. All Dad cared about was finding the right suit to wear to his graduation. There was no acknowledgment that Peter and I rented a truck and drove a thousand miles to pick him up. There were no words of appreciation for Peter agreeing to let him move in when we'd been married only a year and lived in a studio apartment.

On the drive back to New York, I could see the worry etched in Peter's face as he pondered what he'd signed up for. It turns out he was right to be anxious. Dad ended up living with us for six long, nerve-racking months.

Dad slept on a futon couch in the space that functioned as our living room. Our bed was separated by a shelf where I'd stacked a bunch of books. We ended up putting up a piece of fabric to try to create some semblance of privacy, but that was pretty much a joke. A piece of plywood was no way to carve up five hundred and fifty square feet.

My dad and Peter's already-fragile relationship was now all the more precarious because the tables had turned and my father was the one needing Peter's acceptance. I was just waiting for something to blow between these two very different men.

Dad did at least try to cook for himself. Tasting his omelet and soups, which weren't half bad, I couldn't help thinking that maybe if he'd cooked more and performed a few other tasks around the house, he'd still have a marriage and a home with my mother in Colorado Springs. But when it came to cleaning up, Dad was a disaster.

Peter and I would come home from work and the kitchen galley would be a scene of total destruction, with tomato sauce spilled into the cracks of the stove and oil splattered on the floor. Peter wasn't the neatest person in the world, but compared to my dad, he was fastidious.

The kitchen wasn't the only tension spot. The smallest things also became potential flash points. My father bathed at night, and Peter showered before he left for work in the morning. I had to keep reminding Dad to make sure he didn't leave the soap sitting in a dish full of water because it would become soft on the bottom, turning into a mushy mess, which drove Peter crazy.

And Dad liked to spend money that he didn't have, something he and I actually had in common. He'd splurge impulsively, like when he bought a Mercedes SUV that he drove from Colorado to North Carolina and then to New York. I think the payment on it was equal to what Peter and I paid in monthly rent.

Because we lived in Manhattan and didn't have a garage, Dad parked on the street, moving his Benz from one side to the other early every morning. When he overslept one day, he got a big fat ticket that Peter and I had to pay. Peter was furious.

There was no separation, nowhere to go. Dad would prop his laptop on the kitchen counter and spend hours searching the internet, trying to find a job. In between, he watched CNN, sometimes on mute, but often at full volume, virtually twenty-four hours a day. Peter would have to negotiate when he could use our one TV so that he could watch his beloved football and baseball games.

"Okay," Peter would say, exasperation creeping into his voice. "The Niners are playing the Giants, so we have to turn off the news so we can watch the game . . ."

What was even worse was how my father would try to bond with Peter over the game though he didn't know a quarterback from a Quarter Pounder. He would pepper Peter with questions, and while it was kind of sweet that he was attempting to be Peter's buddy, Peter just wanted to enjoy his football games in peace.

"Why are they coming out of the hole?" Dad would ask, mislabeling the dugout while the two watched a Boston Red Sox game. "Why is that guy running?"

Nomar Garciaparra was Peter's favorite player. Every time he got a hit, the crowd roared his name.

"Nomahhhhh," they yelled, their Boston accents tossing the "r" to the wind.

Peter would scream. Then Dad would join in, not knowing what he was yelling, or why.

That year, 2004, the Red Sox won the World Series for the first time since 1918. Peter probably missed most of the plays because of Dad blabbering in his ear.

I was stressed the fuck out. My eyes twitched. My shoulders ached. I was exhausted from constantly looking out for any spark—a misguided word, an annoyance that went too far—in case I needed to stamp it out.

I also continued to carry the burden of being my father's emotional support, giving him comfort. I'll never forget the day he got the final divorce papers in the mail from my mom not long after my second wedding. I believe there may have even been a moment when they lay on the counter right beside my marriage license, which I had yet to put away. I still hold some resentment toward my mother for that—for how I couldn't fully enjoy the first days of my own marriage because I had to pick up and mend my father's broken pieces.

And, of course, I was also stressed because in the first year of my marriage, my husband and I couldn't get it on whenever we felt like it.

As newlyweds, we wanted to make love all the time. But that was now a no-go. Peter and I were grabbing quickies when my father went for an evening walk, took a shower, or moved the car. There was no more easy love, no more Sunday mornings, when we could burrow into each other, lie there, get up to make breakfast, and then go back to bed to make love some more. Now it was furtive, secret. We were married, grown-assed people who had to steal moments of pleasure in our own apartment.

The one exception was on our one-year anniversary. Peter and I went back to the Beekman, inviting friends to fill our room and celebrate with us over a spread of Indian food and prosecco. We invited Dad too. But that night, he had to go back to the apartment and leave us in peace. We made the sweetest love ever.

. . .

When Peter and I finally bought our own apartment, I knew that my dad couldn't come with us. I felt deep in my gut that if he did, he would be with Peter and me forever, preventing us from moving fully into our future. But I still believed I was responsible for him. I was the oldest child, and while he could be exasperating, he was still my father.

I called my sister Alua and told her I didn't know what to do. Like she would so often do in the years to come, Alua came to the rescue. She was renting a guest house in Los Angeles. Dad could come live with her and stay on the ground floor.

When I told Dad the plan, he seemed to take it in stride. He didn't say he felt rejected or shuffled or pushed out, and I was too relieved to probe.

I suppose Dad, the motherless child, simply drew on his past, his experience of being the boy absorbed into his mother's sister's household. Maybe he felt that this was just the way of his life. Even though we were the family that he had made, that he had borne, once again he had no choice but to move on. "I can't be here anymore. So I'll go over there." And he would be all right.

Dad did move on, though he never had steady work again. After he stayed with Alua, he took on a series of short-term consulting projects, bouncing from Atlanta, to Los Angeles, or anywhere else one of my sisters was living. Although he's since remarried, I still help him out financially. For sure it's easier now that I have the means to do it.

When I look back on those six months he lived with us, now able to view them for all that they were in whole, versus a single frustrating day at a time, I realize it was the first time I saw my dad as fully human, as fallible, as maybe even a little weak. His contradictions were startlingly clear: The disciplined thinker who was reckless with money. The keeper of tradition who stayed in no job for long. The gregarious storyteller who always felt alone.

It's a harrowing moment when you see your parent as something other than the all-knowing, powerful protector. Perhaps that's why you try as long as possible to deny what's in front of your eyes.

. . .

I don't remember our goodbyes as Dad headed off to be with Alua. I suppose it's because I was swept up in the excitement of Peter and I having a home of our own, to ourselves, at last.

Peter's uncle, who'd taken over the construction business Peter's grandfather started, loaned us forty thousand dollars to use as part of the down payment to buy a one-bedroom at the corner of 110th

Street and Central Park West, right at the edge of Frederick Douglass Circle. We moved in on New Year's Eve 2004.

It wasn't much bigger than our studio, but we now had actual walls to separate the spaces where we lived, ate, and slept, and that made it feel like we'd leaped into the lap of luxury.

The place needed work. Luckily Peter's dad was handy and helpful. He put in wooden floors made of beautiful blond planks. I picked out new cabinets, and we doused the walls with a new palette, gold in the living room, burgundy in the kitchen, blue in the bedroom, while we left the bathroom a dazzling white.

I had gotten a new job, working for Pepsi; Peter was still doing great, working as a creative for DDB. It felt like the world was our oyster.

As my parents' marriage fell apart, mine took flight. I resented them for giving me even a moment of doubt, for making me wonder, as steadfast as Peter's love was, if he could ever fall out of love with me. But like the weathered floor spruced up with fresh wood, and the cracks hidden beneath fresh paint, that worry was easy to ignore. Just like any other tiny irritation in our marriage.

Everything felt brand-new. For now.

7

Cracked Wide Open

P eter could barely swallow.

The toast I'd butter for him in the morning, the omelet I'd whip up with onions and bacon—no matter what I prepared, every bite was a struggle, a reminder that his reflexes were withering, that life's smallest gestures and pleasures—eating, standing, heading out the door for a quick walk—were slipping away.

One evening, watching Peter painstakingly nibble on a wheat cracker, I suddenly knew what I had to do. I needed to make a lasagna.

It was Peter's favorite dish, and I realized that soon he might not be able to eat it. I rushed to the grocery store to get everything I needed before it closed. I wouldn't use sugary sauce from a jar or that powdery Parmesan so processed that it could sit in a pantry for years and never go bad. I cheated with the noodles, grabbing a box that were premade, but everything else had to be cooked from scratch. I stuffed the cart with fresh tomatoes and basil, mozzarella and ground beef. When I arrived home, I got to work.

It took hours to chop the vegetables, simmer the sauce, and sear the meat. Peter just sat on the couch, smiling with delight as he watched me hustle around the kitchen.

It was after midnight when I finally pulled the pan out of the oven. Lasagna's supposed to sit for a while so the juices and spices can settle, but Peter said he couldn't wait, not even twenty minutes. We both knew his impatience wasn't just because lasagna was his favorite and the aroma was so intoxicating. He was anxious because everything in our lives had become urgent. We had to make haste, whether that meant moving back in together after being separated for years, booking a trip to our favorite getaway, or eating lasagna before it had time to cool.

I cut two chunks, the layers so hot, they slid off the spatula. It wasn't pretty, but Peter didn't care. Because he had to take such tiny bites, it must have taken him an hour to get through a single piece. But he and I ate every bit of that lasagna. And it was damn delicious.

. . .

"Boz, you know how to make lasagna, right?"

Peter and I were visiting his parents on one of our first trips to Massachusetts after we got married.

We'd just finished breakfast and I was sitting in the sun, feeling happy and full, when Peter's mother unleashed that question, seemingly out of nowhere. I immediately tensed up. Was this a test? Or a trap?

"No," I answered with a little trepidation.

"Well," Peter's mom said, a look of "I knew it" smugness settling on her face, "you'll have to learn. It's Peter's favorite. He grew up on good homemade lasagna. No Stouffer's or any of that frozen stuff. You'll need to cook it from scratch."

That got my back up a bit. I liked to cook, but I didn't *have* to do anything.

I looked at Peter. "Do *you* know how to make lasagna?"

Peter just shook his head no. Since he wasn't going to speak up, I did the talking for both of us.

"Peter doesn't know how to make it either," I said crisply. "And it's his favorite."

"Well," his mother said again, "you're going to learn. Today."

Interestingly, my lesson didn't come that day. Everyone seemed to forget all about the lasagna challenge as we went about our weekend. It was on another visit, a couple of months later, when Peter's mother suddenly stood up and told me to follow her into the kitchen. She asked me to chop up some onions. Then she grabbed a pot, filled it with water, and put it on the stove to boil. I knew then that school was about to begin.

It was more me watching than her teaching. I followed her lead and listened to her stories, about how she'd learned to make lasagna when she was a girl, about how when you put the sauce on the stove, you have to be careful not to turn the heat up too high because you don't want it to burn.

I was too nervous to reflect on it in the moment, but in the years to come, I would learn to appreciate the beauty of making lasagna. It is akin to meditation. There is no rushing it. You have to rely on your senses and trust that a cookbook can't teach you more than your memory can hold. Whatever the step—mixing the cheeses for the topping, putting the seasonings in the sauce—everything has to be done with precision and intention.

I could understand why Peter's mother enjoyed making lasagna for Peter and why, once I learned, I cherished it too. It was an act of love. By sharing the recipe with me, Peter's mother was saying in a roundabout way that she cared for me as well, or, at the very least, she had come to accept the woman her son adored.

. . .

I'd never cooked for my in-laws, so I think she may have expected me to struggle to keep up, but I actually felt very comfortable in the kitchen. My mother prepared every meal for our family when I was a kid, and for as long as I could remember, my sisters and I had been her helpers.

Mom didn't even have to ask. It could be early on a Saturday morning, when we wanted to loll in bed, but we'd hear her banging pans and pots, and we knew we'd better get up, wash our faces, and hop to the kitchen in a hurry.

Jollof rice is the Ghanaian dish most comparable to my mother-in-law's lasagna. Every West African woman worth her salt knows how to make it. There's even a rivalry between Ghanaians and Nigerians about who cooks jollof best. Like its Italian counterpart, jollof is all about skill, patience, and a little bit of chance. And when you were finally done, ladling it out of a giant pot, it felt like a timeless gesture of love.

We were visiting my in-laws on yet another trip when I got the bright idea to cook dinner for the family.

"Oh?" Peter's mother said, a little skeptically. "What are you going to make?"

Nope. I didn't say jollof.

"I was thinking lasagna."

My mother-in-law arched her brows ever so slightly.

"Hmmmm. Okay," she said as she left the kitchen.

Don't ask me why the hell I thought making lasagna for my

mother in-law, Peter, and his dad was a sane idea, but now that I'd offered, I had to deliver.

I was extra careful. The boiled noodles had to be al dente because the juices would continue to cook them in the oven, and if they were overdone, they'd turn to mush. I turned the stove's flame down to a flicker to make sure the sauce didn't overcook, and constantly checked to make sure the meat didn't edge beyond pink before I put it in the casserole dish.

Peter came into the kitchen at one point to make a salad and then ran to the store to buy a beautiful bottle of red wine. When the lasagna was finally finished and I'd taken it out of the oven to cool, the four of us sat down in the living room. The TV was on, but I don't think any of us were paying attention. All eyes were burrowing through the walls to the kitchen counter. After what seemed like an endless twenty minutes, Peter's mother stood up.

"It should be ready," she said, as she walked toward the dining room table.

I carried the dish in from the kitchen. You can taste many Ghanaian dishes along the way, dipping in a spoon, dabbing the concoction in your palm, then taking a lick. If it wasn't quite right, you could add a few more tomatoes, toss in some more pepper. But just like jollof, lasagna's flavors have to sit and meld. The meat can be perfect, the cheese mixture can be on point, but you can't be sure how the flavors ultimately jelled until you cut it and put that first forkful in your mouth.

We all knew that I'd set myself up to be judged, and the odds were not in my favor. I could have drunk that entire bottle of red wine by myself as I watched Peter and his dad dive in.

"Mm-mm-mmm!" Peter's dad grunted. "That is good!"

"Yeah, sweetie," Peter mumbled, his mouth full. "You did great!"

Meanwhile, Peter's mom hadn't touched her plate. Neither had I. I couldn't breathe, let alone eat.

She looked down at her lasagna, then over at Peter, then at her husband, chewing furiously. I wondered if she was thinking the same thing I was. That they were putting on quite the show so they wouldn't hurt my feelings.

Finally, I picked up my fork and sliced off a corner. I took a bite, the tomato and spices exploding in my mouth.

It. Was. Slamming.

The noodles were silken. The sauce was rich. The cheesy top was golden. That damn lasagna was perfection.

I'd done it. The odds weren't in my favor, but I'd won.

Of course, I didn't say any of that out loud.

"It's not as good as Mom's," I said casually. "It could have used a little more Italian seasoning. And probably some more salt."

If my mother-in-law wore glasses, she would have been peering over their rims. "Oh," she said, picking up her fork at last. "I'm sure it's fine."

She took a taste, chewing slowly.

She looked at me again. "It's perfect, Bozoma."

• • •

That dish of tomatoey beef and noodles became a symbol in the first years of my marriage. It was a covenant of sorts, a reminder that Peter and I were eternal newlyweds who didn't wait for Valentine's Day to express our love or Christmas Day to give each other gifts. As laborious as lasagna was to make, I'd come home from work in the middle of the week, change into my sweats, and get busy in the kitchen. Peter could smell the lasagna as soon as he got off the elevator, and his first words as he swung open the door were "I know you're cooking something good!"

We ate our meals looking into each other's eyes or out of the window framed with the curtains I'd sewn myself. If this wasn't bliss, I thought, I didn't know what was.

But inevitably, real life began to creep in. They were small irritations, but like a growing web of tiny cracks, too many of them could eventually lead to a collapse.

Peter rose with the dawn, and I liked to sleep in. He'd want to go for a bike ride, and I'd suggest we kick the car into cruise control and take a drive.

And then there was Peter's faith. I'd always found his commitment to Catholicism endearing. It showed his dedication to tradition. But I didn't like some of the church's beliefs, like the way it frowned on being gay. Peter never said anything derogatory about gay people, but I knew that his faith made him feel conflicted, while I was totally steadfast in my belief that God made us all the way we are. So Peter would head to mass early every Sunday while I asked him to pick up brunch as I stayed in bed.

Ambition also formed another divide. Peter's just didn't match mine. He was slow to switch positions or agencies. He'd encourage me, praising my talents while polishing my résumé. But he constantly warned me to be cautious.

At first, I thought it was cute. I had my father's impulsive nature, and I'd watched Dad's sometimes reckless choices compromise the stability of others around him. I appreciated that Peter could be my ballast, the compass to steer me away from a bad decision or the safety net to catch me if one of my spur-of-the-moment career leaps failed to work out. But I wanted what I wanted when I wanted it, ever eager for the next challenge. When I didn't get my way, I got angry, and Peter's tentativeness began to get on my nerves.

Peter did support my restlessness at times. When I finally quit Spike's advertising agency, unable after a couple of years to take the petty behavior of the company's president anymore, Peter paid the bills as I figured out what I wanted to do.

For a second, I tried to be a writer. I became a walking and talking cliché, literally wearing a beret and hanging out at cafés, where I mused about the world. Then I briefly worked for an after-school tutoring program. Finally, I took a job at a recruiting firm.

I hated it. I was making around thirty-five thousand dollars a year, more money than I'd ever been paid, but I found the work—making cold calls and matching candidates to jobs—tedious and dull.

One day, Spike called and said his agency had won a pitch with Pepsi and he wanted me to come back, not as an assistant, but as an executive who would have a key role overseeing Pepsi's campaign. It would mean a five-thousand-dollar pay cut, and the woman who'd been my nemesis was still the company's president. But I'd always had a great relationship with Spike, and the fact he was asking me to come back only deepened it. Working again with him, and also for an iconic company like Pepsi, felt like an exciting opportunity.

I called Peter to tell him about the offer. It was like he poured cold water all over me.

"Don't you think you should stay where you are?" he asked. "You're making more money, and you've got a chance to rise up there. How far can you go with Spike?"

I'd grown up in a home where my father had the final say. My mother abided by his decisions, even when she didn't agree with them. I knew I was lucky to be married to a man who was financially stable and much more deliberative than my dad.

He was talking sense. He was trying to look out for my best interests. Still, I wanted out of that job.

"But," I sputtered, "I hate it!"

Two days later, I quit the recruiting agency, and within a week, I was back working for Spike.

That professional push and pull kept happening. I'd get a job offer and want to leave my current gig, and Peter would urge me to push pause and stay.

Maybe it was because my career was so important to me. Maybe it was because my ambition was so intense. But I began to wonder why Peter so often advised me against following my gut.

Perhaps it wasn't just about being protective, I thought. Maybe Peter just lacked vision. Maybe my contributing a big paycheck to our household was more important to him than my being happy in my job. Maybe, I thought, he was just weak.

I wasn't so sure how well I really knew Peter after all. I began to be resentful of his caution. And soon there would be even bigger challenges to feed my doubts.

. . .

For a long while, Peter's comfort around Black folks made me just shake my head and smile. His life had been monochromatic before me, but he blended into my Black world seamlessly.

Not long after we got married, Peter and I went to a golf tournament hosted by *Black Enterprise* magazine. One of the events on the itinerary was a version of the Newlywed Game, where the host asked sometimes raunchy questions to see how well couples knew their partners. We wrote our answers on pieces of poster board, then displayed them at the same time to see if our answers matched.

Peter was the only white person among the three couples. We were ahead, with one question left to go.

"What," the host asked, pausing dramatically for effect, "is your favorite part of your wife's body?"

Oh man, I thought. *I think we got this.*

Peter loved my butt. He'd watch me admiringly as I walked across the room, give it a pat every chance he got, and always wanted me to put on the tightest jeans I could find. He and I scribbled furiously with our black markers.

"Peter and Boz," the host bellowed. "What do you have to say?"

I wanted to win, but if Peter and I had both written the truth, I knew I was also going to be more than a little embarrassed.

I held up my board. "My butt," I said a little sheepishly.

When Peter revealed his answer, he wasn't so shy.

"The bootayyyyyyyy," he said, dragging the word out with a huge grin on his face. The audience went wild. And we won.

I knew this sense of ease, on display on the nights we went to a Black club and during family dinners at my parents' home, was due in part to his simply being a white man who felt intuitively that the world was his. There was no place that would deny him entry, no space where he couldn't go. The idea that he might be excluded or mistreated never entered his consciousness, whereas it lurked on the edge of mine nearly every day.

But I felt Peter's comfort also was a testament to how much he loved me. Of course he embraced Blackness, I thought, the culture that had shaped me. How could he not?

Outsiders, however, continued to ask questions.

. . .

I stayed at Spike's agency for about two years in my second go-around, and then I got itchy again for a different experience. I'd honed my pop culture bona fides, blending my understanding of contemporary music and art with a distinctly Black aesthetic. Now I felt it was important to get my card stamped in a more mainstream agency to open up other opportunities.

I landed a job working for Arnold Worldwide, a global advertising agency, and my first account was working on smoking-cessation products. It was quite a shift from what I'd been doing, but a part of me still wanted to make my father proud, and using my advertising talents to promote medical aids seemed like the perfect compromise.

I had a white female manager during the three months that I was there. From practically our first meeting, it was clear we couldn't stand each other.

She was right out of central casting: tall, reed thin, blond, and blue-eyed. When she ate her no-crouton salad for lunch, instead of pouring the dressing over the lettuce, she dipped her fork into the little cup tucked on the side.

Yep. She was *that* chick.

I'd worn braids or extensions for longer than Peter and I had been together, and I had a weave trailing down my back at the time I applied for this particular job. But one day, when I was going to my scheduled hair appointment, I had a Halle Berry moment, and just like that, I decided to lop off all my hair.

Let me emphasize here that hair is deeply personal for Black women. Our coils are like pieces of sculpture that can be shaped in a million ways, but they are also fraught with unwarranted symbolism and baggage. There's pressure to mimic the textures and styles of white women to be seen as respectable in white spaces and even among some affluent or aspirational Black folks. I've usually changed my hair to reflect my creativity or mood, but I can't lie. Sometimes my style and texture of choice was more to satisfy society's expectations than my own desires.

The day I decided to cut off my hair, however, was not one of those times. I plopped down in the salon chair and told my hairdresser that I wanted the extensions gone.

"Are you sure?" he asked.

"Yes. But do it quick, before I change my mind!" I said.

My hairdresser stripped out the weave, gave me a brisk shampoo, then cut my hair into a short pixie cut.

That day, Peter and I were preparing yet again to go to Massachusetts, this time to celebrate Thanksgiving. He was getting off work early, and we were going to meet for a late lunch. But first I had to stop by the office to grab some paperwork to read over the long weekend.

Pretty much everyone was gone, but not my boss, Miss Priss. She walked past my cubicle just as I was taking the papers off my desk.

"Boz?" she said, her voice rising several decibels as she did a double take. "Oh my God! You cut off all your hair!"

"Umm, yeah," I said, touching the nape of my neck self-consciously.

"What does Peter think?" she asked, looking at me like she'd seen a ghost.

"I don't know," I said, becoming annoyed. "He hasn't seen it."

"Well," she said, "you know guys like Peter like long hair."

Guys like Peter. I knew what that meant. Guys like Peter, who were tall, well-built, white. The kind of guy she believed should have been with a woman who looked like her. *Those* guys liked long, straight hair.

I'm usually quick with a comeback. But right then I had nothing. She'd hit on an insecurity that was lurking in the back of my mind. Would Peter be attracted to the Boz with the short pixie cut who looked so different from the long-haired Boz he'd fallen in love with?

I grabbed the papers I'd come for. "Happy Thanksgiving," I mumbled as I rushed toward the door.

I thought about her petty warning all the way to the restaurant. When I arrived, Peter was already there, sitting at the table. When he turned around and I saw the look of shock cross his face, it was all I could do to not run to the nearest hair supply store, buy a packet of extensions, and glue them to my scalp myself.

"Oh my God!" he said.

Why did everybody keep saying that?

"I didn't even recognize you," he said. Then he smiled. "You look beautiful."

I searched his face. Was he trying to make me feel better? When he stood up, caressed my neck, and gave me a kiss, I knew: Yes. He still thought I was beautiful. I didn't think I could possibly love him more.

Still, I never cut my hair that short again. I did abandon chemical relaxers as I grew out my hair, wanting to get back to my natural texture. Having held on to Peter's attraction and love the first time I did something unexpected, I wondered how he would react this time.

He was okay with the big chop, I thought. *Now, let's see if he's cool with me going full-on Black girl, kinky hair and all.*

By that time in my life, I was more confident than I'd been the day I first sported my Halle Berry cut, but I was definitely still a little insecure. I was always very aware that Peter had never been with anyone like me before. I never yearned to be with anyone else, Black or otherwise, but I sometimes worried Peter might one day decide he wanted someone who felt more familiar, a girl like the ones his mother and sister sometimes mentioned, with the same background as his cousins and childhood friends.

What if he woke up one day and said, "Enough of this. I don't want to worry about hair products, or 'the rules,' or my wife yelling out that I'm her man because she feels slighted? I want some peace"?

Yet, Peter held me through my uncertainty. As my kinks bloomed into a full-on Afro, his love was steadfast. I felt sure it could never fade.

. . .

On a day in 2006, Peter and I went to a casino in Connecticut with my best friend from college, Leander, and her husband, Ray. They both loved Peter. We often vacationed together, and that particular weekend we were celebrating Leander's birthday. After losing a little money on the slot machines, we made our way to the casino's restaurant to get a bite to eat.

My memories of the incident are muddled now. I know there was a skinny white waitress with a scowl on her face. I know we repeatedly tried to get menus as she took the orders of others who'd arrived after us. Then finally, she hurled a rude comment toward Ray.

She didn't want to wait on us. She didn't want us there. We knew it was because we were Black.

Ray rose from the table, and Leander quickly followed, trying to calm him down.

Peter, often clueless, totally got it this time.

"I'm going to go over and let her have it," he said angrily.

As a Black woman, I understood when to confront something and when to let it go. I had to tap into the rhythm, the knowing, already inside of me. That's how we survive.

It was Leander's birthday. People were staring. Ray, a proud Black man, wouldn't want someone else to fight his battle.

"Don't do that," I said quietly to Peter. "Don't make it worse."

"I'm so sorry," Peter said, becoming emotional. "I want to tell Ray I'm sorry."

I told him he had no reason to apologize. He wasn't the stupid racist. "Let's just salvage the rest of the day," I said.

After talking to the manager, Ray and Leander finally came back to the table, and we nursed our drinks. But Peter couldn't let it go.

"I'm sorry about that, Ray," he finally blurted out.

Ray put down his iced tea.

"Don't apologize," he said. "Don't apologize like you're one of them. You are one of *us*."

That's when it happened. I'm sure Ray and Leander didn't notice. Even I wouldn't have been able to articulate it at the time. But I could feel it. I could see it.

Peter's eyes didn't well with tears of gratitude. Instead, they widened with alarm. He didn't smile in solidarity. Instead, Ray's message of solace and brotherhood seemed to make Peter shrivel.

Peter always sat ramrod straight. Now, he literally sank into the vinyl seat, pulling within. It was like his entire spirit crumbled.

Peter's countenance told me what he could not say. He had empathy for Black people's struggle, appreciation for our resilience. But he wasn't one of us. And he didn't want to be.

The disconnect was something I'd always feared. I'd worried that there were aspects of my existence that Peter simply couldn't bear. Sometimes, I made a conscious choice to not express to him the most painful things about being Black, like how I tensed up whenever I saw a cop, or how I braced for a challenge whenever I settled into a first-class airplane seat.

Peter and I could discuss *Song of Solomon*. He could feel a pang of pain when he saw Ray being mistreated. But while he recognized injustice, Peter couldn't really feel its sting. And he never wanted that to change.

. . .

When Peter and I first began dating, I used to say I didn't fall in love with a white man, I just fell in love with Peter. But I did fall in love with a white man and all his white-man things. And the thing I'd loved most was the way Peter moved through the world.

I remember when Peter and I traveled to Paris together for the first time. One night, buzzed and unsteady, Peter wanted to take a shortcut through a dark alley on the way back to our hotel. I sobered up quickly. The Black girl in me sensed danger and felt it was a bad idea. But Peter insisted that we were going down that alley. His fearlessness may have been the result of the half bottle of cognac we'd drunk. Or maybe it was because he was six five. But I think it was mostly because he was a white man and he felt in full command, even on a strange street in a foreign land.

We walked down that alley and emerged safe. *How I wish I could bottle up some of that white-man bravado*, I later thought, *gulp it down, and use it for fuel.*

But the wholly different ways we viewed and experienced the world also divided us. I've often wondered what Peter would have thought about this moment in time. Where would he stand as this country is forced to confront the ugliness of its past bleeding so profusely and profoundly into its present?

A couple of months after George Floyd's murder, it became difficult for me to go on Facebook. Members of Peter's family were posting that "Blue Lives Matter," "All Lives Matter"—everybody else's life seemed to matter except those of the Black people who were regularly being executed by police officers and white vigilantes. It was infuriating. I didn't know how to respond when all I wanted to do was scream and punch the air.

Then one day Peter's fraternity brother Mike, whom we called by his college nickname, Mecca, sent me a picture. Mike had an upbringing and personality very similar to Peter's, and he lived in a mostly white rural town in Pennsylvania. But the photo he texted showed him carrying an American flag while walking in solidarity with us at a Black Lives Matter march.

I cried, not only because Mike had taken such a stance, but because I wondered if Peter, a staunch Republican, would have done the same. Even though he'd loved and married me, a Black woman, and fathered a Black child, I can honestly say that I'm not sure. And that hurts.

It would be only in hindsight that I could pick apart the flood of feelings I had that day in the casino restaurant. But I know now that it was a pivotal moment. I'd fought my father and even some of my friends when they warned that a love like ours would be hard to maintain. I'd told the doorman in Peter's building that everything would be okay. But that afternoon I started to fear that maybe I'd been wrong and they'd all been right.

I know Peter didn't have the same prejudices as that awful waitress. But I started to believe he identified more with her than he did Ray, Leander, or me. There would always be fundamental things about us that he could not understand. And how could we be Team PBoz, us against the world, if he forever saw himself as one of "them"?

Until then, I'd believed love could conquer all, that ours was a romance for the ages. We didn't have the kind of love that ran hot and cold. It was constant.

But that day in the casino, something ruptured. The cracks, rippling and deep, threatened to become a chasm.

. . .

A year later, Ghana celebrated half a century of independence from Great Britain with months of ceremonies and parties. Peter and I decided to visit, along with my mother, my sister Alua, and Alua's boyfriend, Kip.

Ghana is a place where people get up with the roosters, so the whole country was on Peter's time. When I woke up at my aunt's home, Peter would already be gone. We'd search for him before we sat down to breakfast and find Peter up the street, holding hands and laughing with a group of neighbors he'd just met. At the market, he'd wander off and start haggling over the price of a piece of fruit like he'd been conducting such street-side negotiations his entire life.

"Where's Peter? Where's Peter?" became my family's constant refrain.

I was uneasy. I told him to be careful, that there were customs he had to adhere to so he wouldn't appear disrespectful, like never grabbing anything with his left hand. But Peter would always forget. When I'd smack him as he used his left hand to reach for a spoon at a restaurant or in my aunt's kitchen table, he'd good-naturedly mutter to leave him alone and continue with his faux pas.

I felt my anger before I could pinpoint its root. But slowly I realized that Peter's comfort and privilege were bugging me. It rankled me to see him so confident in a country that wasn't his, when I, a Black woman, remained so uncomfortable back in the country Peter and I called home. I should have been ecstatic that Peter was embracing Ghana. Instead, I was pissed at his white-man arrogance. Every place on the planet yielded to him, while I could seldom walk freely without fear. What should have been a really amazing trip slowly became deeply frustrating, even painful.

The day came when we traveled to the Cape Coast, the part of Ghana my mother's family is originally from. It is an incredibly beautiful place, but also one of immense grief. Historians say that almost 80 percent of all stolen Africans, captured throughout West Africa, passed through the ports of Cape Coast and Elmina Castles.

Hundreds of years later, these castles, the largest and most infamous portals of the Atlantic slave trade, remain frightening places. After dozens of trips to Cape Coast, and up until a couple of years ago, I was never able to bring myself to go down the steps to the dungeons—hollows of agony where men, women, and children had crowded in terror, unable to imagine the harrowing journey they were about to endure and the cruel new world that waited on the other side.

Peter, however, had no problem descending into those depths.

It was yet another reminder of our different places in the world. He was solemn the entire day, respectfully asking questions and sometimes pausing in silence. But this place and its atrocities haunted me in a way that they never would Peter. I felt the pain in my marrow. Knowing Peter didn't—couldn't—just made me more bitter.

I began to lash out, arguing over the silliest of things. When we fought one night before going to bed, I broke down in tears.

Let me say this: I am an ugly crier. My eyes become swollen and red, and if I go to sleep, I wake up with a face that even an ice pack can't fix.

The morning after that fight, I looked horrible.

Peter panicked. "You can't go downstairs like that," he said. But I was still in a bad mood and wanted everybody to see how much he'd upset me.

I got dressed, barely bothering to comb my hair just to add a little extra sauce to the shock I knew everyone would feel when I entered the room.

While I'd struggled to be embraced by Peter's mother, he'd had the opposite experience with mine. From the first night Mom met him at my apartment, Peter could do no wrong. But when she saw me approach the table, a question loomed in Mom's eyes.

"What happened? Did he hurt you?"

I said nothing. I couldn't untangle my complex feelings even for myself. Instead, everyone tried to make it through the uncomfortable breakfast. Afterward, I was more than ready for Peter and me to return to New York.

When we got back, our friends had countless questions. What was it like? What did you do?

I remained, perhaps unreasonably, sensitive.

I wanted to say, "It's not freaking Mars, for God's sake. And there aren't any half-naked women swirling around with waist beads. It's a country filled with cities and people just living their lives."

Instead, I pursed my lips and silently counted to ten.

But Peter couldn't praise Ghana enough. "It was fantastic!" "It was amazing!"

Maybe if he'd felt a little bit as uncomfortable in Accra, as I often felt on the streets of Boston or even Boulder, he'd have a glimpse of my world, of how it felt to be the "other." Maybe then, if Ray ever said again that he was one of us, Peter would embrace those words and not recoil. But even when people stared at Peter on the streets of Ghana, they looked on with curiosity rather than hostility. Peter could stroll through life, oblivious.

Of course, if he'd told his friends he felt like an outsider in Accra, that Africa was off-putting and strange, I would have been even angrier. There was no way for him to win. Peter was in an impossible position.

Soon enough, I would be as well.

. . .

If you have an honest conversation with any married person, they'll tell you there are hurdles you can't anticipate. It took my parents divorcing for me to discover that Peter's idea of responsibility was different from mine. It took the stream of professional opportunities that began to flow my way for me to see that Peter and I had starkly different expectations of what we wanted from our careers.

But some things are too monumental to not discuss before you say "I do." Like whether you want to have children.

We'd been married about four years when Peter began to say he wanted us to start a family. I was in no hurry and wasn't really sure I wanted children at all.

It was startling for those realizations to emerge so late in our marriage. How did we overlook discussing something as life-altering as children? Questions began to eat at me. Was it pride that made us get married? Did we just want to prove everyone wrong? What else did we not know or comprehend about each other? I began to doubt my judgment, and most frighteningly of all, I began to wonder if Peter and I were really meant to be.

I didn't straight-up refuse to have a child, but I kept right on taking my birth control pill every morning. Then, in early March 2008, my period was late.

It can't be, I thought. My cycle had always been regular, so I bought a pregnancy test. When the two pink stripes appeared on the tiny screen, I continued to tell myself that this was impossible. I'd been so careful. But I made an appointment with my doctor.

It couldn't be, but it was. Peter and I were going to have a baby.

I tried to reason through my fear. If I could get pregnant, even while on birth control, even with all the doubts I was beginning to have about my marriage, this must be what God wanted. Right?

God had given me the answers to all my questions. Now, I believed, I had to stop asking them.

8

The Choice

During one of my visits to the hospital, I was sitting beside Peter's bed, watching him sleep, when I first smelled it. I wondered if someone had tossed a bouquet of flowers in the trash or perhaps spilled something on the floor.

The scent was sweet but also tart, so thick I could almost taste it. It was the kind of smell that seeped into the back of your throat, and if you held on to it too long, you felt you might choke. *What is that?* I wondered as it enveloped me, at the hospital, in the living room, in the hallway, before it disappeared.

Soon, I realized the source. The scent was coming from Peter. It was the smell of dying.

When I finally knew what it was, I'd get a whiff and want to run away. I'd put a sleeve up against my nose or press my face into my pillow. Sometimes, lying in bed with Peter, I'd have to get up and go into another room.

Sometimes I thought, *Is that the smell of God?* The idea that it might be gave me comfort. But it also scared me, because I knew its presence meant Peter was getting closer and closer to the end.

. . .

I cried for days after I found out I was pregnant. I cried when I was alone in the bathroom. When I was in the shower. While I was on my way to work. I'd known I was pregnant a week before I finally picked up the phone and told my mother.

Peter, meanwhile, was elated. When I took my first pregnancy test, he'd wanted to call his mom with the news practically before I got off the toilet. Now that my doctor had confirmed we were having a baby, he seemed to no longer just walk around our apartment. He leapt with joy.

I didn't want to be pregnant. I wasn't sure anymore that I even wanted Peter. Had we really thought about what we were getting into? Should we have gotten married at all?

I was starting to hit my stride professionally, filling in the boldest colors of my fabulous New York life. Having a child meant I'd have to stay in a marriage I was beginning to doubt and maybe jobs I'd begun to hate. I liked being able to go to a resort in the Caribbean or Mexico on a whim. Now, I would be fully responsible for another human being.

My self-image as Peter's wife had already started to blur as I adjusted to his cautiousness, seeking counsel and sometimes compromise when I was used to doing whatever I wanted. I feared motherhood would shrink me further. All I was missing was the minivan with the parent and kid stick figures stuck to the window.

I'd read that women needed to get past the three-month mark to make sure their pregnancy was viable, so in those initial weeks, I only told my immediate family and closest friends that I was expecting. But when I crossed into my second trimester and my stomach began to push past my waistband, I began to tell my coworkers.

I was now working full-time for Pepsi. I'd made a lot of contacts when I worked on the Pepsi account for Spike's agency, and those eventually led to the company offering me a job in its marketing department. To a person, my colleagues were thrilled that I was pregnant, and slowly their giddiness began to make me more excited. Outside, on the street, I went from being just any random New Yorker to being an expectant mom. People treated me more delicately. At a restaurant, other patrons would let me cut the line. And when I rode the subway, commuters who might have bumped me without a second thought said excuse me and offered up their seats. The world tilted toward me seemingly overnight.

Still, my emotions remained complicated. I struggled to come to terms with the idea of being someone's mother, and I continued to worry that Peter and I weren't ready to build a family when our relationship wasn't as perfect as I'd imagined.

Yet each time I went to the doctor, the seconds Peter and I waited to hear the baby's heartbeat felt like hours. My need to know that life was pulsing inside me began to overwhelm my uncertainty, deepening my bond to my unborn baby.

My obstetrician was the opposite of the stereotypical stern clinician swathed in white. He cracked jokes as he checked my blood pressure or examined my sonogram. I, however, was never nonchalant when I went to the doctor. Perhaps it was because of my breast cancer scare in high school, but I was a bit of a hypochondriac. I peppered him with questions. Were there certain foods I should avoid eating? Was it normal for the baby's heartbeat to be so rapid? If I felt a cramp, did that mean something was wrong?

"Don't worry so much!" he told me, waving his hand. "Every woman has a different pregnancy. You're young. You're healthy. Everything will be fine."

But I wasn't so sure. I felt like something was off, like something was coming.

. . .

When I was about six months pregnant, the doctor decided to give me a relatively routine test to check the level of my amniotic fluid. The results, received a few days later, showed that my fluid was low.

The nurse who phoned us said that wasn't necessarily a bad sign. Still, they asked me to come back on Monday so they could check the fluid again.

Peter and I didn't panic. The nurse said they were just being cautious since I was approaching my last trimester. We wanted to believe her.

We were heading to Cape Cod for the Fourth of July that weekend. Peter's brother David owned a beautiful home there, and every summer it became a gathering spot for all the Saint Johns. You didn't even have to phone David to say you were coming. You could just show up. That made for a stream of wonderful surprises as people popped up on the doorstep, and before you knew it, the house was bursting with family and fun.

As we prepared for the drive, I noticed that my sandals felt a little tighter and when I put on my lipstick in the passenger mirror, my face looked puffy. I shook it off, resolving to just drink more water.

When we arrived, we didn't tell the family about the results of our amniotic fluid test, seeing no need to worry them with news that, while not great, wasn't automatically bad. Still, David was dating a medical assistant and throughout the weekend she constantly asked me how I was feeling. I hoped it was just general concern and not her professional instincts telling her that something was wrong.

I had the second amniotic test when we got back home. We found out that not only was my fluid low, the baby didn't appear to be developing like it should. Our doctor continued to be nonchalant. Some people had low fluid, he said. And yes, the baby wasn't quite the size that it should be at this point in the pregnancy, but the heartbeat was still strong, and everything else looked normal. Really, he said, I shouldn't worry.

Meanwhile, I was getting more and more swollen. I'd look fairly normal when I woke up in the morning, but I was retaining so much water that by nightfall, you could poke my arm with your finger, and it would leave an indentation. My doctor wasn't alarmed, so I chalked it up to being yet another unpleasant aspect of pregnancy, like having to go to the bathroom twenty times a day. I continued going to work.

The morning of July 10, I walked by the desk of our vice president's assistant, Melissa.

"How are you feeling?" she asked me.

I hadn't told anyone what the doctors said, and normally I would have just tossed out the obligatory "fine" and kept walking. But the truth was, I didn't feel so well. She was a young mother, and I knew she would understand.

"Umm, a little slow," I said, offering her a wan smile.

I made my way to my desk and sat down. A short time later, Melissa walked over.

"You know," she said, a bit hesitant, "you don't look well."

"What do you mean?" I said, my heart beginning to pound harder. "I definitely feel fat and not that comfortable."

"I know," she said. "I've been there. But—I know this isn't something you want to hear when you're pregnant—you really just don't look good to me. I think you should go to the doctor."

Pepsi's corporate campus in Purchase, New York, was a city unto itself, with a bank, a dry cleaner's, and a doctor's office on-site. But I tried brushing her off. Yes, I was a little tired, but that was all. Besides, I had an appointment with my own OB-GYN in a couple of days.

"No," she insisted. "You should go see our doctor. Now."

I stayed put, and she walked away looking concerned. But half an hour later, she was back.

"Humor me," she said. "I'll even go with you."

This is a pain in the ass, I thought as I grabbed my purse and waddled down to the clinic, Melissa walking beside me. I had meetings in the afternoon and notes to review.

When we walked into the clinic, we were greeted by Jane, the type of sweet, old-school nurse who talked about her kids and would give you a lollipop even though you were a grown woman. You'd breeze in wanting to quickly get a flu shot and wind up sitting at the clinic for two hours, held captive by Jane and listening to her stories.

I might as well cancel my meetings now, I thought when I saw she was on duty. *I'll be here all afternoon.*

"Hi, Boz and Melissa," Jane said brightly. "Why are you guys here?"

Melissa told her that she didn't feel I looked well. Jane cocked her head. "She looks okay to me," she finally said.

"I don't know," Melissa said. "Just take her temperature or something. I've got to get back to my desk, but, Boz, let me know later how you're doing." She turned around and left.

Jane sat me down, then took my temperature. It was 98.6 on the nose, so no problem there. She weighed me. I was enormous, so as she balanced the scale, I told her to please not bother telling me the number. She laughed but obliged my request and kept me in the dark. Then she took my blood pressure.

"Hmm," she said, worry lines creasing her brow. "Here," she said, walking over to the water cooler and bringing me back a cup. "Sip this."

I asked her why, and she said my pressure was just a little high. But I noticed her whole demeanor had changed. She was no longer chatty Jane. She was serious, concerned. I drank the water, and we waited a few minutes before she took my pressure again. Then she asked me to lie down. She left the room, and when she came back, she was accompanied by the doctor.

I've never understood why people taking your blood pressure tell you to relax when the first reading is high. Don't they know that just makes you more nervous and causes your pressure to spike even more? Sure enough, Jane told me to be calm. She just wanted the doctor to check me because she wasn't sure she'd done the reading correctly.

I knew that was bullshit. Jane had been a nurse longer than I'd been alive. She knew how to apply a blood pressure cuff. Now, I really began to get anxious.

The doctor asked me a bunch of innocuous questions. What was I working on? What did I do for the Fourth of July? I knew he was trying to distract me. "Can you just take my blood pressure?" I pleaded.

He did. A few seconds later, he asked for the name of my obstetrician.

He quickly left the room, and when he returned, he told me he'd called an ambulance.

The room started to spin. My blood pressure was way too high, he said. I needed to go to the hospital. I jumped up and reached for my cell phone to call Peter. He was as confused and scared as I was.

It's crazy now when I think about it, but I didn't want to wait for an ambulance. I insisted that I could drive myself to the hospital. Jane and the doctor were frantic, trying to make me wait, but I rushed out of the office and got in my car. I called Leander as I drove, needing someone to talk to. My words spilled out in a rush.

"Hey," I said. "I'm scared. I don't know what's going on. The doctor at Pepsi said that my pressure is high. They wanted to call an ambulance."

"What the hell are you doing driving?" Leander yelled.

I didn't know. I guess that was something I could do for myself when everything else was spiraling out of my control.

When I arrived at the hospital, I drove around for several minutes, looking for a parking spot before pulling into a garage. Maybe I was in denial. Maybe I was in shock. When I finally walked into the emergency room, there were doctors and nurses waiting with a wheelchair.

"Are you Mrs. Saint John?"

"Yes," I said, bewildered. What on earth was going on?

As they pushed me through the hallway, they wouldn't give me much information, only that the doctor at Pepsi had phoned ahead, my blood pressure was really elevated, and they wanted to make sure the baby and I were okay.

More people seemed to suddenly appear out of thin air, first my doctor, then Peter. I was in a panic as the medical staff hooked me up to a monitor and took samples of my blood. Peter kept telling me to relax, but how could I when nobody was telling me anything? I could hear people outside the door, speaking in rushed whispers. I felt like everyone but me knew the truth of what was happening. Finally, I made a commotion, tossing something off a side table to get my doctor's attention and force him to tell me what was going on.

For once he wasn't cavalier. I had full-blown preeclampsia. My blood pressure was so high I was probably going to have a stroke. They had given me medication, but nothing was bringing my blood pressure down.

Preeclampsia. It was the reason my amniotic fluid was low. It's why the baby was smaller than it was supposed to be.

I unleashed my fury. "What are you talking about?" I yelled. "I've been asking you questions for months, and you told me everything was fine. I didn't just get this sick today. When did this preeclampsia happen?"

My doctor literally began to back up, edging toward the door. "Well," he said haltingly, "sometimes these cases, they just flare up. Anyway, I'm sorry, but we can't wait another month for you to have this baby. You won't survive."

The words didn't compute. Somehow, in the fog of my mind, I figured the medical team was still trying to find me the right medication. Or maybe they'd put me on bed rest until my pregnancy reached full term. I wasn't thinking about dying. I was just thinking about how to make sure my baby lived.

. . .

Over the next few hours, I began to drift in and out, sleepy from the medicine they'd given me to try to reduce my blood pressure. When I woke up, I saw my mom. Where had she come from? Wasn't she in Colorado? How had she gotten here? How much time had passed?

Soon, another nurse entered my room. There was a new flurry of activity. Something had changed. Again, I asked, "What's happening?"

The nurse appeared surprised that I didn't know. They were getting ready to induce me, she said.

Induce me? I hadn't agreed to that. I was six and a half months pregnant. It was way too soon to have my baby.

Then, Peter spoke up.

"Boz," he said gently. "You have to have the baby today. There's no choice."

"There is a choice," I said desperately. "There's always a choice."

"The choice is either we save you or we save the baby," he said.

"Well," I said, "then it's the baby." Peter just shook his head. I began to sob.

Was there anything else we could do? I asked him. His answer was chillingly to the point.

"No," he said. "One of you will die. I had to make a decision."

Suddenly, our roles had flipped. However indifferent I had been when I first got pregnant, now I would give my life for my baby to live. That was the right choice, I believed. But Peter, who'd been so elated, who'd literally counted the days until he could hold our child in his arms, had made a different decision. And I'd had no say.

Of course, I realize now that Peter had to do what he did. If I'd died, he would have lost us both. But I could not see that then. I wouldn't be able to see it for a long time. There was no logic, just despair. And love.

The medical staff gave me Pitocin and I felt my abdomen tighten as my contractions began. The baby began to kick. *Oh God,* I thought. *The baby knows it's too soon and is fighting not to come out. Maybe I can hold off. Maybe I can control it.* We were in this battle together.

But my body was moving without me. My stomach became taut as a drum as the baby kicked and kicked and kicked. It was torture, feeling how alive my baby was and knowing it was too soon for it to come into the world. The labor seemed to drag on for hours. Then, finally, I felt the need to push. I tried not to, even though it seemed every cell, every fiber in my body, was against me. My child and I were fighting forces more powerful than us. We were battling the inevitable.

I became quiet while the machines, with their clicks and beeps, screamed around me. My obstetrician, who I would have punched in the face if I'd had the strength, loomed at the end of the bed.

"Boz," he said. "It's time to push."

The pain of the contractions was nothing compared to the pain in my heart.

"No," I said, pleading as I looked at Peter. "Tell him. Tell him it's not time."

Peter was silent. So was my mom, tears streaming down her face, as she held me. Why didn't they speak up and tell that doctor no? Everybody was conspiring against me. Nobody was helping.

They sat me up. I couldn't fight anymore. Yielding to the pressure in my womb, I held tight, then released.

My daughter came out with one push. I felt relieved at first. She and I had given it all we could, and now the fight was over. I waited for her cries. But the only one I could hear crying was me.

Peter held me tight. I kept asking, "Is she alive? Is she alive?"

Peter got up to block my view. I struggled to peer around him. It sounded like they were working on her. If they were trying to revive her, if there was still a chance, I needed to know.

"Is she alive?" I screamed.

My doctor walked over. "No," he said quietly. "Not anymore."

A few minutes before, she'd been inside me, kicking furiously. How could so much life go away so quickly?

"I want to see her," I said finally.

A nurse placed her in my arms. I thought about how much she looked like Peter, a scrim of golden hair framing her beautiful face. I counted her tiny fingers, her tiny toes. Everything about her was perfect.

Throughout my pregnancy, I'd thought I was carrying a boy. When I'd told Peter and we began to sift through names, we settled on George, my father's English name and the name of Peter's father.

But George didn't show up. Staring at my daughter, I decided to name her Eve, in honor of my mother, whose English name was Evelyn, and because she was my first girl.

I let her go just long enough for Peter to hold her. While we sat there, Peter's parents arrived. Then my father, and finally, a priest, to give last rites. The scene was upside-down. Everybody showed up as expected for Eve's birth, but the tears were of sadness instead of joy. There was no celebration, only unbearable grief.

I was still in the maternity ward, where I could hear the other newborn babies crying, so I asked if I could be moved to another floor. As the hospital aides placed me in a wheelchair and took me to my new room, I continued to cradle Eve. At one point, I looked up and met the eyes of a stranger. He was maybe in his thirties, probably an expectant father.

He smiled. I began to wail.

When it was finally time to hand Eve over to a nurse, I couldn't do it. So, I handed her one last time to Peter. He carried her out of the room, and I never saw my daughter again.

. . .

I had to stay in the hospital for a couple of days. There I met another one of my angels whose name I never learned or can no longer remember. She was a Jamaican nurse, and she would tell me to go ahead and cry as she massaged my shoulders.

"You know," she said, rubbing my head, "your milk will come in. I'm telling you so you'll be ready. When it does, you will feel the loss all over again."

Why would my milk come in if my baby was not here? I asked. How cruel could God be? She gently explained that my body didn't know what had happened. My breasts would hurt if I didn't expel the milk, but if I pumped, they would produce more, so I would need to massage my chest just enough to give me relief but not enough to keep lactating. It would take a few weeks, she said, but eventually it would stop.

I wasn't home for more than a day when, as I lay on the couch, trying to lose myself in some silly show, I looked down and saw two damp spots on my blouse, each as big as a silver dollar. I went to the bathroom and squeezed my nipples over the sink. I watched my mother's milk slip down the drain.

. . .

We decided to cremate Eve. I found a beautiful tiny urn, in the shape of a heart and colored a pale green. The service, on July 29, eighteen days after her birth, was at a beautiful Catholic church in Manhattan, the kind of sanctuary where we might have held her christening. It wasn't where Peter worshipped, and I can't even remember why we chose it, but the priest gave the most beautiful eulogy, saying how though it wasn't her time, Eve would always be our daughter and we would one day see her again.

I wore pink heels and Ghanaian fabric colored blue and white. Those were the traditional colors our family would have worn at the baby's naming ceremony. Though we were putting Eve to rest instead of giving her a name that would carry her through the world, my mother and I still wanted to honor her in that way.

Back home, there weren't many reminders of her. I hadn't gotten around to creating a nursery, and I'd picked up one simple beige outfit from Gymboree. A few other items my mother-in-law sent were stuffed in gift bags. Still, Eve was all I could think about.

Feeling like I was losing my mind, I decided to go back to work only three weeks after her birth.

Melissa and one of my good friends at the office knew what had happened and told our team. I dreaded the looks of pity I was sure I'd encounter, and I braced myself as much as I could. I wore a tan dress in honor of Eve—my own private homage. It had gold details and a cutout at the waist. If you didn't know me, you might not even know that I'd recently given birth or that beneath the double-breasted buttons, my heart was shattered.

After attending a couple of meetings during my first day, I slowly began to calm down. No one mentioned my loss, and that's the way I wanted it.

I was sitting at my desk when one of the vice presidents from a different division wandered by. He had an office filled with pictures of his brood of children, and he'd been thrilled when he found out I was pregnant. "How are you feeling?" he yelled out merrily every time I walked by.

He stopped at my desk. He didn't know.

"Boz!" he said, grinning when he spotted me. "You're back! Congratulations! Can I see some pictures?"

A second later I saw my face reflected in his. He started to back away. "I'm so sorry," he said, his eyes wide and mournful. "I'm so sorry."

I called Melissa's extension, tapping the buttons on the phone through my tears. She'd tried to tell everyone, she said when she ran over, hugging me. She must have missed him because he worked in a different department.

That night, I went home and barely left the apartment for the next six weeks.

Home held little peace. My feelings for Peter ebbed and flowed. I was so angry at him when I was in the hospital, but at the same time, he was my only comfort. The person I was holding responsible for deciding to deliver our daughter far too soon was the only person who understood the depths of my grief. I could be laughing, watching a comedy skit on *Saturday Night Live,* then I'd burst into tears. He'd never ask why. He'd just hug and comfort me. Sometimes he cried too.

Once, we'd been able to chat about pretty much anything, from the momentous to the mundane. We'd gossip about the coworker who'd pissed one of us off or the book review we'd read in the Sunday

New York Times. Now, those conversations just dried up. The simple had become too trivial in the wake of what we'd been through. We hovered instead in an uneasy quiet, reaching for each other only because there was no one else to hold on to.

. . .

Peter finally suggested we go to therapy, not just to talk about Eve, but to figure out all the smaller things we seemed to be losing.

At first, it didn't go so well. I was ashamed to tell a stranger that for a time I'd been ambivalent about being pregnant. And then, there was the betrayal. How could Peter have decided to basically end our daughter's life and not even shake me from sleep to ask what I thought?

But gradually, as the counseling sessions and weeks passed, a clarity began to emerge. I hadn't fully forgiven Peter, but I wanted to have another baby. Right away.

Our therapist didn't think it was a good idea. Neither did Peter. But I was determined. Pregnancy became a north star, both a goal and a cure.

I was at my doctor's office for a postpartum checkup when I told him I wanted to try again. He echoed everyone else, saying I should give myself some time, but in my mind, no one had less credibility than this guy, who I'd renamed Dr. Dumbass. *He wasn't even able to diagnose preeclampsia,* I thought. *Who gives a damn what he thinks? Fuck him.*

I went back to see him only because I wanted all the details on what exactly went wrong during my pregnancy. He gave me my medical records, and I pored over the file. Apparently, in addition to preeclampsia, I had a protein deficiency that caused my blood to clot more easily during pregnancy. That blocked the blood flow to my placenta, and the combination of problems led to Eve being unable to thrive.

I began to call every obstetrician in Manhattan. I read that Hasidic Jewish women often had a similar medical condition, and I found the name of a Hasidic doctor who was highly sought after to deal with those challenges. When I called, his receptionist said he was booked for months and not taking new patients.

But I was relentless. I was the Boz who let Spike Lee know exactly who she was, who'd worked up the courage to defy her father's dreams and pursue her own. I called that doctor's office every day. I told his receptionist that I needed to see him. Now.

Whether my insistence made them worry that something was seriously wrong, or they just grew tired of my constant calls, the office finally gave me an appointment. The doctor's bedside manner was so awful I almost missed the corny jokes and nonchalance of Dr. Dumbass.

His questions were dry, his attitude cold. But when he did an ultrasound of my uterus and told me that I could definitely have another baby, I was determined to have him guide me through my pregnancy. He gave me one medication to regulate my hypertension and another to thin my blood.

When I got home, I got down to business. I told Peter we were getting pregnant. Immediately.

"No," Peter said, shaking his head. "We need to wait."

"Nope," I said. "Lay down!"

He reluctantly agreed.

I was going to be a mother come hell or high water. And anyone who knows me knows that when I make up my mind to get something done, it's happening.

I tracked my cycle religiously and took my temperature every day to know the optimal time to try to conceive. In addition to taking my medication, I ate raw garlic because I heard it was good for steadying blood pressure. And I bought every supplement you could find. There was fish oil in the morning for my cholesterol, as well as another little mountain of vitamins to make my future baby strong.

After Peter and I made love, I would lie in bed, my legs pointed straight up in the air.

Please, I'd think, my eyes squeezed shut. *Please let something stick.*

Peter would look at me and just shake his head. I'm sure he was worried. The therapist was too. But I knew I was ready. I even started taking prenatal pills before I was actually pregnant. I was calling our baby into existence.

. . .

One night, after one of our purposeful rendezvouses, I lifted my legs into the air like I had so many nights before, and I knew. I just knew.

"I'm pregnant," I whispered in Peter's ear.

"Okay," he said, humoring me as he got up, put on his boxers, and went to watch some game on TV in the living room.

I lay there in the darkness, my whole being filled with joy. I was ready to leap through our apartment. But not yet.

I called in sick the next morning because I wanted to lie down as long as possible to make sure everything stayed on track. For the rest of the day and through the weekend, I only got up to use the bathroom, asking Peter to bring me my vitamins or something to eat and drink. I debated staying home again Monday as well, but

Peter had had enough. I reluctantly got up and went to the office. But my countdown had begun.

My period was due in two weeks. Already certain, I grew only more confident when the designated day arrived, I checked my underwear, and there wasn't a speck of blood in sight.

On November 9, 2008, the anniversary of Peter's and my first date, he wanted to go out and celebrate, but I hadn't put on a pair of heels in weeks, and I didn't want to risk tripping over a crack or spending half the evening dodging in and out of Manhattan traffic. I would order takeout for us instead.

That afternoon I went to CVS to buy a pregnancy test. I didn't tell Peter.

I sat in the bathroom, gazing at the tiny screen. The two lines appeared slowly, then all at once.

Barely a year before, I'd taken a similar test, and when I saw that result, I put the stick in the trash and tried to forget it. This time I got my phone and took a picture. I still have it. In the selfie, I'm holding the test in my hand, and I'm kissing it, smudging it with my lipstick. I put the positive test, smudged lipstick and all, on Peter's pillow.

I was sitting in the living room when he walked in. I'm sure he knew that something was up because I hadn't been calm in weeks. I was always rubbing my stomach, taking pills, or eating garlic.

"Is everything okay?" he asked gingerly.

"Everything's fine," I said, picking up the remote. Peter walked into the bedroom to change. I sat there, waiting for him to notice my gift. When I didn't hear anything, I decided to move things along.

"What's up?" he asked, a little annoyed, as he changed his clothes and I stood in the doorway. I told him to look at the pillow. He turned toward it and saw the stick. Then he looked at me.

"What?" he said, his eyes wide. "Is this a trick?"

"No, babe," I said triumphantly. "We're pregnant."

Once again, our roles had flipped. This time, I was the one who was overjoyed, and Peter was the one who cried. He was scared.

"Why do you want to do this?" he asked quietly, as he wiped his eyes and sat on the edge of our bed. "After all we've been through, you want to do this again? So soon?"

But this was our healing. I knew it. Just like I'd known that I was pregnant. We needed this baby. Otherwise, we'd remain broken.

9.

The In-Between

When Peter's doctors said there was no hope, my sister Alua's best friend Magda said we should all gather and pray.

I'd been praying constantly. While Peter slept and I held his hand. When I stood at the sink and washed dishes. Whenever I got in my car and drove home or to the hospital.

Yet it had never occurred to me that all of us together—our parents, our siblings, our friends—should pray at the same time. My conversations with God were private. I'd never been eager to share them with anyone else.

But as Peter grew sicker, it was clear my singular prayers were not working. How did that old adage go? That God is present wherever two or more are gathered? Maybe Magda was right. It was time to make it biblical. Maybe if we all cried out in unison, our collective prayers would finally break through.

Magda put the date and time for the vigil on Facebook, and

someone else set up a conference line for the call. Peter initially planned to join us so he could thank everyone for taking part, but when the day came, he was too tired to talk, too weak to even listen. I told him I'd jot down every word and relay them to him later.

At first, it was just me, Alua, and Magda on the call. But after a few minutes, I gave up taking mental notes for Peter. There were too many voices, too many pleas.

Magda, who'd had a strained relationship with her own father, wanted Peter to be alive for Lael. Another friend prayed for Peter to feel no more pain. Some shouted into the phone: "Cast out this cancer! Cast it out now!"

The vigil went on for what seemed like hours. It was so moving, so powerful. For the first time in days, I really believed Peter would be healed, that we were all about to witness a miracle.

And I didn't say a word. God already knew what was on my heart. I had prayed enough.

. . .

Throughout my childhood, my parents, sisters, and I spent Sundays immersed in church, the fulfillment of our familial pledge of gratitude for my father surviving prison in Ghana. But our Ghanaian beliefs stood fast. We didn't overtly talk about it, but I understood that juju, hexes, ancestors, and demons were also ever present. Even my name, Bozoma, connected me to the spirit world, so similar to Bosum, which in the Akan language means *goddess*.

All of that made me feel I had a very personal relationship with God, one that didn't rest on ritual or require me to constantly be on the lookout for retribution. To make it plain, I felt like God and I were homies, that I could commune with the higher power anytime.

And when Eve died within minutes of gasping her first breath, I felt God owed me. I could love God, without liking God; and I didn't have to believe that God's will should always be done. What was done had caused me pain, and I didn't know if I could ever forgive God for that. But I wanted to be a mother again, so I had to work with God to believe that miracles were still possible. And a few months later, I was pregnant. God came through.

I knew I would have to be vigilant, but I couldn't see spending the next nine months dealing with the callous specialist I'd found to help me diagnose my medical challenges. I quizzed friends and scoured the internet to find another doctor, and I soon discovered someone I really liked.

The doctor I landed on was a little sprite of a woman, and I immediately dubbed her Dr. Sprite. I appreciated her frankness, as well as her warmth. She began tracking my blood pressure right away and told me to buy a cuff so I could check it myself at home.

Every morning, when I tightened the band around my forearm, my heart raced as my mind flashed back to that day in the campus clinic when a super-high reading meant the beginning of the end. From the start my blood pressure was elevated, though not out of control. Then, in my eighth week, not long before Peter and I headed to Florida to celebrate Christmas, I did my daily reading and my eyes popped at the high number. I called Dr. Sprite, and she told me to come in right away.

I told her that wasn't happening.

I wasn't heading to her office so she could tell me I was too high risk and that I needed to get rid of my baby. But she reassured me that she just wanted me to come in to be monitored. We'd known all along that my blood pressure could become a problem, she reminded me. Now we needed a plan.

I called Peter, then drove myself to the hospital. There was no medical team waiting for me at the door, and that alone made me feel better. I actually had to wait quite a while to be seen, an annoyance that was also reassuring. As high as my blood pressure was, it clearly wasn't an emergency. I breathed easier.

But when I did finally get checked, my lingering worry was confirmed. I had preeclampsia. My lab results also revealed the same protein deficiency I'd had when I carried Eve. Dr. Sprite put me on a different blood pressure medication and said I would have to inject myself every day with a blood thinner to prevent clots.

I was all in for downing vitamins, eating herbs, and trading in my beloved pumps for sneakers and flats. I would take my blood pressure a dozen times a day if I had to. But now I had to give myself a shot? That freaked me out.

Peter got my prescriptions from the pharmacy, and the next day I tried to inject myself for the first time. I was shaking so badly, he decided that he would do the injection for me.

He picked up the needle and poised it near my abdomen. His hand began to tremble. He turned super pale, then bright pink.

"I can't do it," he finally said.

"Just do it!" I yelled. "Don't think about it. Do it fast!"

"Okay," Peter said meekly, picking up the needle. A few seconds later he set it down. "I can't!" he said.

Our back-and-forth must have gone on for something like three hours. Peter would approach me with the syringe, then turn around and flee. I'd suggest we take a break to gather our nerves. Then we'd try again. Finally, I grabbed the needle, took a deep breath, and poked my abdomen myself. After all that, the shot didn't even hurt.

The shot soon became as routine as brushing my teeth. I'd take my shower in the morning, lather myself with lotion, then grab a

 THE URGENT LIFE

cotton ball bathed in alcohol. I had to alternate where I'd inject, sticking the needle on my left side one day, on the right side the next. Sometimes, after I'd pushed the syringe, I'd pull out the needle and point it at the mirror like it was a pistol and I was a cowboy in an old Western.

Yes, I'd think. *I've got this. I'm a badass. I'm a mom, doing whatever it takes to care for my baby.*

I began to talk to my little buddy. "This is our morning cocktail," I'd say as I unwrapped the syringe. Sometimes, I even spoke to the medicine, rubbing the spot where I'd delivered the injection. "Okay," I'd say. "You get in there and do your magic. Work for us. Keep us healthy."

It was a prayer, a command, a battle cry all in one. When we got to Florida for Christmas, we finally told Peter's family I was pregnant. They beamed, slapping Peter on the back, congratulating the two of us. I felt like I was carrying the golden child.

But remembering how some of those family members had been by my bedside a few months before also reminded me of Eve. My pregnancy was still so early, and I had so far to go. I wanted to celebrate with them, regaining the momentary lightness I felt the night I knew in my soul I was pregnant again. But I couldn't help worrying.

The day after Christmas, I had another scare. When I went to the bathroom, I looked down at my panties and saw blood. I screamed. Peter came running. Unable to get the words out as I fumbled and cried, I finally just pointed at my underwear. He looked at me, terrified, then we both raced to the phone and called my doctor.

Dr. Sprite asked a bunch of questions. How much blood? Did I feel any pain?

I answered: A little bit, and no. I actually felt fine. When I grabbed a tissue to check again, I discovered only a trickle. Dr. Sprite instructed me to lie down and to not move for an hour. Then I should call her back.

I went to the bedroom, where Peter lay beside me. My mother-in-law had heard the ruckus and was there when we called Dr. Sprite. As we lay still and waited, she poked her head in the door every few minutes to see how I was feeling. In between, she paced outside, wringing her hands.

The next time I checked, there was even less blood than before, which my doctor assured me was good news. Since I wasn't feeling any cramping, she told me to just monitor myself and to take it easy the rest of the day.

She didn't have to tell us twice. Afterward, everyone treated me like a porcelain doll, practically jumping out of their chairs if I even clicked my fork against my teeth as I was eating.

By the time I returned to New York and went in for my checkup, I wasn't bleeding at all. My doctor said the spotting had probably been caused by a slight vaginal tear. The baby's heartbeat was strong, and the ultrasound looked good.

But that positive news carried me only so far. While the moment I gave myself the blood-thinning shot had become the best part of the day, the rest of my waking hours were filled with fear.

The terror was waiting for me as soon as I threw the cotton ball in the trash and opened the bathroom door. I'd imagine my blood pressure soaring or the medicine missing a clot that would deprive my baby of nutrients and snake its way toward my heart.

As much as I loved a good party, I refused to allow my friends or family to throw me a baby shower. And I was so afraid of jinxing my pregnancy, I once again wouldn't set up a nursery.

Yet, as cautious as I was, I was also becoming annoyed with Peter's constant hovering. He called me at the office so many times a day that when I saw his name pop up on my caller ID, I'd occasionally refuse to answer.

I knew I was being unreasonable. Of course Peter was concerned. What loving husband and expectant father wouldn't be? But my irritability just showed how complicated my emotions remained after losing Eve. Peter's worrying exacerbated my fear of losing another child, anxiety that I carried like an anvil.

And perhaps most painful of all, I continued to feel I couldn't completely trust him because of the decision he'd made about Eve. When he and I went to my checkups, I watched Peter like a hawk, yelling that I needed to hear what was being said when he huddled alone with the doctor. This time, I vowed, there would be no decisions made without my consent. There'd be no decision to sacrifice this child's life to spare mine.

Paradoxically, I also worried Peter might be similarly judging me. After all, I thought, it was my body that had failed.

We continued going to therapy, knowing that we definitely needed it.

When my pregnancy entered its second trimester, our therapist gave us an assignment. She wanted us to go out and buy baby clothes.

Now, remember I was the expectant mother who didn't even want to decorate a nursery. In my opinion, buying baby clothes was a crazy, unnecessary way to tempt fate. But after we told his family and I got through that bleeding episode over Christmas, Peter was doing his best to push through his apprehension and to just be excited about our child. He thought going shopping was a good idea.

Literally an hour before our next session, he dragged me to a small shop near our therapist's office. Looking at all the pacifiers and mobiles, the stuffed animals and rompers, I felt like I was suffocating. Peter, meanwhile, was like a kid in a toy store, picking up onesies decorated with footballs and dresses splashed with pink bows.

"Maybe we should get one of each?" he asked excitedly. "Or maybe we should go for one that's unisex. Maybe yellow or green!"

I just wanted to get out of there as quickly as possible. I was distractedly riffling through the hangers when I glanced toward a corner of the store. It was the section for clothes that could fit a baby born prematurely.

"Maybe we should shop over there," I said.

Peter took one look, then shook his head furiously. "No," he said firmly.

"But the doctor said there was a chance the baby could come early," I said.

"Nuh-uh!" Peter said. "The baby will be fine. We're staying right here!"

We settled on an outfit. Like everything in the store, it was adorable, a tiny tan getup with a matching hat and socks.

"Is this a gift?" the saleswoman asked as she rang us up.

"No," Peter said, happily, rubbing my still mostly flat stomach. "It's for us."

His declaration startled me. The saleswoman was the first stranger we'd told about our pregnancy. I wanted a baby so desperately, but at the same time I felt the need to keep quiet in case tragedy struck again. I veered between talking to my unborn child and trying to not imagine it living inside me because the thought of it not surviving was too much to bear.

But gradually my stomach began to curve into a small mound. And my baby began to dance.

I remember the first time. There's this very spicy hot sauce we make in Ghana. It's smoky, peppery, and tongue-scorchingly hot.

It's meant to be eaten in small portions as an accompaniment to a meal. I couldn't get enough of it, and one night I was eating it by the spoonful when the baby just started going nuts. It felt like it was about to shimmy right out of me. I ran into the bedroom, where Peter was lying down.

"What were you running from?" he asked when he realized I wasn't bleeding or in some other form of distress. "You realize that you can't run from the baby, right? It's inside of you."

I stared at him. Then we both burst out laughing.

I began to do things on purpose to get the baby to move. And like everything else that had to do with this pregnancy, what started out as a lark edged toward obsession.

If I went more than ten minutes without feeling the baby push or shift, I grew concerned. I'd grab a glass of ice water, sip a fizzy soda, or eat some hot chicken soup.

"Are you in there?" I'd ask, poking my belly to get a rise.

And the cutest thing began to happen. Sometimes in response to my various elixirs and jabs, the baby would get the hiccups. I'd rub my stomach, trying to soothe it, and I could imagine rocking her or him in my lap, calming their intermittent, tiny gasps. It was starting to feel like a real baby, a child I would soon hold, and not something I had to live in constant fear of losing.

It was a terrible bind to be in, fear always lurking on the edge of my happiness. I read *What to Expect When You're Expecting,* the go-to primer for new mothers, absorbing the how-tos and what-fors like a lusty teenager imbibing her first Harlequin novel. I'd give myself my daily injection and feel triumphant. But then I had to work to stay in that positive space.

"Your blood pressure is fine," I'd recite like a prayer. "You took the medicine. Everything is under control."

It was easier to utter my mantras and distract myself when I was still going to work each day, but with my blood pressure fluctuating, my doctor decided in my fifth month that I needed to go on bed rest. Lying in bed or on the couch, I spent most of the day and half the night battling to stay positive, wading through fear, trying to latch on to joy.

Movement wasn't the only thing my doctor restricted. My longtime breakfast standby of two fried eggs on a cinnamon raisin bagel with extra crispy bacon was off the menu. I couldn't have anything with salt or anything fried. I still craved booze, so Peter would buy me nonalcoholic beer and then when my doctor gave the okay, I began to have half a glass of red wine once a week as a treat.

I was almost thirty-one weeks along when my blood pressure shot up into a danger zone. Dr. Sprite was on vacation, so I went to the emergency room at NewYork-Presbyterian Hospital. I'd been on bed rest for a month and a half, getting up only to use the bathroom, so there wasn't any particular trigger for the spike. They decided to admit me and observe me overnight.

Usually after a night's sleep, your blood pressure dips. But the next morning we discovered mine had inched higher. The dreaded conversation about whether I could carry the baby full term began again, and I was determined to stay clearheaded so I could be a part of any critical decisions.

I remembered being told that Eve's lungs hadn't had time to develop, so I asked the obstetrician on duty what we could do to make sure this baby would be able to breathe if it came early. He suggested steroid shots to strengthen the baby's lungs. We began that treatment right away.

When my overnight stay grew to three days, Peter finally decided to return to work. But only a couple of hours after he left, my blood pressure shot up again. It was May 28, two months too soon, but I would have to deliver the baby.

Despite the urgency, this time felt different. Instead of being worried, the nurses cheered me on, saying my baby was coming and everything would be fine. And even though some things felt the same—like Peter hurrying to come to the hospital and my mother arriving from Colorado—this time, my sister Alua was bringing celebration with her, as she boarded a plane from Los Angeles with her own pre-birthday cocktail in hand. Alua's birthday was May 29, so she just knew that her new niece or nephew was about to be a spectacular birthday gift for herself. Nothing and no one could tell her differently.

I asked for an epidural, which actually slowed down my labor, and the three of us sat there waiting, literally for hours. Peter even went to get a burger, and as he noisily munched on his sandwich and the nurses happily scuttled about, I felt like I was hallucinating.

Really? I thought, as Peter sipped a milkshake and exchanged high fives with the nurses. *They're having a ball and I'm lying here terrified.* We were having two totally different delivery experiences.

"Don't y'all know what I've been through?" I wanted to yell. But I held my tongue, trying to absorb their optimism.

Finally, it was time to push. They had oxygen and an incubator in place, and a whole medical team in the room. They were ready to do their job. Now I had to do mine. This baby had to live.

The doctor warned that the baby might not make a sound when it came out, and to not be afraid. He also told me I might not be able to hold the baby right away.

My mother stood on one side of me, and Peter stood on the other. I squeezed my insides.

And—nothing.

A few minutes later, I gave another squeeze. Again. No progress. *Where the hell is this baby?* I thought.

I gave it two more tries, pushing as hard as I could. And then, at last, she came.

Our baby. Our second daughter. Lael. La El. "Belonging to God" in Hebrew. Her name signified a prayer and a warning to anyone or anything that would try to take her away from me.

She came out hollering. It was like a church bell, the clearest, most beautiful sound coming out of a girl so tiny she could literally fit in the palm of my hand. I reached for her, and when they placed her on my chest, she felt as light as air.

It was my turn to cry and scream when they took her away. But at least this time I could watch every move they made. No one blocked my view. They cleaned her up, then attached monitors to her little frame. When they said they were taking her to the neonatal intensive care unit, I yelled that I was going too. They didn't argue, wheeling me behind her incubator.

Lael's skin was so thin, I could see her heart move with each heartbeat. I asked if I could touch her again, and they opened the incubator. My finger was too large, but she was able to grab hold of my pinky.

I knew then that she was a fighter. *We* were fighters.

"Okay," I said to the nurse. "You can take me back to my room."

. . .

Have you ever spent time in a NICU? It is shocking that a place of such miracles, a space where nurses and doctors do the most delicate and sacred of work, is also so morbid, a unit where the newly born tread the thin line between life and death. That ward was about to become my second home, and my days there would become some of the most trying of my life.

The NICU is full of babies, yet there's no sound of children. That's what I found most striking. They're too sick to coo or cry. All you hear are the machines keeping them alive. The beeps. The clicks.

Then there's the flapping of the scrubs as the nurses rush to feed this child or check on another. Rushing. Always rushing. And there are the constant whispers. I don't know why the nurses don't speak in their normal voices. Maybe it is to protect the babies' delicate eardrums. In between those discordant sounds there is just an eerie silence.

When Lael was born, parents weren't allowed to stay in the NICU overnight. You had to leave at midnight and could return at 6:00 a.m. But the limited hours didn't seem to matter much to really anyone but me. Rarely did I see another mother or father, though there were ten or eleven other babies being cared for. I understood. It was just too sad, too scary.

Sitting there with Lael, I began to make up stories in my head about her and her little playmates. That's how I wanted to think of all those sick babies. I wanted to imagine them as healthy kids in a playgroup or day care.

All the babies had their names written on their incubators. I memorized them. But sometimes when I returned in the morning, one of Lael's little neighbors was gone. I hoped they'd gone home, but I doubted there'd been a happy ending. So I never asked.

Our goal was to get Lael to five pounds. That's when she could leave the hospital. She weighed 3.4 pounds when she was born, so we had a ways to go.

Sometimes, as midnight approached, I'd pretend to be asleep so they wouldn't kick me out. I'd squeeze my eyes tightly, but inevitably I'd feel a gentle shaking of my shoulder.

"Mrs. Saint John," a nurse would whisper. "It's time to go."

I'd trudge to the subway or occasionally hail a cab. Then, as soon as I walked in my front door, I'd be on the phone calling the hospital. "What is she doing now?" I'd ask.

"Sleeping," they'd say gently, "like she was twenty minutes ago, when you left."

The next morning, at 6:00 a.m. sharp, I'd be waiting outside the NICU door.

"Good morning, Mrs. Saint John," the receptionist would say as she gave me an understanding smile.

"Good morning!" I'd say quickly. Then, I'd take my perch.

There was a rocking chair for me to sit in, and it was unbelievably uncomfortable. But even though I'd just given birth, I'd sit in that hard-assed chair for eighteen hours a day, gazing at Lael.

Like me, the nurses knew she was a little warrior. At one point, she developed jaundice, so the medical team placed a UV light over her incubator. Usually Lael was pretty restrained because she was connected to so many monitors. But one morning, when I walked in, Lael's little arms had broken free and the doll-size shades that were supposed to protect her eyes were off. She was staring straight into the light.

My screams ricocheted around that quiet place. "Her eyes!" I yelled. "What if she's blind?"

The nurse on duty said that her eyes would be fine, but she and Lael had been fighting all night. She just wouldn't keep those sunglasses on. "Watch," she said.

She put the glasses on Lael's face. Sure enough, not more than five seconds later, Lael scooted them off.

I marveled that she had the strength to do that. It spoke to her spirit. I was so proud.

. . .

Over those long weeks, I sat and watched Lael's eyelashes come in and her fingernails grow thicker. Her thin, pale skin began to gain color, so after a while I could feel her heartbeat but no longer see it.

I thought about how all those things would have happened inside my belly if my pregnancy had gone full term. Instead, I got to see my daughter transform right in front of me. It was something most mothers would not experience. It was another gift from God. For all the pain, for all the fear, I got Lael, and the opportunity to see my little miracle become more miraculous every day.

Still, my vigil in the NICU began to create another fault line between me and Peter. I was on leave from work so I could be with her every day while Peter had gone back to the office. When I returned home late at night, I would tell Peter how Lael had changed, the progress she'd made. He would eagerly listen but felt he was missing so much. I believe he became a little resentful.

It didn't help that I remained fiercely overprotective. I knew what times Lael was supposed to eat. I monitored whether she burped and on which side she turned to curl up and sleep. And because the staff let the parents participate as much as possible, I was usually the one who weighed her. You could push a button on the incubator to see how much she'd gained.

Peter would often stop by the hospital in the evening when he got off work, and sometimes he wanted to do the weighing. I was irritated that he was messing up the routine.

"It's too tight," I'd whisper when he'd put on her diaper. "Loosen it a little bit."

Or, "Be careful! You have to center her better on the scale."

He didn't say anything, but I could see the frustration on his face.

Finally, in early July, after five weeks, Lael was able to leave the hospital. We'd return once a month, until she was one year old, so the doctors could chart her weight, height, and overall development.

Once we got Lael home, my favorite time was late at night, when Peter was asleep and I would bring Lael into the bed to lie with me. It was our "kangaroo time." I would undress her, take off my nightgown, then place her on top of me. My breasts were huge. I'm talking triple-H boobs trying to balance on top of this narrow rib cage. Lael would snuggle between them as I nursed her. It gave me a feeling of such peace.

It also gave me time to reflect. The scar from the biopsy I'd had in high school stretched along my engorged breast. One night, as Lael nursed, she slid her hand across my chest and her finger touched it. She began tracing the mark, perhaps wondering exactly what it was. I was amazed that she'd noticed it. And knowing she'd felt it made me sad as I thought how she would eventually have to learn about the frailty of life and all the disappointment and pain it could bring.

Eventually I had to face the fact that I couldn't stay in the apartment with Lael forever. I'd used up my six weeks of maternity leave when I was on bed rest and then gone on short-term disability, which gave me only three additional months off. In a few weeks my leave would be done, and if I didn't go back to work, I'd lose my job.

It was excruciating. Lael had reflux, and when she spit up, I'd hover to make sure she didn't choke. Like so many new moms, I would peer anxiously into her crib several times during the night to check that she was still breathing. I was terrified to leave her.

But Peter and I couldn't afford for me to quit. And as much as I wanted to be home with Lael, part of me also still wanted a career.

Lael's immune system was too fragile for her to be in day care, so I had to find a nanny I trusted to be as much of a guardian as I was.

I put four or five cameras up throughout the apartment and let every nanny Peter and I interviewed know they were there. We also had all kinds of sanitation routines in place. We forbade people from wearing shoes in the house. You had to leave them outside in the hallway. And I was a drill sergeant with the Lysol, cleaning every surface at least twice a day. When Peter rode the subway home, he had to change his clothes before he could come near the baby.

We must have interviewed a dozen women before we found Salematou Salam. I believe to this day that she was someone who'd always lingered at the edge of my existence, waiting for when I most needed her to come into my life.

She was from the francophone African country of Cameroon. Her gentle spirit reminded me of my sister Aba. And Sale immediately did everything right, washing her hands before she approached Lael, singing her a song as soon as she met her.

While Sale's love for Lael made it easier for me to leave each morning, it was still hard at first to concentrate at the office. Work had once been a central part of my life. Now I would spend part of the day crying, wishing I could be at home. I called Sale constantly.

My colleagues tried to make my transition back to work smoother. They eased my workload and were understanding if I got to the office a little late or rushed out the door a little early. And then there was Melissa, the executive assistant who'd stepped in during that first pregnancy, and Jane, the chatty nurse. Melissa always checked to see if there was anything extra that I needed, and Jane would bring a concoction every day to help with the flow of my breast milk.

I'd sip the beverage before I went to the lactation room to pump, which I did faithfully twice a day. The cold suction device was nothing compared to cuddling with my sweet Lael, but knowing I was continuing to make sure she had breast milk, even when I was working, made me feel attentive and purposeful.

. . .

Meanwhile, Peter and I continued to engage in a subtle battle of wills. He tried to tell me what to eat, getting tips from both of our mothers. When a girlfriend told me I could have a glass of wine, then pump and dump my milk to make sure it didn't contain traces of alcohol before I fed Lael, Peter would sit and watch while I drank. He wouldn't say anything, but it was clear what he was thinking. The chastisement was in his eyes, the judgment all over his face. I would pretend I didn't notice, but his hard stare made it impossible to enjoy that little reprieve. Sometimes I would drink not because I wanted to but simply because I wanted to annoy him.

Peter would also try to do his own version of kangaroo time, but his chest was hairy and Lael would squirm. He'd ask for a blanket to make her feel comfortable, but I told him with more than a little satisfaction that a cotton barrier defeated the purpose. Then, I'd snatch her back.

I knew I was being selfish. But nourishing Lael held an importance for me that was hard to explain. It was like an apology from the body that betrayed me and failed Eve, that didn't allow Lael to fully grow, then kicked her out before she was ready. My abundant production of breast milk was something my body was finally doing right. I wanted so much to hold on to that, and I felt like Peter was encroaching.

Those were the invisible things, the irrational things, that slowly challenged our bond. The cracks spread. Rather than bringing us together, having a child who lived ironically, unfathomably, was tearing us apart.

Instead of sharing Lael, we competed for her attention. And the apartment where we were raising her, the place that once was a haven, now felt claustrophobic. There was so much emotion, so much pain packed between those walls. It held memories of losing Eve, of misunderstandings and missed opportunities. Peter felt it too.

One day, he suggested we move.

I was a bit of a New York City snob, but Peter felt that buying a bigger place in New Jersey was the natural progression of things once you had a family. We put our Manhattan apartment on the market and moved into a spacious three-bedroom condominium in Edgewater, New Jersey.

Edgewater was a compromise because New York remained in sight. We could see the glorious span of the George Washington Bridge and the spiky tops of Manhattan's skyline from our living room window.

We moved in shortly before Christmas. And for those first few weeks, it felt like old times. We bought new furniture and picked out curtains. In between, we made forays into the city, to see the Christmas tree in Rockefeller Center and the Rockettes kicking in synchronicity at Radio City. Somehow, we'd never done those things before, but now that we were a family of three, it felt comforting and right.

Peter and I also made an effort at rekindling our romantic flame. We enlisted Salematou and my sister Alua to watch Lael and booked a Caribbean cruise hosted by the legendary radio personality Tom

Joyner. It was the first grown-up alone time Peter and I'd had in almost a year. After my guilt-laden teetotaling, and nearly three years of vigilantly monitoring everything I put in my body, I was able to drink with abandon, and I took full advantage. The first night I got completely smashed.

Peter and I partied for five days, and on the ocean, under a blazing sun, we were able to retrieve a bit of our spark.

When we returned home, we began making plans to celebrate Lael's first birthday and I focused all my energy on her party. Peter was as excited as I was, talking about the decorations, and everyone we would invite.

But once that day passed, I was stuck again. I realized that I was starting to live for the special occasions, whether it was a cruise hosted by a radio DJ, a long holiday weekend, or my daughter's birthday. There was no urgency, no living in the moment. I was always looking off into the distance, searching for anchors, waiting for joy.

After Lael's party, the commute from Edgewater to Purchase, New York, loomed longer. And Peter and I talked less and less.

At the time, we were friends with a couple who fought constantly. When we went on double dates, we could feel their anger, left over from the quarrel they'd had as they dressed or drove to the movie theater. Peter and I didn't bicker with their frequency or ferocity, but I felt we were slowly becoming like them—people who were more at peace when they were apart than when they were together, tethered more by habit and obligation than passion. We were becoming those people we'd never imagined we'd be.

"We're a lot like Kerry and Artie," I said to Peter one night after we'd sat in silence for most of the evening. "Half the time we don't have anything to really say to each other."

Peter shrugged. "Well," he said, picking up the remote, "my parents sometimes go a whole day in the same house without talking. And most of our friends argue, just like Kerry and Artie. Maybe that's what marriage is."

I was dumbfounded. Was that what he was willing to accept? I wanted butterflies and romance. I knew that wasn't realistic to have all the time. But I wanted to feel that giddiness more days than not.

It was another way we were fundamentally different, looking at the world, our lives, our marriage through completely separate prisms.

I was frustrated. I was unsatisfied. I knew I didn't want to whittle away my life waiting for the next extraordinary moment. You had to live, and to try to be happy, in the in-between.

I didn't know how I would tell Peter. But I was beginning to realize I wanted out.

• • •

Around Labor Day, Peter and I left Lael with our nanny, Sale, and we went to our favorite spot for Indian food.

Sitting there, I thought about Fashion Week. About Thanksgiving. About the next anchor. And it all just felt too far away. I thought once again that I didn't want to sleepwalk through my days, glancing at the calendar in desperate anticipation of the next distraction.

I had to say it. It was time.

"I don't think I want to be married anymore," I blurted out.

Peter looked at me like I was a stranger. All the blood drained from his face.

I tried to flip it. "You've got to feel the same way," I said. "Neither of us is happy. There's no way you want this."

He stared at me, still stunned. "Why would I not want it?" he finally asked. "Even when it's hard, this is all I've ever wanted."

Seeing his pain hurt me. But I couldn't turn back. I wanted what we had before, but too much had happened. Too much sadness. Too much blame. Too much regret. And every time I looked at Peter, I saw Eve. I couldn't go on living like that.

We'd been so worried about my blood pressure and strokes and the terror of having two pregnancies that might kill me. But in the wake of all that, I'd come to a harsh realization. While I was willing to die for those babies, I was not willing to die for this marriage. I was not willing to die for Peter. And shouldn't I be, if this was a marriage worth fighting for?

I was no longer the same person Peter met in a cafeteria ten years before. I was a woman who now knew what it was to face death and constant crippling fear. The tenuousness of my own life was ever-present because I now so desperately wanted to be there to shepherd the life of my only child.

And yet I didn't want Lael to grow up knowing this version of me, the version that was frightened and unsure. I wanted her to know the Boz who headed to New York with barely any money in her pocket, certain that she could carve her future into the shape of her dreams.

Somehow, I knew she'd never know that person if I stayed. I didn't know how to get that person back without leaving Peter.

Years later, looking back on that interruption and the precious time it cost us, I still respect my decision, because ultimately you have to live in your truth, even when it breaks two hearts. At that moment, I felt I had to leave so I could continue to breathe, so I could continue to be.

"You're like sand," Peter said, his eyes welling with tears. "I try to hold you, but you just keep slipping through my fingers."

I understood what he meant. But I didn't want him to try anymore.

10.

Healing from the Break

C alling off our divorce was the easiest thing.

It had taken me months to ask Peter for it. But making the decision to officially begin our love affair again was wonderfully simple, especially compared to everything else we had to confront in the face of his illness. When your to-do list includes writing a will, planning your husband's burial, and mapping out your four-year-old child's entire fucking future, putting the brakes on a divorce is a breeze.

It was simple for me emotionally too. Whatever time Peter had left, I wanted to be there with him. Like the early days of our romance, when we professed our love for each other within weeks and decided to move in together after mere months, our decision was spontaneous.

Peter and I simply did what we felt was right.

Still, with all the pressing tasks we had at hand, it took a few days for us to call our lawyers. I finally just phoned each of their offices and left a message that we'd decided to stay together and would no longer proceed. Likewise, there was no dramatic announcement to our family and friends. There didn't need to be. They knew we were back together. They would look at Peter, then me, and simply smile. Or someone would walk over and suddenly swallow Peter and me, together, in a hug.

Without words, they were offering us congratulations. It was another incongruous moment, a celebration in the midst of our terrible sorrow.

. . .

Years earlier, as our marriage deteriorated and Peter and I learned to care for our new baby, we had to deal with yet another layer of stress. My father was back living with us. Dad suffered a stroke while working as a consultant in Atlanta, and my sisters had a litany of reasons why they couldn't take him in. They didn't have the space, or the time, or the extra money since our father would have to leave his job. Once again, I felt I had to be the dutiful eldest daughter and have Dad come stay with me. At least this time our three-bedroom condo was big enough for Peter, my father, and me to each maintain a bit of privacy.

I didn't tell Dad that Peter and I were separating until a few days before Peter moved out. I didn't want to give him time to try to change my mind. I delivered the news like I might mention I was ordering Thai food for dinner, then quickly went to check on Lael. I largely sidestepped my father for the rest of the week.

As painful as the decision to part had been, the process of Peter and me separating our lives was surprisingly calm. We simply decided it would be easier if Peter was the one to go. He quickly found a small apartment down the street so he could continue to see Lael every day. I was relieved we could make such a big step without a lot of drama, because at that point, every other aspect of my life was full of it.

I'd left Pepsi nine months earlier to become head of marketing for the fashion company Ashley Stewart. It was the first time I'd held such a senior role, and the company had a wonderful mission, making beautiful clothing for fuller-figured women, particularly Black customers in urban communities.

But the executives were old-school. Facebook was quickly becoming a phenomenon, and I thought it would be a great way to market our brand, but I was trying to tap into social media at a company that in 2010 still didn't have computers in its stores. The pay was good, but I quickly grew miserable.

I was in a job I didn't like, my marriage was in free fall, and my father was back, living under my roof.

The day Peter finally left, near the end of September, was surreal, with everyone acting as though nothing out of the ordinary was going on. Will, one of Peter's best friends, was there to tape and haul boxes, and my girlfriend Erika came by because she and I were going to a fashion show.

The four of us, along with Will's wife, had hung out a million times. Erika asked Will about his new baby, born a couple of months after Lael. Will gave Erika a hug and chatted with her about work. And I spritzed perfume and wrestled on my heels. When Erika and I grabbed our purses and headed for the door, Dad ducked his head out of the guest room just in time to tell us to enjoy ourselves. The whole scene was bizarre, and Erika said as much when we finally settled into her car.

"What the fuck?" she asked.

Yep. That about summed it up.

When I got home later that evening, Dad was in the living room, watching CNN like always, and Lael was down for the night. The only hints our lives had shifted was the half-empty closet in the master bedroom and Peter's shelf in the medicine cabinet that had been scraped clean.

Actually, there was one other clue. Salematou was there to watch Lael while I was out, and one look at her big sorrowful eyes told me there had been an earthquake even though everything appeared in its rightful place.

She asked if I needed anything, and I knew she wasn't checking to see if I needed her to put away the laundry. I wanted to tell her yes, to confess that sometimes I didn't know what I needed. Instead, I just said no and that I'd see her Monday morning.

When Sale left, Dad turned from the TV.

"What are we going to do?" he asked quietly.

The relationship between Peter and my father had evolved from the early days, when Dad so viscerally disapproved of us being together. Still, I knew he was less sad that Peter was gone and more worried about me facing the world as a single mother. Not only did he figure it would be difficult, I'm sure he was also concerned that it just wasn't a good look, another glitch in the perfect vision he'd once had for his oldest daughter.

"Well," I said, taking off my shoes, "I'm going to make dinner." I changed into a pair of sweatpants, tied back my hair, and went into the kitchen like it was any other day.

In a weird way, Dad's plaintive question underscored the unease I'd begun to have in my marriage. There was an implication in it, an assumption that I needed a husband to be complete. I was a grown-ass, capable woman, taking care of my baby and my father too. I earned as much as Peter. I'd moved alone to New York City and made my life happen. I didn't want to be seen as a piece of a whole when I was more than enough all by myself.

Yet at the same time, I did worry about what people would think. I'd hesitated to tell old friends and many of my relatives about the separation because I didn't want to be pitied or judged. And, of course, I still cared about Peter. Nothing was simple: Peter was gone. My dad was recovering from a stroke. Lael was freaking teething. I was just fighting to not be strangled in my tangle of emotions.

Even after separating, I was still searching for anchors every day. *Let me make it to tomorrow,* I would whisper to myself. *Let me make it to next week.* I would do the laundry, rock Lael to sleep, watch an episode of *Grey's Anatomy.* Every mundane thing took on extra importance, becoming a buoy in the dark to keep me from becoming undone.

Then I lost my job.

. . .

They called me in on a Friday afternoon. Things weren't really clicking. They'd expected more. Something, something. Yada, yada. I could barely respond because I knew they were right. It had been a while since I'd given my best. I was too distracted by all the off-key notes in my life, from my struggling marriage to my father's halting recovery. Still, I wanted so badly to prove myself, to show haters like that awful woman at Spike's agency that I had what it took to be a leader. I wanted to win. Instead, I was losing everything.

They gave me a couple of weeks' pay as severance. I stuffed a small box with the photos on my desk and imagined my father's face as I rode the elevator down to the street. "What are we going to do?" he would surely ask me again.

It was around this time that I began to wake up at dawn.

I'd always been a night owl. Before I became a mother, I waited impatiently for dusk, that last glimmer of light that meant the workday was over and it was now time for cocktails and laughter at hot spots like Nell's and Balthazar. When Lael came, night became the time for nursing and cuddling. Once she was asleep, I'd click on the local news, leaf through a novel, or jot my plans down in a notebook. Mornings were always a struggle, coming too fast and heralding a day that I'd barrel through, impatient for night to come again.

Now I suddenly no longer needed an alarm clock. I woke up on my own, in time to see the sky streaked pink and gold. At first, I started the day worried. I had some savings and that small severance, but my money could stretch only so far. And I dreaded seeing Peter every day. He would show up to see Lael looking so pitiful, I often had to leave the room.

But one morning, about two weeks after I was fired, I was lying in the huge bed Peter and I once shared that now held only me. I couldn't sleep, so I sat up.

As I rose, so did the sun, giving Manhattan's craggy skyline a copper sheen. *Why am I here in New Jersey, looking at this view from across the Hudson?* I thought. *The city. New York. That's where I want to be.*

Then, I heard it. God's voice.

It wasn't a rumbling bass that spoke in riddles, like in *The Ten Commandments*. Instead, words that I knew weren't my own permeated my entire being.

"Dawn always comes," it said. "And I will always take care of you day after day."

I don't remember the rest of the words, but I still get goose bumps recalling the message. That dawn signaled a new day, a new chapter, like the promise Nina Simone sang about in a song I love so much.

"Sun in the sky, you know how I feel . . .
It's a new dawn . . ."

God's words gave me power. I got up that morning feeling like nothing could go wrong, like I was invincible.

After that day, I went from dreading the morning to reaching for it. I took solace in the dawn. Instead of seeking out anchors to keep me afloat, I could sit in the darkest of moments and know that another moment was just over the horizon, one that had the potential to be so much better, so much brighter. I just had to look for it.

There were still times when I had to fight for that feeling of peace. When I had no leads for a new job or when I longed to fall asleep in Peter's arms, I had to will myself to look for that pinpoint of brightness. I would remind myself that if I could just hold on, that tiny light would become a blinding sun. I leaped from dawn to dawn, waiting, hoping. The anchors I grasped helped me to survive. But the promise of dawn lifted me.

Near the end of the year, an old colleague from Pepsi sent me an email. One of the women I'd previously worked with was going on maternity leave, and they needed someone to cover her desk while she was out. Was I interested?

Though I'd called a few old contacts to look for a job, I'd deliberately avoided reaching out to my former colleagues at Pepsi. I'd left there in a blaze of glory, headed to this new senior position at

Ashley Stewart, and I was too embarrassed to tell my old coworkers that not only had I been fired, I was on the verge of divorce.

Yet Pepsi had called me. A temporary gig meant I could pay another month's rent on my own and fill the grocery cart with a few more steaks and maybe even some gourmet treats. This was a miracle. I didn't pose or front. I said yes immediately.

It got better. The manager asked me my rate. Up to that point, I'd told my prospective bosses what I'd made before, they offered me a salary, and, grateful for the opportunity, I accepted. Now, I had a chance to dictate what I wanted to earn, to articulate what I was worth. It was like God was standing there with an open checkbook, ready to take care of me.

I slept on it. When I woke up at dawn, I had a number in mind. I grinned as I got ready to face the new day.

And the salary I asked for? They gave it to me, and then some.

. . .

Peter and I had always been New Year's Eve people. We'd get dressed up, buy sparkly hats, and practically bathe in champagne. But we were heading into 2011 leading separate lives. It was his night to be with Lael, so they were going to ring in the new year together, and Lael's godfather, Mecca, who was Peter's best friend from college, drove up from Pennsylvania to be with them.

Meanwhile, Erika had invited me to a house party. As I dressed, ticking off the friends she said were going to be there, it startled me to realize that not only were they all single, I was now single too. Sort of. I was nervous and also excited. Peter and I had been separated for nearly four months, and I still wore my wedding ring. That night, for the first time, I took it off.

Peter was subdued when I dropped off Lael, which wasn't out of the ordinary. I hugged Mecca and said a quick goodbye. But when I walked out to the hallway, I heard a strange sound behind me, like a whimper. I froze, thinking it might be Lael. Then I heard Mecca's voice. It was probably just the TV.

The party was at the apartment of a guy I didn't know. People were dancing along to a video on the big screen, and most of the folks were already a few drinks in. Eager to catch up, I made my way to the bar. I spotted Erika, and we gave each other a big hug.

"Holy shit!" she said, glancing down. "You're not wearing your ring!"

I was about to respond when my phone began to buzz. It was Peter. My heart pounding, I ran to the bathroom to shut out the noise.

"Where are you?" he yelled as soon as I answered.

"I'm with Erika at a party," I said. "What's wrong? Is it Lael?"

"Who's there?" Peter asked, ignoring my questions.

Was he serious? "Nobody you know. I don't even know these people," I said. Now I was getting pissed.

"Why aren't you wearing your ring?" he yelled. Then he started to cry.

Because we've been separated for four months, I wanted to say. *Because our marriage is over, and I just don't want to wear it anymore.*

But it was New Year's Eve. Peter was crying. And I didn't want him to hurt.

"I don't know," I said. "I don't know."

I heard Mecca's voice in the background. I'm sure he'd spent the last hour trying to convince Peter not to call me before giving up.

"I won't be here that late," I said, trying to get off the phone. "I'll see you and Lael tomorrow."

I hung up, distressed and exhausted. I no longer wanted to be with Peter romantically, but I still loved him. Hearing him sound so broken was too much for me to bear. I'd never heard him cry like that.

What we imagine is often so much worse than what's real. I'm sure Peter thought I was attending some big orgy. If only he knew I was surrounded by a couple dozen people playing video games and cards and that none of them was showing the slightest interest in me.

That night, I stayed just long enough to hug Erika at midnight, then headed home.

I wanted to be honest with Peter, to always speak my truth, but I knew now I wouldn't be able to. We would be co-parents, and maybe even friends, but our relationship could go only so deep because I couldn't stand the thought of saying something, doing anything, that would break his heart over and over again.

. . .

I spent the winter focused on getting comfortable with my new routines. Dad's health improved, and he found a new consulting gig and moved out. Meanwhile, my job at Pepsi was extended. And I finally took the plunge and decided to move back to Manhattan. I'd no longer be around the corner from Peter, but I was determined he'd still be able to see Lael whenever he wanted, even if I had to constantly drive her back and forth to New Jersey.

Most of my friends lived in Harlem, so I responded to a listing for a sublet on 115th Street and Fifth Avenue. The owners were a young Latino couple who looked like a mirror of Peter and me when we were happy. I fell in love with them, and with their apartment.

The building was a contemporary high-rise that towered over Harlem's brownstones. There was a gym and dry cleaner's next door, and I even had my own parking space, which I didn't have to pay extra for, a perk that was practically unheard of in Manhattan. It was another miracle.

Lael and I moved in just in time to see the first buds of spring. I watched my new neighbors peel off their down jackets, swapping boots and scarves for T-shirts and sandals. When I boxed up my gloves and winter coat and pulled out my shorts, I felt like I was shedding my old self.

In Manhattan, I felt my most beautiful, my most powerful. I wasn't the mother of a dead child. I wasn't an estranged wife. I was just Boz, living her best life with her little girl. And boy did it feel good.

I would plop Lael in her stroller and we'd take long leisurely walks up St. Nicholas Avenue or over to Morningside Park. Because I was tall, thin, and dark, the Senegalese brothers selling cloth on the streets or grabbing a plate of yassah at a restaurant in Little Senegal assumed I came from their part of the world.

"*Bonjour, belle. Viens ici,*" they'd sing as I walked by.

"I don't speak French," I'd yell back playfully, before sashaying away with a smile. I felt seen. I felt free. It was as though all the frustration, fear, and sorrow that had shadowed my pregnancies and the last years of my marriage lifted and disappeared. I felt so liberated that one afternoon I literally skipped down the block in my Louboutins.

• • •

One early summer night, Lael was spending the weekend with Peter. My new single crew and I were getting ready to see Sade perform in New Jersey, but first we had a party to go to. It was one of those fetes that made Manhattan feel like the coolest place in the world, a celebration on a rooftop with New York City buzzing below.

We were young, successful, beautiful, and Black. They never showed women who looked like me and my girlfriends on *Sex and the City*, but we were totally about that life. Swaying on the rooftop to spin after spin of neo soul, I sipped a rainbow-colored cocktail and counted down to Sade.

Then I saw him. This tall brown-skinned man with striking eyes and a whisper of a goatee. He caught my stare and walked over.

His name was Lamar. He was ex-military and a burgeoning entrepreneur and was the friend of a friend of a friend. I don't know what made me more tipsy, the drinks or the thrill of a new overwhelming attraction.

Talking to Lamar was easy. I didn't tell him I was separated. I didn't tell him that I had a child. In that moment, on that rooftop, I was just a fly young Black woman wearing a sexy, midriff-baring blouse and having a hell of a good time. It was magical.

Then, one of the people in our group suddenly had to take care of something and couldn't attend the concert. Lamar eagerly took the spare ticket. The night was shaping up to be so perfect, I thought for a moment that Lamar and I might be at the beginning of a fairy tale. Everything was so spontaneous. There was no stress, no deep conversation, just laughter and light. We piled into somebody's car and headed to the Izod Center across the river.

Of course, we had box seats because it had been that kind of evening. Lamar sat beside me, his leg brushing against mine. About halfway through the concert, the band began to play a song that I recognized from the first note.

It was Peter's song. My song. Our song. "By Your Side." We'd danced to it at our wedding and etched its lyrics inside our wedding bands.

When Sade began to coo the words, I didn't drift down from my high. Rather, I crashed, weighed down by the pit that suddenly ballooned in my stomach. Lamar leaned over.

"Is everything all right?" he asked. I guessed he could see a change in my face, feel a change in my energy.

"Oh yeah," I said. But that song marked the end of my magical night. It was a searing reminder that I could escape reality for only so long. The fact was my life was too complicated to be completely carefree. I was estranged from a man who didn't want our marriage to end. He and I shared a child. And together we had endured unimaginable grief.

That song reminded me that I had failed at love, and if I couldn't make it work with Peter, who I once felt I couldn't live without, how could I ever make love work with someone else?

. . .

I'd given Lamar my phone number, and a few days after the concert, we went to dinner. I told him I'd been separated for several months, that Peter and I had a young daughter, and I was still trying to figure things out. Lamar had also recently left a relationship and had three sons. Again, it was so easy to offer up my truth with him.

It wasn't that way with Peter, though. I still couldn't bring myself to tell him that romantically, I was moving on.

Within a few weeks, Lamar was occasionally spending the night when Lael was over at Peter's. He usually left first thing in the morning.

On one particular Saturday, though, before Peter was due to

arrive, Lamar was still chilling, sipping a glass of orange juice, chatting about this and that. I became anxious.

Peter would be at my door with Lael any minute. I was trying to figure out how I could convince Lamar to run to the store—or maybe hide in the closet—when Peter called and told me he was having trouble finding a parking space so I'd have to come downstairs.

Whew, I thought as I headed to the elevator. But when I got back to the apartment with Lael, I could feel Lamar's mood had changed.

"He doesn't know about me, does he?" Lamar asked after Lael went into her room.

Oh God, here we go. I didn't bother lying.

"No," I said. "He doesn't."

"Well," he said, folding his arms across his chest, "you need to tell him."

He was right. Peter and I had been apart for a year, but we'd established the kind of rhythm and rapport that could easily have led him to believe that we would eventually work things out, that this break was only temporary.

We'd landed in a softer place after the initial awkwardness. We made small talk and laughed. Sometimes we even hugged. I didn't want to lead him on. I didn't want there to be any misunderstanding.

A few days later, I asked Peter to go out for something to eat. I picked a random restaurant rather than one of our old favorite spots so there was no mistaking our outing for a date.

But when Peter showed up, he was wearing cologne, which was rare. He had a fresh shave, and months after we split, he was still wearing his wedding ring.

Oh no, I thought. *This is going to be bad.*

Peter was fidgeting, repeatedly asking me the same silly questions.

In some ways, the scene reminded me of the night that he proposed. That realization finally gave me the courage to cut to the chase.

"I'm seeing somebody."

Peter looked down at his plate, quiet for a few seconds.

"Who is it?" he asked

"No one you know," I said hastily, picking through my appetizer. "It doesn't matter."

"Well," Peter said, his voice hesitant, "tell me about him."

I wanted to say that he was African American and so I didn't have to translate my Blackness. I wanted to say he allowed me to forget my past trauma, for at least a little while, and to just have fun.

"He's a nice guy and I like him" was what I finally came up with. "You should think about seeing someone too."

Peter looked me in the eyes. "I'm not going to see anybody," he said. "You're my wife."

There was nothing else to say.

Peter never asked about Lamar again, and a few months later, it became moot when Lamar and I stopped dating. Peter and I just went on, maintaining our awkward pas de deux.

Every once in a while, when he dropped off Lael or I picked her up, I'd jokingly ask whether he'd found the girl of his dreams yet. He'd roll his eyes but no longer got upset.

. . .

The summer after I found the lump in my breast, my mother's younger sister Auntie Amma was diagnosed with breast cancer. Desperate to comfort her, I flew to London for her birthday as a surprise. It was frightening to see her so weak as she went through radiation and chemotherapy, but Auntie eventually made a full recovery.

But cancer wasn't done. When Lael was two, it came knocking on my mother's door. Mom and Dad were divorced, and she was working at a department store and living in a beautiful townhome in Colorado Springs that she decorated with photos and Ghanaian sculptures that symbolized piety and love. Then she discovered a small swelling in her breast.

My sisters and I created a schedule, each of us spending a week at a time with her. Lael wasn't in school yet, so I would take days off from work, pack a small bag, and take her with me.

Looking back on the many difficult episodes in my life, Mom's battle with breast cancer oddly doesn't stand out as especially bad. Of course, I hated to see her suffer, and it was certainly jarring to fly to Colorado every month or to wait for updates from my sisters and my mother's doctors. I was working at Pepsi at the time, juggling meetings, conference calls, and campaigns. Still, despite such a heavy load, it somehow seemed manageable. Auntie Amma was all right. I'd had my own scare when I was seventeen, yet I was all right too. I always believed that Mom would be fine.

Thankfully, she did go into remission, but in early 2013, Mom received yet another diagnosis. This time it was uterine cancer. Peter and I were separated, Lael was in day care, and I'd moved back to New York City. Flying to Colorado every few weeks would be too difficult this time around, so I asked Mom to move east.

After so many years taking care of my dad and her daughters, Mom still yearned to have her own space, and Manhattan was terribly hectic and expensive. So, we got her a short-term rental in Jersey City and found her an oncologist nearby.

I went back and forth across the George Washington Bridge, often staying at Mom's place overnight when she had her chemo treatments and couldn't summon enough strength to even open the blinds. This second bout of cancer scared me more because I wondered if we would be fighting this disease forever. Would we win one round, only for it to come back again, attacking another part of her body or another person we loved? Peter's mother had also survived breast cancer. Where would cancer pop up next?

Still, though Mom's ongoing chemo was debilitating, her surgery was successful. She was pulling through.

. . .

During this time, Peter didn't live far, and he was incredibly helpful, checking on my mother every day and even occasionally picking her up groceries. I'd had two relationships in the nearly three years we'd been separated, but in so many ways, Peter was still acting like my husband. We talked all the time, about our extended family, about Lael. I guess the anger, over Eve, over slights big and small, began to diminish, allowing us to embrace each other again.

Then, in February or March 2013, I went to Peter's apartment to drop off something for Lael and I glimpsed a pair of women's shoes. I knew Lael, not yet four years old, couldn't fit in them. And those flats definitely weren't mine. Not my size. Not my style.

I was surprised. I'd really believed that Peter was never going to move on. But now another woman's shoes were sitting in his entryway.

My feelings were unexpected. First there was the gut punch. I felt a little possessive. Then I was elated. Whoever fit those shoes was going to free me from this weird limbo. I started to smile, then wiped it away. I didn't want Peter to know I'd seen the mystery shoes. I'd wait for him to tell me about their owner.

I was getting ready to leave when he kicked the shoes inadvertently. I looked down, then up at him. We smiled at each other, but he didn't say anything. I turned and left.

Days passed, and I grew tired of waiting for his revelation. The next time I dropped off Lael, I asked Peter whose shoes I'd seen.

"I've met someone," he said a little shyly. "Her name's Angela." He paused. "Do you want to meet her?"

It was so interesting. Though Peter knew I was dating, I still hid my boyfriends, never introducing any of them, not just because I didn't want to hurt Peter but because none of my relationships had been special enough to warrant it. Even I knew the guy I was currently dating wasn't "the one."

Now, here was Peter being up front about his new girlfriend from the beginning. *This must be serious,* I thought.

I wondered if she was Black. I didn't want to ask Peter directly, but I was curious. I didn't want her to be, because somehow, weirdly, that would feel like he was literally replacing me. But at the same time, I didn't want the white girls to win either. Whenever Peter and I walked arm in arm past a group of them, like the girls in that SoHo store so long ago, I'd felt a little victory.

I didn't want her to be a Black girl, and I didn't want her to be white. So, of course Angela ended up being both.

She was at Peter's apartment the next time I dropped off Lael. She didn't rise from her chair so much as bounce. Wearing leggings, what looked like a sports bra, and big fuzzy socks, the word that best described her was *lovely*. Not striking. Not beautiful. She was just—lovely. Not just in her appearance, but in her spirit.

Angela was biracial, a yoga instructor who I think grew up in the New York suburbs. Tall, graceful, with ringlets of dark curls that cast a shadow over her almond skin, she and I were nothing alike. That made me feel good and at the same time made me look at Peter with a question. Why her?

She didn't have on a stitch of makeup and literally smelled like Ivory soap. She was natural and earthy. In that way she did make sense for Peter. She was the kind of woman who would eagerly accompany him on a hike or camping trip.

This is what I'd wanted, I reminded myself, for Peter to get involved in a new relationship. And Angela's affection for Peter was palpable. I ignored my twinges of jealousy and tried to focus on how good it was that Peter had found someone else who could make him happy.

Things were finally working out.

• • •

A couple of months later, in May, I was picking up Lael. She was grabbing her backpack when I glanced at Peter and saw a small growth on his neck. I'd noticed it before, but now it seemed to be getting bigger.

"What is that?" I asked him. He brushed it off. He never got sick, not even a cold, so it was probably nothing, he said. But the lump's growth seemed to escalate over the next couple of weeks, to the point that Peter finally couldn't ignore it.

He went to our family doctor. He examined him and diagnosed it as tonsillitis. I made fun of him endlessly. What person made it to adulthood with their tonsils intact? I teased. He had them removed in an outpatient surgery that also required him to eat his favorite food as medicine: ice cream. We laughed at how lucky he was that even his illness still ended with a lucky strike.

But a few days later, the doctor called and said that his tonsils looked odd, so he was sending out a sample to be examined.

After a battery of tests, Peter got his diagnosis. Burkitt's lymphoma. A rare form of cancer.

Cancer. It was always on our tail, clutching Auntie Amma, catching Peter's mom, plowing its claws into my mother not once but twice. And now it had grabbed hold of Peter.

In that way it seemed cancer was almost inevitable. But precisely because Peter and I knew so many survivors, it also seemed beatable. Yes, it sucked. Yes, it was serious, but Peter would get treatment, maybe even surgery, and he'd be fine. There was no reason to believe otherwise.

The only thing that made me worry a little more about Peter was how much pain he was in almost from the start. Like on Lael's fourth birthday.

We threw her a party in the park. The lump on Peter's throat formed a blot beneath his chin, but it wasn't so big that a stranger would necessarily notice it sitting on top of the collar of his shirt.

But Peter was hurting. He helped supervise the kids' games and made it through our singing "Happy Birthday," but at one point I looked at him and saw him grimace. He didn't want to go when I suggested he head home.

"She's four," I told him gently. "She won't remember that you had to leave before it was over. And she's going to have plenty of other birthday parties where you'll be there the whole time."

Peter relented. He was in so much pain he couldn't drive, so I asked my cousin Tina to take the wheel and get him home.

I would never have guessed as they drove away that Peter was right to want to stay, that he wouldn't live long enough to see Lael turn five.

. . .

I began to juggle caring for my mother and Peter. When my mother had to get chemo, I would take Lael to day care, then drive Mom to the facility for her treatment. I'd call and check on Peter, then sort through emails as I waited in the lobby. When Mom was done, I'd drive her home, get her comfortable on the couch, set up her food and water, then put in a full day's work on my computer. Around 5:00, I'd pick up Lael, get dinner ready, check on Peter, then go to sleep.

The next day, I'd run the same marathon all over again.

My managers were understanding and let me work remotely most of the time, but sometimes I had to go into the office and work from there. I didn't tell many of my colleagues what I was dealing with. Somehow, the idea of giving voice to it all, actually hearing out loud what I was living through, seemed too overwhelming. But my silence left me lonely too.

I was so tired that I was numb. If I thought too hard about it all, I wouldn't have been able to get out of bed. In hindsight, if I told them, my colleagues would have helped me. Maybe they would have volunteered to bring dinner over some days or set up a delivery service. Maybe they could have recommended a part-time caregiver.

But somehow, I felt that I couldn't ask for help. This was my lot, my burden. I was being the dutiful daughter my parents had raised. And in hindsight, maybe I also felt this was my penance.

Perhaps I'd been selfish in breaking up with Peter and wanting a less complicated life. Now, ironically, I was fulfilling my marital vows after all. To have and to hold. For richer and for poorer. In sickness and in health.

Maybe caring for Peter and my mother, enduring those grueling days, would be the sacrifice that allowed me to find peace on the other side. Maybe suffering alongside Mom and Peter would save them and me. They'd get better, and I'd never have to hear a similar, devastating diagnosis after one of my annual mammograms. I would have paid my dues.

I wasn't completely on my own, though. Peter's girlfriend, Angela, and I previously had little to say to each other beyond hello and goodbye. But once Peter was diagnosed, she and I exchanged phone numbers. Soon, instead of sidestepping each other, Angela and I became partners, trading shifts during times when Peter had to stay in the hospital and exchanging updates on how we felt Peter was doing as he underwent radiation and chemotherapy.

Since I was also caring for my mother, it was an immense relief knowing that Angela was there to help look after Peter. She'd go with him to the doctor, then send me a selfie of the two of them sitting together after he'd had a round of chemo with feel-good exhortations like "Yeah!" and "Good job!"

When I visited Peter during his stints in the hospital, Angela would jump up and give me a hug before stepping out of the room to let me take over. And on days when Peter would feel really ill and call to talk about what else he should do—"Take vitamins? Eat more herbs?"—I'd inevitably ask, "What does Angela think?" I was grateful for her presence.

I'm sure to outsiders it sometimes looked a little crazy.

There was a day when we were all crowded in Peter's hospital room. Angela was literally lying in the narrow bed beside him, Peter's parents had come down from Massachusetts and were sitting in chairs, and I was there too. The doctor came in, looked at this multicultural, multigenerational gathering and tried to hide his confusion.

"Umm, I need someone to sign off on these papers?"

There was an uncomfortable pause. Then Peter looked up. "Give them to my wife."

It was awkward, to say the least.

. . .

Peter, thankfully, was getting better. When his cancer appeared to be in remission, we gathered a couple dozen friends at Peter's favorite Italian restaurant to celebrate.

His parents and sister, Debra, also came. There were too many of us to sit at one table, and I felt a ripple of jealousy when Angela was the one who got to sit beside Peter, giving him soft kisses in between sips of wine while I passed rolls to Peter's mother. But Angela was his partner now, not me.

When Peter stood to thank everyone for their support, he talked about me first. He told a story about how when he started to lose his hair, he'd called me in a panic. Peter loved his golden locks. He went to the barber every other week and used a special shampoo. Seeing clumps of hair fall into the sink after he started chemo was traumatic. He'd been afraid, angry, and I'd reassured him that certainly he had a right to be mad about losing his beautiful hair. And it was okay to be sad too. Faces swiveled toward me, their eyes filled with tears and appreciation.

Then Peter turned to Angela and talked about how much fun she was and how she made him feel so alive. I sunk into my glass of Cabernet Sauvignon, feeling the start of a sulk. When someone suggested we hit a nearby bar for one more round of drinks, I couldn't stand the thought of watching Angela and Peter cuddle as they got more and more buzzed. I told everyone good night and went home.

I'd never mentioned divorce before. I didn't want to be the one to ask for it and make Peter upset. Fiercely Catholic, he didn't really believe in it, and for the longest time I think he thought we'd get through this phase and work things out.

But that night convinced me it was time. Peter's health was rebounding, and I didn't want to continue sitting in this awkward void. I'd rather be the ex than this weird in-between wife. The next day I called Peter and told him we should go ahead and file.

He didn't sound happy, but to my relief and surprise, he agreed. After nearly three years, he'd finally faced what I'd known since the day I told him I wanted out: we weren't going to reconcile.

I think we both figured we could divorce the way we separated, the way we'd lived and loved. We would be reasonable. We would be partners. We would be friends.

We were so naive.

· · ·

I suggested Peter and I each get lawyers to draw up the paperwork, not because we really needed them but because I assumed that was just what people who divorced did. I didn't know that getting our own attorneys meant Peter and I would be on opposite sides, literally and figuratively.

I remember the first time I went to Peter's attorney's office for what I thought would be mere formalities. Peter and I had figured out custody years before. Lael spent equal time with each of us, and if he wanted to go out of town with his friends on a weekend he was supposed to have her, I had no problem switching. That didn't have to change. Neither of us was looking to the other to provide financial support. We'd already worked out our rules and boundaries. Now we were just trying to make it legal.

But when I walked in, Peter and his lawyer were sitting on one side of a large conference table and my lawyer was sitting on the other, an empty chair beside him. Looking back, I wish Peter and I had taken a stand right then, rearranging the seating so we could be together. Only thirty minutes earlier, Peter texted me to hurry up because he knew I was going to be late, a good-natured ribbing he bracketed with smiling emojis.

Now, in this office, something felt off. And the only additions to our equation were that table and those damn lawyers.

Peter's attorney was combative from the start, and my lawyer picked up the scent and responded in kind.

"What happens if Peter decides to move to Spain?" Peter's lawyer asked, leaning back in his leather chair.

I smirked. Early in our marriage, Peter and I actually talked about one day moving to Barcelona.

"Well," I said, "then I would go with him."

It was Peter's attorney's turn to smirk as he scribbled furiously on a notepad. The hypotheticals kept coming from both sides of the table.

Who was going to pay Lael's college tuition? Who would pay for the ballet classes and violin lessons?

Peter and I looked at each other. What the hell was going on?

These lawyers didn't know us, how we interacted, what we'd been through. But they seemed determined to rile us up.

Peter and I had always been really good at sharing money. During our marriage, we had several joint accounts. There was one for the must-haves, like paying the light bill and buying groceries. We had another to cover outings to the movies or vacations. We had one for our savings. And whatever income we had left went into each of our own personal accounts, so if I wanted to buy a Fendi purse or Peter wanted a new bike, that was our business.

Even after we separated, Peter and I continued to pay our individual rent and other bills out of that same joint pool of money. Our lawyers thought that was crazy. So we started questioning that arrangement as well.

Peter and I had known each other for thirteen years, gone through some of the most harrowing experiences a couple could endure, and come out friends on the other side. Yet soon we refused to talk about anything significant without our lawyers.

A few months earlier, I wouldn't have hesitated to call Peter and ask him to pick up Lael from day care if I was running late from work. I'd just swing by his apartment to bring her home. Now I felt that would give Peter some example he could use against me, a piece of evidence that would show I was an unreliable mother. It was ridiculous.

The divorce was causing me to lose touch with Peter in a way I'd never anticipated. I'd thought the happily ever after that eluded us in marriage could be our destiny in divorce. But the gulfs that divided us when we were together were widening again. It hurt because I still loved and respected Peter. I just didn't want to be married to him anymore.

And, of course, when my interactions with Peter changed, so did my relationship with Angela. I still worried about Peter's health, but the messages Angela and I exchanged about Peter's illness and progress became snippy and terse.

"How's Peter today?" I'd ask Angela in a text.

"Why don't you call him?" she'd respond.

That was it. No more selfies. No more happy-faced emojis. Our days as sister wives were done.

I also wondered if there was another gripe fueling Angela's attitude. I heard through friends that when Peter was complaining about all the shit we were wading through with our lawyers, he blamed me. I wanted the divorce. Not him. I'm sure he didn't say that to Angela. That would have been cruel. But Angela wasn't stupid. I wasn't particularly sympathetic at the time, but in hindsight, it must have been incredibly hard to be in love with a man who wanted to stay married to someone else. She couldn't take her anger out on Peter. So, she took it out on me.

But then came the day of the call, the day I learned Peter's cancer was terminal.

All of a sudden, our insecurities and grievances no longer mattered.

• • •

I was obviously no stranger to death. I'd lost Ben and Eve. But my mother was in remission. Peter's mother had been cancer-free for years. I never thought Peter's story would be different.

Believing there was a light at the end of the tunnel gave me fuel when Peter first got sick. *Dawn is right there,* I'd say. *When morning comes, I'll be able to sit down and celebrate with the biggest glass of champagne.*

But that day Peter's mother called me at my office, when I rushed to the hospital, into his room, and Peter told me he was dying, the light went out. Not with a flicker, but with a gasp, like a candle extinguished in a hurricane.

I haven't used the phrase *light at the end of the tunnel* since that day. I realized that when you're in darkness, instead of waiting for a ray of sun to appear, you sometimes have to find the light within. You have to conjure the match, spark the flint, and ignite it yourself. I learned that it was up to me to create the dawn.

11

Sugarman Gone

W hen we found out Peter was dying, we knew we'd have to tell Lael.

He and I were still grappling with our own shock. But the doctors said Peter might have only days, and at most a few weeks, left. We couldn't put it off.

Lael knew Daddy wasn't feeling well and sometimes had to stay at the hospital. But, of course, she was only four—she didn't understand what was really going on. The day we moved Peter home, Lael twirled around his room, so excited that her grandparents, cousins, Uncle Mecca, and Aunt Debra were all suddenly there.

We had a friend, Melissa, who was a psychologist. She was one of the many people I needed to call. I asked her if she had any advice on how to tell a four-year-old that her daddy was dying.

"Don't say that he's sick," she warned. If we did, any time someone caught a cold or the flu, Lael would worry that like Daddy, they'd go away. "Just tell her the truth," Melissa said, "clearly and plainly."

I whispered Melissa's advice to Peter. We didn't rehearse or write out a script. We just asked our family members and friends to give us a few minutes alone with Lael; then we sat her on Peter's bed and each took one of her hands. I couldn't say it, so Peter did.

"Honey, Daddy has cancer," he said softly. "I'm not going to get better. I'm going to die."

Lael was more puzzled than alarmed. "Why?" she asked. "Why is your cancer not going to get better? Why are you going to die?"

Why? It was the simplest question in the world and the hardest to answer. I thought about how I'd been asking God the exact same question, and like Lael, I could not fathom why this was happening.

But unlike Lael, I knew what was coming. I envied her innocence, because I understood all that she would miss, not just on her next birthday, but for the rest of her life.

It's so wonderful to have your children look at you, believing you know it all. It hurt that Lael had to begin to face the most devastating of losses that day, and that she also learned that there were puzzles her parents couldn't solve. I grieved for all of that too.

Why? There was only one answer we could give Lael. We didn't know.

She scanned our faces, as if she was looking for more. We had nothing else to say, so she stopped asking questions.

Later, when I reflected on that devastating moment, I saw a beauty in it too. It was so difficult to speak to grown-ups about Peter's illness, detailing the treatments we'd tried, listing the alphabet soup of medicines that had too many consonants and not enough vowels. But when we spoke to Lael, we stripped what was happening down to its bare essence. With Lael, there was no beating around the bush, no denial. There was only the truth.

We could have detailed Peter's deterioration, explaining that Daddy was having trouble swallowing, that his legs were getting weak. We could have pretended there was still a chance Daddy would survive. But if we went round and round, we'd still have to circle back to the reality that Daddy was going to die.

I have applied the lesson I learned that day to virtually every other aspect of my life. When I'm in the midst of my hardest conversations, I speak as if I'm talking to a four-year-old. We spend so much time burying the truth in a bunch of excuses and rationales, trying to make ourselves feel better or to skirt the uncomfortable. But why add all that extra fluff when the truth is simply what it is?

It's like when you quit a job. So many people trot out a long explanation. I did the same thing when I left Spike and the first time I left Pepsi, ticking off a laundry list of the opportunities I didn't get here, and the perks I would get there, trying to justify why I was leaving.

But when you got right down to it, the simple answer was I just didn't want to be there anymore. Period. That was the truth of it, distilled to its core.

I've learned to be just as straightforward when dealing with friendships that have run their course. You hope that when a friend invites you to get together, and you say no enough times, that they'll get the message and there will be no need for a final farewell. But if they ask why—"Why aren't you speaking to me anymore? Why aren't you calling me?"—there are two ways to answer.

You can trot out the reasons—"Because you offended me, because you work my last nerve, because we are too different now and no longer enjoy the same things"—or you can make it simple: "I just don't want to be your friend anymore."

I choose simplicity. I don't explain away the inevitable. I don't

waste time. It may seem abrupt, even hurtful, but there's no misin-
terpretation. It is what it will be.

That's what I learned when Peter and I told Lael the bitter truth
that day in the hospital. She couldn't hide from it, and neither could
we. There was no turning away. It was just a fact. There was nothing to do but accept it.

. . .

My reconciliation with Peter was a stunning reminder of the fickle-
ness of fate. How just as life could make your knees buckle, leaving
you to grapple with how a man could receive a death sentence in the
prime of his youth, life could just as quickly hit rewind and flip your
emotions upside-down.

Who could have imagined that grief and loss, which had nearly
destroyed my marriage, would now be the forces that put it back
together? Sorrow and pain, bound up with love and appreciation,
would become the new foundation of our relationship reborn.

Sometimes, when you look back at a situation you were desperate
to escape, you wonder what could have been so bad. Before Peter
and I separated, I felt like I would suffocate if I stayed. But when I
had to stare fate in the face, I wondered, *Couldn't I have stuck it out?*

It was easy to berate myself, to feel I'd been selfish and weak, to
resent the interruptions that had robbed us of time.

But the grief I felt when looking at him but seeing Eve, the pain
I felt being battered by a society that made me feel our marriage
was constantly under attack, created a valley so deep, I just couldn't
summon the energy to climb out of it. Who's to say I wasn't strong
enough? Who's to say I gave up? Maybe I wasn't a quitter. Maybe

I recognized my exhaustion and decided that I needed to save myself.

That's the reasoning I'd reach in the years to come. But at that moment, all I wanted was to save Peter, or at least fight until the looming end.

. . .

It was time to tell Angela.

Peter hadn't called Angela the day we got his final diagnosis. But the day he left for home, she was back at the hospital, milling among our growing crowd of relatives and friends. At one point, in the midst of all the energy and emotion, I lost track of Lael. I nearly lost my mind.

I rushed down the hallway. Then back to the room. I'm sure only a few minutes had passed, but my nerves were ragged. Then, I looked up and saw Angela and Lael getting off the elevator. They were holding hands, and Lael was licking a scoop of vanilla ice cream. I went off.

"What the hell are you doing?" I yelled. "You don't just take off with my daughter! Stay away from Lael!"

Lael's eyes welled with tears. So did Angela's. I'd overreacted, but I was raw. Angry at the world. Angry at Angela being in the middle. She turned and practically ran away.

I marched into Peter's hospital room with Lael on my hip. I knew everyone had heard my outburst, so I didn't need to raise my voice much above a whisper when I commanded that everyone should clear the room. They obeyed silently, shuffling out, interrupted conversations left hanging in the air. In the process, someone took

Lael from my arms, knowing that whatever I had to say didn't need additional ears besides Peter's.

"You've got to tell Angela it's over," I said plainly. "Maybe I'm being selfish. But I can't do this—*we* can't do this—with her around."

I knew I wasn't being fair. Angela loved Peter, and she'd been an integral part of his life for months. At one point, she'd even been a partner to me, helping to take care of Peter when I was juggling so much. But this was urgent. Peter and I had only a little time left, and now that we'd decided to get back together, I didn't want to share.

He looked at me like he'd known this moment would always come if only he was patient. He once said he'd wait his whole life for me to come back. Neither of us knew that we wouldn't have to wait decades for his wish to come true.

I don't know what Peter said, but no more than fifteen minutes later, I got a text from Angela. There was no trace of her trademark sweetness. Instead of the terse talk that briefly flowed between us when Peter and I were in the midst of our divorce, Angela let me have it in message after message. I was manipulative and mean. I was taking advantage of a terrible situation. I didn't deserve Peter.

I hit back with some fire of my own. Our exchange was sharp, ugly. I regret that. I know she must have been in great pain, and I could have been more understanding.

But at the time, I was thinking only of Peter. He wrote on his Facebook page to make our reconciliation official: "God has given me time to spend with my family and friends, and has also given me back my kingdom, which is the greatest gift I could ever get. And it doesn't matter for how long . . ."

Now our ending could begin.

. . .

When I started waking up at dawn, I found that was the time I felt closest to God. Sometimes the conversation would go one way, with God talking to me and me sitting there quiet, like a child. Other times I'd rattle off questions, seeking answers. Even when I heard nothing, I felt that I could always be honest, that I could bare my soul. God wasn't judgmental. God was a friend.

And so, I was able to tell God something that until now I've never told anyone. I had yet another fear.

If Peter was able to beat this disease after all, if the doctors were wrong, would the sweetness of our fresh start wear off? Would I again be trapped in a marriage that I wanted badly to get out of?

One morning, I returned to my apartment. I'd been over at Peter's place, packing. We'd decided that he would move back to New York, and I briefly left him with his parents and drove home. It had been a while since I'd been all alone, and I filled the silence with that pesky, eternal question: Why? Why was this happening to me? How could I lose someone else?

My questions were more a mental refrain than a direct query to God. Still, God answered.

"You didn't appreciate them," the voice said.

I knew it was God because it was a truth I didn't want to face. I knew it was God because the voice filled the apartment, like surround sound streaming from a giant speaker.

I literally collapsed to my knees. Because I knew. I knew that it was about Ben. I knew that it was about Eve. I knew that it was about Peter. I hadn't appreciated enough being Ben's love, being Eve's mother, being Peter's wife. My gratitude for them deepened only when they were gone or on the verge of being taken.

227

I should have turned around and picked up the phone the last time Ben called. I should have loved Eve as intensely when I learned she was growing inside me as I did when I lay in the hospital ready to sacrifice my life for hers.

And even now, in the back of my mind, I was still having doubts about Peter. Did I love him? Yes. Did I want him to live? Desperately. If he survived, would I want him constantly and all consumingly? I didn't think so.

It was all so confusing. At times, I sometimes felt in the throes of new love. Peter would text me cute messages, and I'd send him songs. I literally felt light-headed, like when I climbed Pikes Peak in Colorado without drinking enough water and began to giggle and say stupid stuff, drunk on the altitude. My reborn romance with Peter could feel like that, effervescent.

But other times, the butterflies in my stomach would drift away as I remembered the abyss we were approaching.

When the oncologist said Peter's blood count had slightly improved, or when Peter seemed a bit stronger, I sometimes felt the prick of a different kind of fear amid my hope. A fear that if he made it, I might regret a pledge I made when I believed he wouldn't. I wanted him here for me, for Lael. I would always be by his side. But I still wasn't sure I wanted to be married.

And so, I felt guilty. Sometimes I still do, wondering what I would have done if he had survived. Would I have stayed married, to the detriment of my own happiness? Would I have caused Peter another heartbreak?

But that morning, when God spoke to me in my apartment, I knew I had to focus. Whatever doubts I had about my marriage, I resolved to ignore them, to not let them obscure the lesson that was coming into view. Faced with the truth that I'd lacked appreciation, I staggered to my feet, understanding that from now on, the only way I could live my life was with full gratitude.

I owed that to Peter and God. I owed that to myself.

I would no longer take anything for granted, not a love, not a moment. From then on, I would live every day of my life with urgency.

I vowed to actively demonstrate my thanks for every breath, not with a passing thought or a glib remark that I said but didn't mean. My gratitude was going to be intentional. I didn't want to gaze at the light as it began to dim. I wanted to cherish it all along the way.

. . .

It's a complicated gift, knowing the end is coming, fretting about how soon it will arrive, but also being pushed to make the most of every hour.

It means savoring a soft kiss and a hamburger grilled just right. It means lingering over a butterfly until it flies away. But it also means embracing the hard parts too. Like making sure you've jotted down your partner's final wishes. Like asking for the details of that funny story you love so much because soon your loved one won't be there to share them.

Too often when we think about gratitude, we want only to reflect on the good stuff. But I believe it's important to reckon with the hard things as well, and to tease out what those tests of will are trying to show you.

That was one of the lessons I grasped when we had to stuff years' worth of memories into Peter's final days. I cataloged it all with my phone, memorializing every meal, capturing every burst of laughter.

One of the many items on the lists he'd compiled was to take Lael fishing for the last time. I didn't want to let either of them out of my sight, but Peter insisted that he needed to have some time with Lael alone.

He wouldn't even tell me where they were going. I knew I'd worry incessantly, but I understood his need to connect and for Lael to have a memory that would be hers alone. I kissed them both as they clamored into the car, fishing poles in tow. I just asked Peter to be sure to take a picture.

They didn't get lost. And in the photograph, smiling side by side, I'd rarely seen either of them look so happy.

Another one of Peter's to-dos was to eat gelato. Actually, I was surprised that particular task wasn't number one.

I've bever been a fan of that Italian dessert. I preferred the vanilla swirls you got from trucks that roll through neighborhoods on burnt-orange afternoons. But Peter thought gelato was nectar sent straight from heaven. A couple of summers before he and I met, he and his nephew, Scott, traveled throughout Italy, tracing their family's roots. I saw plenty of photos of them roaming around, wearing sunglasses, chilling in shorts. And I think in almost every shot, they were eating gelato. Lemon. Chocolate. Butterscotch. They ate it morning, noon, and night.

After that trip, Peter compared every gelato he bought, whether it was at a street fair in Boston or in the Ironbound section of Newark, to those creamy cups of goodness he'd had in the motherland. Of course, they never measured up. And how could they? Gelato in Italy had ingredients that were impossible to replicate, like the sweetness of being eaten beneath a Roman sun while hanging out with your favorite nephew.

I thought it would continue to be a quixotic quest to try to find a perfect gelato in the States, but Peter was having more and more difficulty swallowing the store-bought stuff and there was no time to fly to Europe. We had to ferret out a good cup of homemade gelato right here.

We went to Little Italy in Manhattan, a neighborhood where we'd had wonderful times visiting with Peter's parents. By the 2000s it was more a Disneyesque tourist stop than a real community, but we still enjoyed eating our way through its festivals, stuffing our faces with carbonara and cannoli.

During our gelato search, we passed store after store, not even bothering to go into most of them, convinced of their mediocrity just by the look of the dessert encased behind the counter.

Peter tired easily, walking like a man twice his age. I held his hand, and we stopped often so he could gather his strength.

We were almost to Chinatown when we finally saw a tiny shop. Its OPEN sign was faded. I wondered how long it had been there. We'd never noticed it before.

Peter could no longer down a heaping plate of food or a mountain of ice cream. At most, he could probably handle one scoop. If we stopped here, this would have to be it. We decided to go inside.

Typically, Peter would opt for something exotic—the ginger chocolate crumb or the peachy bourbon. But that day he chose my favorite flavor, vanilla. I got a scoop too.

I dipped in my spoon. Maybe it tasted more luscious because we'd searched for it so long. Maybe it was the emotional significance of the day. All I know is that it was delicious. I looked at Peter.

"Your turn."

He plunged his spoon in with a dramatic flourish, then put it in his mouth. He closed his eyes, cherishing the sweetness. He nodded his head, then sighed.

Victory.

. . .

We weren't totally beholden to our notebook ledgers. Peter occasionally went off script, like the evening he said he wanted us to head back to Edgewater to look at the view of Manhattan from there.

We took a beautiful drive along the edge of the Hudson River, then headed to a hillside gazebo we'd often passed when we lived in New Jersey. We always said we should stop with a picnic basket and make an afternoon of it. But we'd never done it, until then.

After we parked and began to stroll, Peter started talking about how grateful he was for our time together and how thankful he was that we'd reconciled. Then he slowly got down on one knee.

I tried to stop him, worried it would be too hard for him to get back up. But Peter insisted, gripping a guardrail.

"I really love you," he said. "I've never met anyone like you. Boz, will you marry me?"

We'd already excavated our wedding rings and were wearing them again. I looked at him with a slight smile.

"We're already married," I reminded him.

"You have to say yes!" he said, starting to laugh.

"Okay," I replied. "Yes!"

I helped him back to his feet and we stopped a stranger to snap our picture. Then we drove to Peter's old apartment. He still had the lease, and his parents were staying there. We rummaged through a closet and dug out our wedding video, then we ordered food and called my mother so she could join us.

We stuck the video in an old player and had the best time, laughing at one of my aunts, who said something ridiculous, and Peter's cousin giving one of countless woozy toasts. Lael was there watching the video with us too. It was sweet to explain to her that this was the day Mommy and Daddy got married. She'd never seen the video before, and even Peter and I hadn't watched it since shortly after our wedding.

There was no cake or champagne, but we had white wine and a package of Hostess cupcakes, those retro chocolate desserts with the cream-filled middle. I'm not sure where they came from. They might have been left over from Peter's three-year stint as a bachelor. No matter. That night they tasted like the finest dessert in the world.

• • •

Every time we checked another activity off the list, it felt like we were watching more sand slip through an hourglass. I thought of trying to trick fate, adding something new to replace whatever we crossed off, hoping to evade the inescapable.

The lists could only distract us so much. Every morning we woke up, it seemed something new had gone wrong. One day Peter said he couldn't feel his perineum.

I tossed him a look. What the hell was a perineum?

"You know," he said, sitting up in bed.

"No. Really, I don't," I replied.

He pointed below his waist. I was still clueless.

Exasperated, he finally just spit it out.

"My asshole!" he said. "I can't feel my asshole!"

We cracked up laughing.

He still had his sense of humor and that beautiful crooked grin. But of course, none of this was funny.

Soon his sphincter muscles began to fail, making it difficult to control his bowels. His doctors said that we could readmit him, but if he wanted to stay home, he would probably need to start wearing a diaper. Peter was humiliated. But honestly, he was eating so little, he hardly needed one.

It didn't take long before Peter was really struggling to walk. Lael was starting a new school, a Catholic academy not far from our Manhattan apartment. I was combing her hair when Peter poked his head in the door. He wanted to go with me to escort Lael on her first day.

The school was only a few blocks away, but I knew that would be too far for him to walk, so I decided we'd drive. There were a couple of spots in front where a taxi or car could drop off a passenger, but you weren't supposed to loiter. I waited until most of the kids were inside, then pulled up and honked to let the school officer know I would need to park. We didn't know him, and he didn't know what was going on, but he smiled good-naturedly and waved as he went inside.

My sister Alua rode with us in case Peter needed help. As we walked in, she snapped a photo of Peter and me holding Lael's hands.

I look at it often. You would think we were just a pair of parents happily celebrating our daughter's milestone. But Peter's legs were so weak, he had to fight to make his way from the car to the steps that led to the school's front door. Once he got there, Peter grabbed the railing and glanced at me. Lael, unaware, swayed happily back and forth beneath our gaze.

Peter was practically bent over. We both knew that for him, walking up those stairs would be like climbing Mount Everest. I saw the fight in his eyes disappear, replaced by a fleeting sadness. I told Lael Daddy needed to get something from the car. I would take her the rest of the way.

. . .

Peter's oncologist had told me to watch for any signs that Peter wasn't doing well, though he was deteriorating so fast, it was hard to figure out what was cause for alarm and what was the unavoidable regression we should just expect and endure.

I didn't bother to call when he could barely stand or to report that it was taking him an hour to eat a small lunch. But right before Thanksgiving, I went into the kitchen to boil water for tea. When I returned to our bedroom, Peter was awake, and I noticed a slight darkening around one of his eyes.

This was new. I didn't want to scare Peter, so I gave him a mug of Earl Grey, left the bedroom, and quietly called the doctor. She said it was a sign that he might be bleeding internally. I needed to get him to the hospital right away.

Again, I was numb. There was no guidebook for this, no primer for how to calmly deliver frightening news when you yourself were terrified.

When I went back into the bedroom, I didn't tell Peter I'd made the call, only that I was a little concerned about his eye and wanted to take him to the doctor to check it out.

He refused. "You know all kinds of things are going on," he said lightly. "I've lost my hair. My asshole's numb. Forget it. Let's have breakfast."

Peter hardly ever looked in the mirror by then, so I snapped a picture of him, dressed in his favorite Superman T-shirt, a faint shadow above his right temple. When he saw it, he still waved me off.

I began to get anxious. I didn't want to frighten him, but I knew we needed to go. He was slowly eating a bowl of watery oatmeal when he finally looked up.

"There's something you're not telling me, and we're supposed to share everything," he said.

I admitted that I'd called his oncologist. He might be bleeding internally. We needed to go to the hospital right away.

Peter didn't seem fearful or even nervous. "Okay," he said quietly. "I don't think you're in any condition to drive. Let's call an ambulance."

I'd taken the photograph to show the bruise not only to Peter but also to his doctor. The darkening was so slight, I thought—hoped—my mind might be playing tricks on me. But it continued to darken, and by evening, Peter looked like someone had punched him in the face.

Peter would have to spend Thanksgiving in the hospital, so I cooked some of the holiday dinner and ordered other parts, then brought it there. There was pecan pie, Peter's favorite, macaroni salad, stuffing, and of course a roasted turkey. Peter's brothers Neil and Steven were there, along with their parents, Alua, Lael, and my mom.

It actually turned out to be rather nice. We spread the food out on our wedding china, in the family waiting room. While we served most of the dinner there, carrying our plates into Peter's room, we knew he wouldn't want to miss the carving of the turkey, so we put the bird on the table where the hospital staff placed his meals and his father did the honors.

By that time Peter was finding it hard to raise his arm. I made him a small plate, with the softest of foods—mashed potatoes, gravy, a tiny bit of turkey—and I fed him.

. . .

During those final days in the hospital, Peter seemed to veer between quiet acceptance and a yearning to do what he had done before. For instance, he still wanted to go to the new jazz club he'd read about to discover what might become a regular hangout spot, even though he couldn't stand for any extended length of time. One day when I arrived at the hospital, he started talking about how he needed to get out of bed and head to the club. I gently steered the conversation in another direction.

Within days, he couldn't walk at all. The lymphoma was attacking Peter's nervous system. He could barely lift his right hand, then couldn't move his left. Soon his eye muscles weakened as well.

Peter always had terrible eyesight. He wore contacts and was so vain, I think we'd been married for years before I ever saw him pull out his glasses. The lenses were as thick as magnifying glasses. I remember joking that he'd lied to me the whole time, never admitting to me that he was blind.

But one day at the hospital, even though he was wearing his contacts, he said everything looked fuzzy. I was across the room, adjusting a calendar on the wall or fiddling with a plant. When I looked at him, I realized one eye was focused on me, and the other was drifting.

He could still see well enough to notice the fear on my face.

"What's wrong?" he asked.

"Nothing," I said. "Maybe your contact slipped. We'll figure it out."

The disease was taking him, piece by piece. My mother watched Lael, and later my friend Leander and her daughter came so that

Peter's parents and I could stay overnight at the hospital. There was a love seat and two chairs that we'd rotate sleeping on.

One night it was my turn on the small couch, but sleep wouldn't come. Peter couldn't really move on his own anymore, and after a while in the same position, he would get sore and need to be turned. He hated being so helpless, so he'd never complain. We'd have to watch for the grimace on his face to know it was time.

I lay there listening. The room was dark, and Peter's parents were gently snoring. I knew how Peter breathed when he slept, so I knew he was awake. I wrestled with whether to say something or to just give him time to be in his own thoughts. During the day we were always all over him, propping up his pillows, trying to stay upbeat. *Maybe*, I thought, *he just needs a little peace.*

After a few minutes, though, I decided to call out to him.

"You awake?" I whispered.

"Yeah," he said quietly.

I asked what he was thinking about.

"Every day I wake up something else is missing, something else is wrong," he said. "What if I get trapped? What if I can't open my eyes and you don't know that I'm still in here? I'll be awake and I'll be able to hear you, but you won't know."

His voice was so small, yet it was filled with a fear so big. *How terrifying*, I thought. *That would be like being buried alive.* I silently prayed to God to not let that happen. If Peter had to go, when he had to go, I pleaded for it to be quick.

Instead of reassuring Peter that he wouldn't suffer that terrible paralysis, I made a vow.

I told him I would never leave. He would never be alone. Even if he couldn't open his eyes, as long as he was breathing, I would sit there every single day and talk to him. I reached out my hand.

He didn't have the strength to squeeze mine, but our touching was filled with a love so strong it was impossible to express. No room was big enough to hold it. There wasn't enough time to fully evoke it.

It was the last promise I would make to him.

. . .

I'd taken time off work so I could be at the hospital as much as possible. Sometimes when Peter napped, I'd sit and read. Searching for solace, I'd plunge deeply into a story to forget my own. A few days after Thanksgiving, I pulled a book out of my purse and read a passage.

I've forgotten the title and who wrote it. But it spoke of how just before a person dies, they suddenly seem well, giving those who love them hope.

When Peter woke up that afternoon, he was different. He seemed stronger than he'd been in weeks, his eyes bright and more focused. He told me he wanted to get all his boys together.

I figured he wanted to have a party like the one we'd had the day he last left the hospital, so I proceeded to make the calls. But Peter told me he didn't want to have a celebration. He asked me to tell his friends that he wanted to see each of them by themselves, one by one.

Over that day, the whole gang, trickled in. We filled the waiting room, making such a commotion that the nurses occasionally shushed us and tossed a disapproving look. It was like sitting outside the Oval Office, waiting to be summoned. As one person went in, another came out. They'd spend fifteen or twenty minutes with Peter, and when they emerged, most left immediately. They didn't stop to say see you later. They didn't linger.

I told myself that Peter probably wanted those one-on-ones so he could have a little personal time with his buddies, just like he'd wanted to take that fishing trip alone with Lael. He was so alert and full of energy I didn't want to believe he might have called them there to say goodbye.

I left to pick up Lael from school and bring her to the hospital for a little while. It was football season, so after Peter's last friend headed out, the three of us sat together and watched the game.

"It was a good day," he said. "It was great to see everybody."

After Leander came to get Lael, I gave Peter a kiss and tucked his sheets around him. His parents, who'd taken a break while he visited with all his friends, eventually came back, and the three of us hunkered down in our makeshift beds.

The next morning, everyone woke but Peter. We washed up, went to get coffee, and Peter still didn't open his eyes. Finally, a nurse came in to give him his medicine. When she returned a short time later, she was accompanied by Peter's doctor.

Peter was still alive. But he wasn't going to open his eyes again.

We didn't know how much time he had left. It could be minutes. It could be days.

I sat by his bedside. Peter's sister, Debra, came to join me and his parents. So did his nephew Scott, the same one he'd eaten gelato in Italy with. He was terrified of Peter's dying. He didn't want to accept it. But we begged him to come. It felt only right; they'd always been so close.

A nurse who did not regularly tend to Peter came to the room. I believe my mother-in-law had found her. She had the most beautiful voice, and she sang a Catholic hymn. It felt solemn, like a funeral. But Peter was still there. The beeping of the heart monitor and the warmth I felt when I touched his arm told me so.

Later that day, Peter's mother suddenly jumped up and beckoned me, Scott, and my father-in-law to come gather at the bed.

I panicked. What was she sensing? The heart monitor was still beeping. Everything was the same as it had been for the last several hours. I looked at Scott and I thought he might faint, but we did as we were told, clutching hands as we circled the bed. My mother-in-law, holding her rosary, led us in the Lord's Prayer: "Our Father, who art in heaven, hallowed be thy name."

I don't know how I envisioned the end would be, but this wasn't it. We must have stood there for something like twenty minutes before I finally said I didn't think Peter was going anywhere that day.

Scott looked relieved. Then he said he couldn't be there anymore. He couldn't sit and watch Peter die. Wiping tears from his eyes, he turned and left.

I was angry. He and Peter had been raised like brothers. Debra, Scott's mother, was grief-stricken, yet she stayed. I was mad at Scott, but I also envied him, because he could go. I didn't want to see Peter die either, but I'd made a promise. I couldn't walk away.

A couple of days passed. Finally, Debra couldn't take it anymore either. Now it was just me and Peter's parents, along with my mother and my sister Alua, who had joined us at the hospital.

Late one night I drifted into a fitful sleep. When I woke up, the clock said it was almost 4:00 a.m.

The heart monitor was still sounding off, but Peter's breaths were shallow. I took his hand.

"I'm still here," I whispered in his ear.

It was almost dawn, and I knew he was going. I woke everyone, and we once again stood around Peter's bed. This time, they all knew it too.

In the medical shows, there's always that dramatic moment when the medical team rushes in with the defibrillator and shocks the patient back to life. Or maybe it's like the show *House*, where the brilliant, eccentric physician comes up with a miraculous cure just in the nick of time. That's what I was hoping for.

I asked Alua to tell the nurses that Peter's breathing was shallow and to ask what they could do. She left but came back quickly.

"Are they coming?" I asked.

"No," Alua said quietly. "They're not going to revive him. He's supposed to die."

I was too numb to respond. Instead, I laid my hand, then my head, on Peter's chest. I didn't want to listen to the monitor anymore. I wanted to hear his heartbeat.

It wasn't like he took one final gulp of air, then let go. The rhythm in his chest just got slower and slower. I waited a minute. Then I looked at his face and I knew Peter wasn't in there anymore.

I thought of *Song of Solomon*, the Toni Morrison novel that had first tied us together.

Sugarman done fly away. Sugarman done gone.

It was December 11, 2013. Knowing death was coming didn't make it any less devastating when it finally arrived. But I also felt if Peter's spirit wasn't in his body anymore, it must have gone somewhere. Peter was free to be, no longer shackled by a broken body that didn't work anymore.

It was complicated, excruciating grief coupled with relief.

The room was quiet. I guess we were all too spent to cry. No one rushed in. When the doctor did arrive, his voice seemed far off in the distance.

"Time of death," he said, "4:44 a.m."

. . .

After that came the cacophony. It was jarring after all that stillness. We'd been approaching this moment for months, but now that it was here, everything was moving too fast.

The doctor and nurses said they would need to take his body. We had to pack up and leave, unceremoniously, like we were being forced to flee after a fire or natural disaster, with just a few minutes to collect our essential belongings.

Peter was wearing his wedding ring and an amulet around his neck for protection. Peter's mother removed the chain, and I took the wedding band and placed it on one of my fingers.

We began to fill our purses and duffel bags. I grabbed our toothbrushes and my shower cap, things that I'd probably never want to look at again. Still, being able to gather those inconsequential items gave me something to do, something to distract me from the grief that stood in the corner, ready to run over me.

I took down the notes filled with affirmations, the cards that wished Peter the best and that he would get well soon. I wanted every trace of Peter, even the socks he'd worn to warm his feet and grip the floor.

At one point I drew my hand out of the bag I was filling and looked at my hand. Peter's wedding ring, far too big for my finger, was gone.

"It's gone!" I yelled. "His ring is gone!"

Alua ran over and quickly retrieved the band from the bottom of the backpack. With the ring recovered and our bags packed, I filled out some final paperwork, and we turned to go.

It was unbelievable knowing that we were leaving and wouldn't return. For the past few weeks, I'd been in and out of the hospital, getting to know the parking attendants. But in the week leading up to this day, I hadn't so much as gone outside for a fresh breath of air. My car had been parked in the hospital's garage, waiting to be useful. I dug out my ticket and handed it to the attendant.

He brought the car up from underground, and we piled in. I got in the driver's seat, turned the ignition, and car filled with Sade's voice.

You think I'd leave your side, baby.

You know me better than that.

It was our song. The song we danced to at our wedding. The song whose lyrics were etched in the two wedding bands I now wore on a single finger.

I broke. All of us did. Peter's parents, my mother, my sister.

Alua went into a frenzy trying to turn off the radio. I finally recovered long enough to locate the volume button and turn it down.

I don't know how long we sat there and cried. Then we all looked at one another in disbelief.

Of all the songs, how could that be the one that was playing on the radio?

It was the first of many signs that Peter's spirit would be with me always.

12.

Signs

As a child, I'd never seen my mother's father. Not even a picture. But I have a very vivid memory of running into his ghost.

I was four, playing in our front yard in Accra. My mom and Mama were inside cooking our midday meal. The sun was high and bright. I must have been sketching something in the grass or imagining that the jasmine flowers were teacups, when I felt someone behind me.

I turned and saw a man swathed in traditional kente cloth. The bolts of fabric were a vibrant orange, green, red, blue, and yellow. He was regal and looked like he was headed to an important celebration. But his feet didn't quite touch the ground. He seemed to be floating. I recall that the man had the most brilliant smile as he reached his hand toward mine.

I so wanted to touch him, but I was suddenly overcome by a chilling fear. I turned from his hand and instead ran into the house.

When my mother asked what was wrong. I didn't know what to say.

"Nothing," I said, my heart racing. "I'm fine."

But Mama knew. "She's seen something," she said.

I was grown when I finally told my mother what happened that day, that I believed I'd seen my grandfather's spirit. It would be several more years, however, before I had proof. Mom didn't have any photos of her parents, but on a trip home to Ghana, she connected with a distant relative who had her father's portrait. She eagerly showed it to me when she returned.

"Wasn't he beautiful?" she asked, tracing her father's face with her finger.

"Yes," I said. He was. And then I knew for sure. That was the man I'd seen in our yard.

The only other person I ever told that story to was Peter, and he immediately told me he'd had a similar vision. It was when he was a little boy, during his grandfather's funeral. As the priest presided over the service, Peter looked up and saw his grandfather standing there, behind the altar. Stunned, Peter grabbed his mother's arm, and after the service he told her what he'd seen.

I always found it interesting that both Peter and I had seen our grandfathers after they moved beyond this physical plane. So many people would hear that and think we were crazy. But Peter and I believed, and that knowing connected us. We understood that love formed a connection that lived beyond death.

. . .

On the morning Peter passed, we didn't tell Lael that he was gone right away. Because my in-laws and I had hardly been home in the past couple of weeks, she was just happy to see us. Not only was her family all around, she had a Christmas pageant at school that afternoon, and she was excited that she was going to get to sing a song.

We were so heavy while she was so light. How would I ever find the words to tell her that Peter was dead? Thankful for the reprieve, I reasoned that I couldn't deliver that devastating news before her big show. I wanted to put off the conversation as long as possible.

Christmas had been Peter's favorite holiday. He and Lael always had matching Santa hats, and Peter would literally wear his until the white cotton edge was ragged. Lael wore hers pretty much around the clock as well, and she was going to have it on during the pageant.

If we were still at Peter's bedside, his parents and I would have missed the show. But now, of course, we'd be able to go. I tried to be upbeat for Lael, picking out a glittery outfit and applying makeup when all I wanted to do was curl up in a ball and disappear. We all made a weary effort, forcing smiles as we choked back tears.

Our crew filled a row by itself in the school auditorium, and we rose to our feet when Lael belted out her portion of "What Child Is This?" When we got home, she was still zooming on adrenaline, chattering about how her best friend had been so nervous, but how everyone did a good job and had so much fun.

As I got Lael ready for her bath, taking off her stockings, tugging the barrettes out of her hair, I kept wondering if one day she'd be angry with me for letting hours, even days, pass before I told her the truth. While I fretted, she splashed in the tub, and I sang her favorite bath-time song to her. The words were in Fanti, and I hoped that she'd remember them.

Yen kita wae chir

Yen kita wo tuun

Yen kita won sa whon

Yen kita won sa whon

Simple in melody with a catchy cadence, I could lose myself in the rhythm, while Lael hit the water with her small fists in time to the beat. She mimicked my words with her little voice, and again I wondered how I would ever ruin this pure moment with the devastation that I held at bay.

I dried her off, gingerly applying shea butter to her caramel skin, while marveling at her eyebrows, which were arched just like Peter's, and her slanted eyes, which always looked surprised, also just like his. It was unfathomable that I'd never see his eyes turned toward me again. As I guided her arms through the pajama top and her legs through the bottoms, I breathed easier knowing that I'd have another night to contemplate how to tell her. But just as I pulled the covers toward her neck and leaned over to kiss her forehead, Lael turned her tiny face toward me.

"Where's Daddy?" she asked.

It was another simple question. I knew it deserved a simple answer. I took a deep breath.

"He's gone," I said.

Lael looked deeply into my eyes. "Okay," she finally said.

It would have been easier if she'd wailed and thrown herself on the ground. Comforting her would have given me something to do, a place to direct my sadness and rage. But hearing her simply say "okay" crushed my heart because I knew she had no understanding of what she'd lost, of how the ramifications of that void would ripple out for a lifetime.

No, I thought, *it's not okay. It never will be.*

I began to cry. Lael touched my face, trying to comfort me.

. . .

The next morning, I was aimlessly wandering around the kitchen when I looked at the counter. What the hell was that?

There were pieces of broken pottery, all that remained of Peter's pill caddy.

I shared my mother-in-law's love of china, and I constantly added to my wedding set and purchased stand-alone pieces over the years. On one of my excursions, I found a beautiful ceramic butler whose delicate hand held a tiny tray. For a long time, it was forgotten, tucked in a corner, but when Peter became ill, it began to serve a vital purpose.

Peter was on so much medication that Alua came from Los Angeles to help me manage it, along with all the other tasks we needed to juggle. We had a case marked with the dates and times he needed to take his assorted medicines, and to make it all less depressing, we'd place the pills on the butler's tray and deliver them to Peter like they were a gourmet meal, and not prescriptions he needed to stay alive.

But mysteriously, the morning after Peter died, the caddy was on the counter, broken into bits. It had been intact the night before, when I'd glanced at it wistfully before heading to bed. When had it broken?

I asked my mom, my friend Lauren, my in-laws, Alua. No one had touched it. It was one of the many puzzles that started to poke through my grief.

I remembered the feeling of doom that struck me the morning of the day I learned Peter's cancer was terminal. I recalled our wedding song blaring from the car radio after he died. Now, the dish that once held his life-sustaining medicine was shattered.

I'd always believed in God, and the ancestors, and magic. But after Peter's death, the spiritual truly became tangible.

. . .

Not long before he passed, Peter looked at me from his hospital bed and told me not to worry.

"I'll go to heaven and take care of Eve, while you stay here and take care of Lael."

He said it with a laugh. He was so thoughtful in that way, trying to reassure me when he was the one facing his own mortality. I managed a weak smile.

"I guess that's one way to look at it," I said.

But a few days after he died, his brother Neil called me. Giavanna, his seven-year-old daughter, had had a dream and she needed to tell me about it.

Gia, as we called her for short, and Lael looked so much alike they could have been sisters. They were tight, and Gia had also been especially close to Peter. When she came to the phone, she was crying.

The night before, Gia dreamed that she was at school, on the playground, and there was a giant tree. When she looked over, she saw Uncle Peter, peeking from behind it. Confused, she walked over. When she rounded the trunk, he was standing there holding a little girl. Gia wasn't sure who the other child was, but she said Uncle Peter smiled and told her to tell me that everything is okay. Then she woke up.

Our families never talked about Eve. I don't even think Gia knew that I'd lost a baby. And I'd never told anyone what Peter said to me in the hospital.

If one of Peter's siblings or friends had called me and relayed that dream, I might have doubted it, wondering if they were just trying to make me feel better. I'm sure that's why Peter picked Gia to come to. She was the perfect messenger.

My eyes welled with tears. And, for the first time in weeks, I smiled.

. . .

Peter was cremated, and we decided to hold his memorial service on December 15, on what would have been his forty-fourth birthday.

I bought Ghana wax-print cloth colored black and red, the traditional colors worn at Ghanaian funerals. My mother, emotionally spent, was in no mood to sew, so I walked through Little Senegal, the diasporan community near our apartment in Harlem, in search of a seamstress. When I came across a woman sitting in a stall stacked with fabric, I told her I would quickly need two dresses, one for me and one for my four-year-old daughter.

She looked at the colors of the cloth. She knew what they meant. She gazed at me with pity.

How I hated that look. I'd seen it so often since Peter first became ill.

The service would be at the same church where we'd celebrated Eve. Peter and I had appreciated the priest who'd presided over her funeral, how he somehow managed to make us smile, even laugh, during such a terrible time. Peter wanted the same priest to eulogize him.

Of course I would respect his wishes, but the thought of going back to that sanctuary also fueled my fury. I felt betrayed, by life, by fate. And I definitely wasn't speaking to God right then. He hadn't performed a miracle. He hadn't spared Peter.

I'd go back to that church, breathing in its musty smell, listening to the father's attempts to somehow soothe us, but I vowed to myself that this would be the last time. After Peter's funeral, I never wanted to see that church again.

The day of the service, I wrapped my hair and body in swathes of red and black while my mother helped to dress Lael. New York was in the grip of a terrible storm, and it was snowing so hard I wondered how many people would show up. But there must have been two hundred people packed in the sanctuary. Folks came from everywhere, people I hadn't seen in years. They were there in their Patriots jerseys and their suits. It was beautiful to see the tapestry Peter had created, that he'd lived the kind of life that brought together so many who had nothing in common but him. I was moved. I was grateful.

I don't remember much. I know I was going to say a few words, though right before I headed to the lectern, I decided I couldn't do it. Alua grabbed my hand and told me I had to or I'd later regret it. I have no idea what I said afterward, only that Alua stood beside me the whole time. I also remember that Peter's mother spoke. I marveled at how strong her voice was as she buried her baby. I had been struck mute when I buried mine.

Then, for some inexplicable reason, when the service ended, we had a receiving line. I numbly absorbed hug after hug. I spotted Angela, Peter's ex-girlfriend, in the crowd, but as the queue formed, I saw her duck out the door.

We'd once been partners. We'd both loved Peter. I would have liked to say hello and goodbye.

Eventually I planned to take Peter's and Eve's ashes to the Saint John's family mausoleum in Massachusetts. But I couldn't bring myself to make the trip right away. Instead, I put Peter's ashes in the crypt behind that church I never wanted to see again.

The day I carried them there, I briefly panicked as I scanned the shelves. Then I spotted Eve's tiny green urn, shaped like a heart. It actually felt good to put Peter's urn next to hers. I decided the two of them could keep each other company until we moved them to their final resting places.

When I went home, Lael was in the kitchen, frosting cupcakes with my mother. I felt like our family was split in half, Eve and Peter together in that musty old crypt, and Lael and I here, giggling as we got high off sugar. But at least neither of our girls was alone. It was just how Peter told me it would be.

. . .

Now, I had to figure out how to go on, how to take the shards of my life and rebuild. I knew that I was lucky to have family and so many loving friends. But I knew that ultimately, Lael and I would have to make peace with our loss and chart a new path on our own.

Everyone made their way home after the funeral, and I wanted a quiet Christmas with just Lael and my mom. I'd bought Lael a dollhouse, the gift at the top of her Christmas list, and she jumped up and down with happiness after she unwrapped it Christmas morning. It was up to me to put it together.

Once, I'd felt so capable. Give me five minutes and I could figure out a solution or come up with a plan. But after Peter died, I often felt helpless. The smallest decisions overwhelmed me. Did I need to get the carpet cleaned? What dress would Lael prefer, the yellow or the green? Peter was the one who was handy. He assembled our furniture and all of Lael's toys.

As I emptied the dollhouse box, I looked at the mess in front of me and thought there must have been five hundred pieces lying there. I sat on the floor, pushing tiny walls into slats, struggling to make them fit. The directions made no sense, and my mom, busy making breakfast, just looked at me occasionally and shrugged.

I cried. I sweated. I cursed, both God and Peter. How was I going to do this? Why wasn't Peter here?

It took me two hours to put that thing together, but finally I did it. The tiny plastic dolls could go about their business inside their tiny rooms, a perfect family inside their perfect home, their make-believe existence so serene compared to mine.

It was a small triumph. I grabbed a glass of red wine and asked my mother to snap a picture.

Later that night, sitting in the quiet, I decided I really didn't want to be in New York anymore. I didn't want to visit my sisters in California or Peter's family in Massachusetts. That would mean having to engage with or sidestep more grief. But I desperately needed to get away. So, just like the day I found out Peter's illness was terminal, I reached out into the void.

I had a former colleague who was the chief marketing officer for the Hard Rock hotels. I sent him an email to see if there might be a room available at their property in Mexico City. He didn't respond, and of course why would he? It was Christmas Day. I continued sending messages.

Finally, I thought of a public relations executive I knew, Marvet Britto. Our paths crossed over the years at various industry events, but we didn't know each other well and had never hung out. Still, we were friends on Facebook, and I remembered she'd posted that she was representing the Caribbean island of Anguilla.

I sent a query via Messenger. My husband just died. I needed to get out of New York. Was there any way for me and my daughter to quickly book a stay in Anguilla?

It was close to midnight on Christmas Day. And she responded right away.

Years later, Marvet would tell me that she rarely checks her Facebook messages, and she certainly never did so on a holiday. But that evening, for some reason, she did. She was actually leaving for Anguilla the next day on a private flight. Her friend, the island's attorney general, had a guest home she'd just finished building. She'd check if I could stay there. And though there wasn't any room on her plane, if I could book my own trip, Marvet would make sure there was someone to meet me and Lael at the airport.

I didn't know the attorney general. I barely knew Marvet. Still, I called Delta Air Lines; threw some random clothes, underwear, bathing suits, and cover-ups in a carry-on; and the next day Lael and I boarded a plane to Anguilla. The trip was so spur-of-the-moment that when I filled out the customs form, I didn't even know what address to put down when it asked where I was staying.

Looking back, I know that I was being protected by a higher power. I walked out of the airport full of grief, gripping the hand of my four-year-old, on an island where I'd never been. A man greeted us with a sign scrawled with my name. And together, Lael and I followed him blindly into our next adventure.

Marvet was one of my angels, and Josie, the attorney general who owned the house, instantly became another. As soon as we arrived, Josie's ten-year-old daughter led Lael into the kitchen to get something to eat while Josie showed me the guesthouse where we'd stay.

She said she'd give me a minute as she shut the door. I flung myself on the bed, thinking I just needed a quick nap to reenergize. I stayed in that bed for the next three days.

I slept most of the time, so tired that I didn't even dream. And I hardly ate during the brief periods when I could bear to be awake, though Marvet and Josie did their best to feed me.

You know that scene in the film *The Color Purple* when Mister and Celie slide trays of food quickly passed through the door to Shug Avery, the blues singer they're caring for? Our setup was something like that. Josie and Marvet would bring me meals, and when they largely went untouched, Marvet would gently knock on the door and encourage me to eat.

Finally, one morning, I woke up, looked out at the ocean, and thought to myself, *What a beautiful place.* I decided I should at least say thank-you to my hosts, who'd welcomed me and looked after my child. I combed the knots out of my hair, brushed my teeth, and showered for the first time in days.

Marvet was visiting with her boyfriend as well as her best friend, who'd also lost her husband to cancer the year before. Her friend had two children, whom Lael was having a ball playing with, and to-gether we formed our own little community, a tiny tribe searching for sustenance and solace under the Caribbean sun.

I began to take frequent walks. One day I had to postpone my stroll while I waited for the rain to stop. When the sun filtered out, I put on a caftan and made my way to the property's edge.

There I saw the biggest rainbow I'd ever seen. It seemed to go on forever, caressing the land on one side of me and the ocean on the other. Then, to my amazement, I saw a second rainbow appear, small enough to hover beneath the other.

There's one for Peter and one for Eve, I thought to myself.

I was kidding. But right after those words ran through my mind, something extraordinary happened. A shape began to appear in the clouds.

There were eyes and a mouth. A man's face. And he had something on his head. It looked like a Santa hat.

I stared. I blinked. I thought I might be losing my mind. I fumbled for my phone to take a picture before the clouds began to shift. Then I ran into the house.

"Marvet!" I yelled, out of breath. "I just saw Peter."

Marvet gave me one of those pitying looks I'd grown so used to. *Poor thing*, she seemed to be thinking.

"No! Really," I said, pulling up the photo.

Marvet looked down at the phone, then up at me, then back down again.

She will tell anyone who asks that she's very afraid of anything that seems ghoulish or ghostly. "I don't want to look at that," she said finally, backing away.

But she'd seen it. Peter was finding every way he could to let me know that he and Eve were okay, and they would always be with me.

• • •

In the weeks and months that followed, I learned so much. And one of the most striking lessons was that relief can be far more complicated than grief.

Grief is straightforward. Maybe there is a little anger wrapped up in it, but for the most part, deep, abiding sadness runs along a single, jagged continuum. Relief, however, can encompass a kaleidoscope of emotions.

I was relieved that Peter was out of pain. It was unbearable those last months, hearing him groan in agony, watching every part of his body fail. But I was also relieved that much of my discomfort was over as well, and that shrouded me in a veil of guilt.

Peter's death meant I no longer had to anticipate the tidal wave to come. I didn't have to pretend I didn't see my in-laws crying in a corner. I was relieved to have a respite from the drone of constant prayers.

Maybe those feelings were understandable. I was tired and wrung out. I didn't want Lael and me to be forever known as the fatherless child and the widow. I wanted us to just be. But feeling that way still seemed like a betrayal of Peter.

. . .

I continued to work at Pepsi, but in my mind, the job was inextricably tied to all the personal tragedies I'd endured while I'd been there. One night when I was attending a Super Bowl event connected to ads Pepsi created for the Big Game, a man I knew casually approached me. He was working with the legendary rapper and producer Dr. Dre and music icon Jimmy Iovine. They'd recently launched a music company called Beats Music. He set down his drink.

What would it take for me to leave Pepsi and come work for them?

I was caught off guard but intrigued. The job would be on the other side of the country, in Los Angeles. It would be quite the leap. But I desperately needed a new beginning. This might be a new dawn, I thought, like the one I experienced a few years earlier when I was fired from Ashley Stewart and got that out-of-the-blue call from Pepsi. I told him I was interested in talking more.

Over the next couple of weeks there was a flurry of phone calls, culminating with a chat with Dre and Jimmy. The conversations went well, and I felt confident that they were going to make me an offer. Then, Judy, the company's human resources person, called to ask if I could send my résumé.

Typically, that would be asked for at the beginning of the process, not the end. I guessed it was a formality, a loose end that needed to be tied up, like calling references or giving a potential hire a drug test. But there was a problem. I had a résumé, but I had no idea how to find it. Peter had always been the one to update and maintain it, even after we separated. It was stored on his laptop, but when I logged on, I couldn't locate it.

You'd think I could just get on Microsoft Word, find a template, and type up all the professional things I'd done. But I was frozen. In the midst of my trauma over Peter's death, a hiccup that I once could have easily resolved became an obstacle that seemed impossible to overcome.

I didn't know what to do. I was too embarrassed to tell my friends that I didn't know how to put together a basic CV. But I worried that failing to deliver a résumé could be a deal breaker.

I'd been mad at God, not speaking to him, but I needed him now. I sat in front of Peter's laptop, closed my eyes, and prayed.

I need this change, I said. *I want this job. Please make this whole résumé mess go away.*

The next day, I sent Judy an email. I didn't have my résumé, I confessed, but could I send her a short bio instead?

She responded within minutes. "Sure," she wrote. "That works. They want you so badly, they won't care either way."

And that was it. A few days later, I was offered the position. Since then, no other employer has ever asked me for a résumé, not Apple when it purchased Beats; not Uber, the unicorn tech company; not the international talent agency Endeavor, where I became chief marketing officer; not Netflix, where I became the first and only Black person in the C-suite. God removed the obstacle, not for a moment, but permanently.

Now I needed to prepare to move across the country. But before Lael and I left for California, I had to do what I'd put off, and that was reburying Peter's and Eve's ashes in Worcester.

. . .

It had been six months since Peter died. My mother, my girlfriend Justina, Lael, and I were going to drive to Massachusetts together. On the day of the trip, I retrieved Peter's and Eve's urns and placed them in my trunk. Then we got on the road.

During the four-hour drive, we reminisced about Peter, sharing stories and telling jokes to distract ourselves from our mission. But when we were only a few miles from Worcester, I began to freak out.

I couldn't catch my breath. My heart began to pound. I got dizzy. My husband's and daughter's ashes were sitting in my car. I was going to have to bury them. Again. I couldn't do this.

I pulled over to the road's shoulder and jumped out, clutching my chest. Justina leapt out behind me. Then a car flew by, blaring its horn.

I looked and saw a Ford. There was a name on the license plate: PETE.

I quickly jumped back in the car. My mother and Justina stared after the Ford. Lael, confused and probably afraid, did as well. I yelled for Justina to take a picture of what we might later not believe we'd seen. Meanwhile, I raced behind, following the car as it took the same exit I'd been heading toward in Worcester.

The Ford made a right turn. I stayed on its tail. And then, suddenly, the car was gone.

I don't think I looked away. All of our eyes had been glued on it. But it had disappeared.

Out of all the unfathomable moments I'd already experienced, amid all the wonders and signs, the sight of that Ford struck me the most. It confirmed one of the greatest truths I've gleaned from this entire odyssey.

When I was at my weakest, reeling, questioning if I could go on, Peter could just show up and give me strength. It just was like the poets say. Love can overcome illness, transcend death, and carry those left behind.

· · ·

Sometimes it's hard to believe that any of this happened. That my college boyfriend died by suicide. That I became pregnant when I didn't plan to and then had to bury a child. That I met a love I thought I'd keep for life and lost him to cancer. But I've had time to take stock and to revisit all the wisdom those experiences had to offer.

From Ben, I've learned to defy boundaries. He was constantly pressured to choose, between Black and white, between his art and his family's idea of respectability. But during his short time in this world, Ben refused to be boxed in. In that I found inspiration.

From Eve, I've learned that love is infinite. She would have been fifteen this year, and I love her more today than when she was born—even though she's not physically here, even though I don't know what her eye color would have been, what she would have loved to eat, or what would have made her laugh.

And from Peter, I learned to live life with urgency: to take the trip; to call a friend; to cut off the toxic person not next week, not next year, but as soon as the thought crosses my heart. I don't delay. I don't count on an unpromised future. It is a gnawing, a knowing, that is sobering but also freeing.

I'd always been impulsive, moved to action by my restlessness. But urgency is not reckless. It is intentional. It is listening to my gut, listening to God, then being fully present as I embrace each step of my journey.

When I got the offer to become the chief marketing officer for Netflix, it meant leaving behind a company where I was valued and felt at home. But I paid attention to my instincts. I sat in solitude. I prayed. Then, because it felt right, I submitted my resignation. Like I learned the day I told Lael about Peter, I kept it simple. I just didn't want to be here anymore. I wanted to be over there. I said my goodbyes and moved on to my next chapter.

Like all of us, my life has been roiled by change. As a child, I was uprooted often, moved from Accra to Washington, from Pasadena to Nairobi. And yet with every loss—of a friend, of a home, of a loved one—I also grew. I've been pushed over emotional cliffs and I've tripped over obstacles of my own making, yet I survived. Maybe I emerged bruised, exhausted, but I picked myself up, found my footing, and went on my way.

Other times, I was lifted by angels, like the women who cared for me and my little girl on a foreign island when I was in the depths of despair, or the wonderful lady in a Harlem bakery who nurtured me with pastries and love.

Still, I have regrets. I wish I'd stayed home the night Ben rang my phone incessantly. I wish I'd known instinctively how to nourish Eve. I wish I'd been a better lover to Peter.

And I have to fight to keep fear at bay, to ward off the worry that there's another tragedy around the bend. Sometimes I feel like I'm trapped in a game of Whac-a-Mole. If only I could cover all the holes at once, I think, maybe I could keep the next bad thing from happening.

I may actually fear death now more than ever because I don't want to leave Lael. I often think when I'm at work, *What is the last thing I said to her?* Before every business trip, I write her notes, especially if I leave early in the morning before she is awake. I place each one on her pillow so that if, God forbid, something terrible happens, she will have that piece of paper and know that the last words her mother thought as she walked out the door was that she loved her.

But tragedy has also taught me resilience, forcing me to dig deep, to find a way forward as a single mother raising a young child while coping with everlasting sadness. It's helped me to redefine success, to know that achievement isn't reaching goals scrawled on a whiteboard but being able to tell your little girl the hardest of truths. It's fighting for love when it might be simpler to walk away. It is carrying on when hope seems hollow, and deciding to embrace struggle, trusting that the knowledge gained from those travails will buoy you for a lifetime.

Loss taught me to live with urgency. Faith taught me that I could survive the unimaginable. And love gave me the endurance to overcome not only fear but overwhelming grief.

I hope God and I are even. I hope God and I are good. That's the way I'm able to be positive, to move forward, by having the pure faith with no proof that something so heart-wrenching won't happen to

me again. My prayer is that any other death in my life will be natural, and after that person has lived a long, fruitful life.

That's the faith that I have.

That is my only prayer.

. . .

On January 21, 2021, I turned forty-four years old. I feared that I
wouldn't make it, that maybe I didn't deserve to. Peter died four days
before his forty-fourth birthday, so why should my destiny be any
different than the father of my children, the man I loved so much?

After Peter's death, at 4:44 a.m., I began to see the number 444
everywhere. I wake up suddenly and it will be 4:44 a.m. I meet
someone I want to mentor, and he'll be wearing 444 on a necklace
draped around his neck.

I've read that 444 is a direct pathway to the spirit world, and
when it keeps popping up, it's a sign to move in whatever direction
you are contemplating. So, four days before my birthday, I got 444
tattooed on my wrist, in honor of Peter. Now I don't have to look at
a clock or to the world outside for that portent. I can turn my arm
and always be reminded of the spiritual forces that guide me.

I continued counting the days until I reached my milestone.
When I had three days to go, I woke up in the morning thinking
that I had lived one day more than Peter. Would I get there? What
would God decide?

On January 20, my birthday eve, my girlfriends and I began the
celebration, downing champagne and shots of Hennessy. I tumbled
into bed, and when morning arrived, I initially felt more tentative
than excited.

I waited all day for some magical feeling to descend. That didn't happen. But slowly I was enveloped by an overwhelming peace. I was so happy to be alive. I wished Peter had lived as long, that he was living still, but for the first time in a long while, I looked forward to the years stretched out in front of me.

My love story with Peter feels unfinished, even if it was meant to end like this, with Peter forever young and frozen in time. I still update his Facebook page. It's not a memorial. His spirit is still so strongly with me I don't want to act as though his presence is in the past. Instead, I post pictures of Lael and catch him up on the latest news. His friends gather there as well, chatting about a promotion, their newest baby, or how the Patriots really blew their last game.

I still wonder, as I watch Lael grow and remember her quiet acceptance of Peter's death so long ago, when the kicking and screaming will finally come. Will it be when she suffers her first heartbreak and just wants her daddy? Will it be when she has children of her own and realizes they will never know their grandfather? Maybe that's also why I try so hard to keep Peter alive, for me, and for her.

I still argue with God from time to time. If there's something you want me to know, I say, can you find another way to teach it? Can I gain wisdom without the sacrifice? I have learned so much, it seems, in such terrible ways. My gratitude for all that I have comes at a heavy price.

But I also know that for me to be who I am today, those things had to happen. I will always feel sorrow that Peter was taken, but I also know that it had to be in order for me to be who I am right now.

There's a Diane Ackerman quote that I love, about getting to the end of life and not having just lived the length of it, but the width of it too. That's what I want, to fill every day, every inch, with gratitude so great, there isn't room for fear or doubt. Even my grief will be pushed to the edge.

...

On my forty-fourth birthday, my friends and I played in the Malibu surf. Mom and Lael joined in the revelry too. And as is now my habit, I took lots of pictures to capture the precious moment in time.

I spent the day loving and being loved; reliving my loss in gratitude instead of sorrow; living my life urgently with confidence knowing that whatever the future brings, I am more than a survivor.

ACKNOWLEDGMENTS

The ancient Egyptians believe that a person dies twice; the first when they die in their physical form, and the second when their name is no longer said. They believed that a person will continue to live if they are remembered. Therefore, it is my intention that Peter, Eve, and Ben will become immortal—in that way, my thanks to them will never know an end. I live an urgent life because they passed through mine.

I give thanks to God, who is as real to me as any other tangible, living, breathing being. Our relationship has had its fair share of turbulence, distance, closeness, trust, and love. I am thankful for the constant guidance that shows up in my gut to lead me, regardless of whether I want to go in that direction. I've come far in my journey, but only by the grace of God.

I'm thankful for my ancestors, especially the mothers who have borne generation upon generation while nurturing us in our present and praying for our future. I honor those who remained on the continent of Africa, and those who were stolen from the motherland's bosom and thrown into distant lands. I am in awe of the beauty that they retained through their own adversity and passed on to me in my spirit, imprinted on my DNA, and saved in my memories. First among them in my gratitude is my own mother, Aba. I am also grateful to my father's mother, Bozoma, who didn't live long enough to see him grow into a boy or become a father. I'm proud that he accomplished all he has in his life even without the physical nurturing of his mother, and although he didn't bear a son to carry on his name, Appianda, I hope that he is proud of the legacy his mother's name will leave behind.

I do not remember time without a sister by my side. And I've been fortunate to have had three sisters walking with me almost all my days. I have not been lonesome because I've had Alua, Ahoba, and Aba, who have loved me when it's been hard to do so, challenged me when it's been for my benefit, and kept my secrets when it's been impossible to tell any other soul.

And there are my chosen sisters, some of whom I have loved for decades and others I've found in recent years, but regardless of time I will love all of them forever: Tina, Leander, Kadian, Erika, Justina, Luvvie, and Cari. We may not share DNA, but my heart is etched with their names. They're ready to pop champagne to celebrate my wins and throw punches at anyone who aims to steal my joy.

For the many family members, friends, teachers, classmates, and colleagues who I haven't mentioned by name but who have left an indelible mark on my life, I am in deep gratitude for the way you've shaped me— whether for a moment or much longer, your presence has mattered.

And even though I'm not one to be easily influenced, the seed of this book was planted by Jennifer Rudolph Walsh, who heard my story and adamantly told me that I should write it. I wouldn't begin writing it for many years after that conversation, but I am in debt to her belief—not just because she said so, but because it matters to me that she thought it was worthy of telling. Suzanne Gluck, my literary agent at WME, took on that belief and counseled me through the process from beginning to end. I have trusted her with every part of this telling and how it is presented to the world (even in choosing the title!), and I am grateful for her guidance and unwavering support.

In the moments when I waited with bated breath for a reaction to drafts, it was in Meg Leder's brilliant hands that my faith lay. She gave constructive feedback that made the writing better, she gave encouragement when doubts clouded my vision, and she shared tears when a particular passage touched her as if she had been in the room with me. I am grateful to her and the entire team at Viking/Penguin Books for their care of me and mine (special shoutout to the marketing and publicity teams led by Lydia Hirt and Lyndsay Prevette, because they know I know what it takes!).

This has truly been a labor of love. I thought I understood what that saying meant, until I had to labor in the love of birthing this book. And if I continue with that analogy, then the midwife who massaged, guided, held, coaxed, and "yes, you can"-ed me through this process deserves more thanks than I can articulate because I am overwhelmed by what has come to fruition. Charisse Jones has been my partner in writing day in and day out. She pushed me further than I thought I could go and allowed me the space to get it all out. There were times when she pulled a thread of a story thinking that it would add more clarity, only for us to end up in a completely different place with more to tell. I went to places I thought I'd left behind but felt brave in the journey because she held my hand there and back.

Even though this book is dedicated to Lael, I still want to take a moment here to thank her for being. It was her heartbeat that surged me back to life when I thought I'd never be able to take another painless breath ever again. It is her laughter that makes me want to chase joy. It is her future that inspires me every day to the best version of myself.

And thank YOU for coming along on this journey too, and for giving me the gift of your time. I don't take a minute for granted so I am blessed that you chose to spend a part of your life reading about mine. My prayer is that my story of love, loss, and survival will open the portal for your own life to be lived urgently. And like the Japanese artform *kintsugi*, I hope you see that the shattered pieces of our lives can be melded back together to make an even more beautiful existence. Today, I can look back at my story and see the beauty beyond what was broken.

Onward!